The English Revolution
c. 1590–1720

MANCHESTER
1824

Manchester University Press

Flag device of Major William Rainsborough, Leveller and Ranter, depicting the severed head of Charles I in 1649, accompanied by the slogan 'salus populi suprema lex'. (Reproduced by permission of the Dr Williams's Library: MS 12.7, fo 115)

The English Revolution
c. 1590–1720
POLITICS, RELIGION AND COMMUNITIES

edited by

Nicholas Tyacke

Manchester University Press

Manchester and New York

distributed exclusively in the USA by Palgrave

Published by Manchester University Press
Oxford Road, Manchester M13 9NR, UK
and Room 400, 175 Fifth Avenue, New York, NY 10010, USA
www.manchesteruniversitypress.co.uk

Distributed exclusively in the USA by
Palgrave, 175 Fifth Avenue, New York,
NY 10010, USA

Distributed exclusively in Canada by
UBC Press, University of British Columbia, 2029 West Mall,
Vancouver, BC, Canada V6T 1Z2

British Library Cataloguing-in-Publication Data
A catalogue record for this book is available from the British Library

Library of Congress Cataloging-in-Publication Data applied for

ISBN   978 0 7190 7707 4 *hardback*

First published 2007

16 15 14 13 12 11 10 09 08 07   10 9 8 7 6 5 4 3 2 1

Typeset 10/12pt Minion
by Graphicraft Limited, Hong Kong
Printed in Great Britain
by Antony Rowe Ltd, Chippenham, Wiltshire

Contents

Preface   *page* vii

List of contributors   viii

List of abbreviations   x

1 Introduction: locating the 'English Revolution'   1
   Nicholas Tyacke

2 The English Revolution and its legacies   27
   Michael J. Braddick

3 'Patriots' and 'popular' spirits: narratives of conflict
   in early Stuart politics   43
   Richard Cust

4 Religion and community in pre-civil war England   62
   Anthony Milton

5 The queen is 'a goggyll eyed hoore': gender and seditious
   speech in early modern England   81
   Andy Wood

6 Politicising the popular? The 'tradition of riot' and popular
   political culture in the English Revolution   95
   John Walter

7 Religious diversity in revolutionary London   111
   Ann Hughes

8 Behemoth, or civil war and revolution, in English
   parish communities 1641–82   129
   Dan Beaver

9 The kings' book: *Eikon basilike* and the English Revolution
   of 1649   150
   Sean Kelsey

10 Public politics in England c. 1675–c. 1715   169
   Mark Knights

11 'My Kingdom is not of this world': the politics of religion
   after the Revolution   185
   Justin Champion

Index   203

Preface

This book derives from the Neale colloquium held at University College London on 21 February 2004, on the theme of 'The English Revolution and its legacies', and incorporates a revised version of the keynote Neale lecture given by Michael Braddick on the previous evening. With two exceptions, the other chapters are based on papers discussed at the colloquium itself. We are very grateful to Peter Lake for his scintillating commentary on that occasion, which has helped shape the present volume, and to Anthony Fletcher and Angus Gowland for chairing some of the discussions. Conrad Russell, the premier figure in the field of English civil war studies, had planned to join us at the colloquium, but was sadly prevented by illness and died the following October. We mourn the passing of a great scholar and a personal friend to many of us.

Random House, successor to the publisher Jonathan Cape, continues to provide vital support for the lecture and colloquium established in honour of Sir John Neale. The British Academy also generously met the travel and accommodation costs of the overseas participants at the colloquium, as well as those of the Neale lecturer himself. In addition the Royal Historical Society provided welcome financial assistance for graduate students attending. Meanwhile much of the administrative burden fell on Nazneen Razwi and Helen Matthews, both of the UCL History Department. We extend them all our warmest thanks. Lastly the editor must record a combined personal debt – to Alison Welsby at Manchester University Press for her patience and to the anonymous publisher's readers for their wise counsel.

Nicholas Tyacke
University College London

Contributors

Dan Beaver is Associate Professor of History at Pennsylvania State University. He is the author of *Parish communities and religious conflict in the Vale of Gloucester* (Cambridge, MA, 1998), and his book on forest politics and the origins of the English Revolution is forthcoming from Cambridge University Press.

Michael J. Braddick is Professor of History at the University of Sheffield. He is the author of a number of studies on the development of the English state, the British empire, and of popular politics in early modern Britain – including *State formation in early modern England* (Cambridge, 2000), and editor (with John Walter) of *Negotiating power in early modern society* (Cambridge, 2001). He is currently working on *God's fury, England's fire: politics and society in civil war England*, to be published by Penguin.

Justin Champion is Professor of the History of Early Modern Ideas at Royal Holloway, University of London. His most recent book is *Republican Learning: John Toland and the crisis of Christian culture* (Manchester, 2003). He is currently working on a study of Hobbes and irreligious culture.

Richard Cust is Reader in Early Modern History at the University of Birmingham. He has published a range of books and articles on early Stuart England, the most recent of which is *Charles I: a political life* (Harlow, 2005).

Ann Hughes is Professor of Early Modern History at Keele University. Her most recent book is *Gangraena and the English Revolution* (Oxford, 2004). She is currently completing (with Thomas Corns and David Lowenstein) an edition of the works of Gerrard Winstanley, to be published by Oxford University Press.

Sean Kelsey has written extensively on the trial and execution of Charles I and the foundation of the English commonwealth. An erstwhile Lecturer in Early Modern History and quondam Post-Doctoral Research Fellow of the British Academy, his current projects, including a biography of Lord President John Bradshaw, proceed at a pace consistent with the pursuit of a legal career in the City of London.

Mark Knights is Reader in History at the University of East Anglia. He has recently published *Representation and misrepresentation in late Stuart Britain: partisanship and political culture* (Oxford, 2005), and has edited a volume of *The Morrice Ent'ring Book 1677–1691* (Woodbridge, forthcoming). He also directs a project to create a 'virtual research environment' for the early modern period, funded by the British Academy and the Joint Information Systems Committee.

Anthony Milton is Reader in History at the University of Sheffield. His publications include *Catholic and reformed: the Roman and protestant churches in English protestant thought, 1600–1640* (Cambridge, 1995), *The British delegation and the synod of Dort (1618–19)* (London, 2005) and *Laudian and royalist polemic in seventeenth-century England: the career and writings of Peter Heylyn* (Manchester, forthcoming).

Nicholas Tyacke is Emeritus Reader in History at University College London. He is the author of *Aspects of English Protestantism c. 1530–1700* (Manchester, 2001) and editor of *The history of the university of Oxford*, vol. 4: *Seventeenth-century Oxford* (Oxford, 1997). His book (co-authored with Kenneth Fincham) *Altars restored: the changing face of English religious worship, 1547–c. 1700* is due to be published by Oxford University Press in 2007.

John Walter is Professor of History at the University of Essex. His books include *Understanding popular violence in the English Revolution: the Colchester plunderers* (Cambridge, 1999) and *Crowds and popular politics in early modern England* (Manchester, 2006). He is the editor (with Michael Braddick) of *Negotiating power in early modern society: order, hierarchy and subordination in Britain and Ireland* (Cambridge, 2001).

Andy Wood is Reader in History at the University of East Anglia. He is the author of *The politics of social conflict: the Peak Country 1520–1770* (Cambridge, 1999) and *Riot, rebellion and popular politics in early modern England* (Basingstoke, 2002).

Abbreviations

BL	British Library
CJ	*Commons Journals*
CLRO	Corporation of London Record Office
CPR	*Calendar of patent rolls*
CSPD	*Calendar of state papers domestic*
HEH	Henry E. Huntington Library
HMC	Historical Manuscripts Commission
LJ	*Lords Journals*
ODNB	*Oxford dictionary of national biography*
TNA	The National Archives

1

Introduction: locating the 'English Revolution'[1]

Nicholas Tyacke

The idea of an 'English Revolution' as having occurred in the middle of the seventeenth century remains controversial. Thus only in the wake of the French Revolution of the 1790s did this usage emerge and it has always been associated with a progressive, not to say radical, reading of English history. During the latter half of the nineteenth century, liberals of various kinds, or 'Whigs' as they are often called, largely dominated the field, especially in the person of the revered Victorian historian Samuel Rawson Gardiner. Although often remembered for his use of the term 'Puritan Revolution', Gardiner in fact came to employ it interchangeably with 'English Revolution'.[2] According to this version, a constitutional rather than a class conflict was involved; absolutism went down to defeat in the civil war, partly thanks to the extremist brand of protestantism known as puritanism, and a system of parliamentary monarchy developed – subsequently to be modified in an increasingly democratic direction.

But just as the French Revolution led to a reappraisal of the nature of the English civil war, so the Russian Revolution of 1917, and its communist denouement, served to breathe new life into the theory that Stuart England had undergone a 'bourgeois revolution' – involving the destruction of a 'feudal' *ancien régime*.[3] From the 1930s through to the 1970s this class interpretation proved extremely influential, the role played earlier by Gardiner now most obviously filled by the Marxist Christopher Hill, who, like his predecessor, was a prolific author. Thereafter, however, a marked retreat set in, with growing numbers of historians abandoning both Whig and Marxist interpretations, a movement epitomised by the leading revisionist Conrad Russell choosing to entitle a volume of his collected essays *Unrevolutionary England 1603–1642*.[4]

Current historiographical trends, however, suggest that the time is now ripe to re-open the whole question. Beginning in the 1980s, a new group of historians has emerged, often collectively referred to as 'post-revisionists'. This label indicates that the writers in question do not simply reject revisionism but rather seek to incorporate some of its insights into their own accounts, which at the same time draw, at least implicitly, on earlier interpretative models in seeking to explain the events which led to the English civil war. A milestone here was the publication, in 1989, of a volume of essays, edited by Richard Cust and Ann Hughes, entitled *Conflict in early Stuart England: studies in religion and politics, 1603–1642*. In the words of the blurb, the book provided 'a vigorous critique of revisionism' and reasserted 'the importance of long term ideological and social developments'. The 'conflict' of the title was a conscious rebuttal of the revisionist stress on 'harmony and consensus in politics' during the pre-war years. On the other hand, the chronological centre of gravity of *Conflict in early Stuart England* is still located very much in the 1620s and the editors fight shy of reviving the term English Revolution. Yet the logic of the post-revisionist approach would seem to call for a more fundamental review of the pros and cons of previously discarded theories – along with a reconsideration of those of more recent vintage.[5]

Although not until after the French Revolution did writers come to talk of an English Revolution as having happened some 150 years previously, it is striking that as early as the middle of the seventeenth century what still remain the three main schools of interpretation had already emerged, at least in embryo. Thomas May, the official historian of the Long Parliament, cast his account essentially in terms of a struggle for 'liberty' against the absolutist ambitions of the early Stuarts, while James Harrington sought to explain the conflict in terms of a prior shift in the 'balance of property' – whence 'came the House of Commons to raise that head, which since hath been so high and formidable unto their princes'. By contrast, Edward Hyde, future earl of Clarendon, emphasised mistakes in policy and the role of accident, which a collection of power-hungry individuals was able successfully to exploit.[6] In more recent centuries Whig, Marxist and revisionist historians have come to ring the changes on May, Harrington and Hyde, whether in hybrid or in purer form.[7]

Nor was the idea of revolution in the modern sense completely alien to Stuart contemporaries. Hence those who executed Charles I in 1649 and dated their letters from the 'first year of freedom' were clearly well aware that they lived in overturning days. Indeed the declaration of an English republic was not easy to reconcile with the claim of simply restoring an immemorial 'ancient constitution'.[8] Moreover there already existed a long-standing tradition of investing protestantism, and in particular puritanism, with radical implications. Thus in 1591 the Italian Catholic Girolamo Pollini had published an account of the English Reformation under the title *Storia ecclesiastica della rivoluzione d'Inghilterra*, while Richard Bancroft in his *Dangerous positions* of 1593 claimed to have exposed the existence of a puritan conspiracy in both church and state – something which was to prove an enduring theme.[9]

Many seventeenth-century contemporaries, including Clarendon, also alleged that the English civil war had split the country along social lines, with a majority of the nobility and gentry supporting the monarch; over against them were ranged 'the greatest part of the tradesmen and freeholders, and the middle sort of men'.[10] Granted that the concept of progress really emerged only later, during the Enlightenment of the eighteenth century, a writer such as David Hume could then adapt with relative ease the views of Harrington to the theory current in his own day that societies develop through a series of stages, going on to argue that the period of the English civil war had coincided with, and was partly explained by, the advent of the commercial epoch. At the same time, Hume recast in a very novel way the ideas of May and his successors regarding the role of both liberty and religion. Far from the absolutism of the early Stuarts being an aberration, Hume argued that this was intrinsic to the monarchical institution which they had inherited from the Tudors. Therefore, rather than defending the status quo, the advocates of liberty were the true innovators, and where May had portrayed James I and Charles I as subvertors of the protestant 'interest', Hume envisaged a much more dramatic clash between the forces of 'enthusiasm' (the puritans) and 'superstition' (the Laudians).[11]

Hume's *History of England*, which began to appear from 1754 onwards, in addition jettisoned the previously dominant historiographical model of an ancient constitution dating from Anglo-Saxon times. This earlier tradition had culminated in the work of the French protestant Paul de Rapin-Thoyras, published in the 1720s. While noting more recent research regarding the origins of parliament, Rapin – as he is usually known – had essentially chronicled the ebb and flow of English liberties as first established by the Germanic invaders after the collapse of the Roman empire. In this scenario the Anglo-Saxon witenagemot was the ancestor of parliament. While the Norman Conquest involved a temporary breach, 'by degrees' the descendants of William I's feudatories 'put on the English genius' and, becoming 'wholly addicted to liberty', they sought to have 'the Saxon laws re-established'. This led to King John being forced to grant Magna Carta in 1215, and its confirmations by Henry III and Edward I. Subsequent violations resulted in the depositions of both Edward II and Richard II. Thereafter, however, Magna Carta in combination with a reinvigorated parliament had proved an effective bulwark against the pretensions of the monarchy until the days of James I and Charles I. Then, as in the past, the great charter provided the basis of constitutional resistance, its principles successfully reasserted in 1640 – and again in 1688 with the ousting of James II.[12]

Hume, however, increasingly came to regard much of this tale told by Rapin and his predecessors as nonsense. The ancient constitution was a myth; parliaments were no older than the thirteenth century, and in their medieval form were 'barbarous' institutions now outmoded by social change. Magna Carta itself was a feudal relic.[13] What had transformed the situation were the developments gathering pace under the Tudors, when the monarchy emerged supreme in the aftermath of the Wars of the Roses. Although Hume applied the term 'revolution' only in passing to mid-seventeenth-century English events, he was adamant that a profound rupture occurred at this time. The growing wealth of the 'middle rank of men' had paralleled the declining fortunes of the nobles, and through the medium of parliament the former had gone on to forge 'a new plan of liberty' – essentially the eighteenth-century constitution.[14] In this regard, so Hume argued, England was a remarkable exception to the European norm of absolute monarchy. Part of the explanation for the difference, he thought, was the late development of an English standing army. But Hume also stressed the role of puritanism, singling out the Elizabethan firebrand Peter Wentworth, and his advocacy of freedom of speech in parliament, as a harbinger of things to come. Wentworth's successors were the 'patriots' who in the early Stuart House of Commons took advantage of the financial weakness of the crown.[15] Moreover, during the civil war of the 1640s 'the commercial part of the nation' was, he claimed, to be found in opposition to Charles I.[16]

Hume's account of the English civil war largely dominated the field for some sixty years,[17] until the mid-1820s when two challengers appeared in the persons of Henry Hallam and Francois Guizot – the latter a French protestant, like Rapin, but also a child of revolution whose father had been guillotined in 1794.[18] Hallam was among the first of a long line of new Whig historians who resurrected the notion of an ancient constitution, despite the previous assault of Hume, by harnessing it to the concept of progress. This school, however, mainly traced the development of English freedoms from Magna Carta onwards. Rather than a story of recurring loss and recovery, the process was now seen as one of gradual accretion.[19] But Hallam had little to say about social change, and the break represented by the civil war was played down. Commencing his *Constitutional history* with the accession of Henry VII in 1485, he wrote of the 'liberty' achieved in England up to that point as 'the slow fruit of ages, still waiting a happier season for its perfect ripeness'. In pursuit of this theme Hallam focused on developments in Elizabethan and early Stuart parliaments, including that of 1601 and the debate about monopolies which generated, so he reckoned, 'more heat than had ever been witnessed'.[20]

The approach of Guizot, however, was very different from that of Hallam, not least in his choice of terminology. Entitling his study of seventeenth-century England, the first two volumes of which appeared in the years 1826–27, *Histoire de la revolution d'Angleterre*, Guizot drew a quite overt comparison with the French Revolution – which in his view shed a 'strong light' on earlier English events. Both 1640 and 1789 belong to the same genus of 'revolution': each 'helped civilization to advance along the road which it has been pursuing for fourteen centuries'.[21] Although Guizot was rather dismissive of Hume, their interpretations share some important features. Absolutism was on the march in early modern Europe and the 'feudal aristocracy' in the process of being broken – their successors becoming metamorphosed into courtiers. But in England, unlike on the Continent, a new grouping had arisen:

> the simple gentlemen, the freeholders, and the citizens, whose only anxiety was to turn their lands or capital to good account, increased in wealth and credit, became daily more closely united among themselves, drew the entire people under their influence, and without noise, without political design, without even a consciousness of what they were doing, concentrated in their own hands all those social forces which are the true sources of power.

These were the purchasers of the land flooding on to the market during the sixteenth century, especially former ecclesiastical property. As a consequence – and here Guizot does indeed cite Hume – by 1628 'the House of Commons was three times as wealthy as the House of Lords'. With this great increase in prosperity, however, the gentry and their allies, like the lords in previous centuries, came to challenge the crown. 'By degrees the memory of the people reverted to thoughts of their ancient liberties, of the efforts by which the great charter had been won, and of the maxims which that charter consecrated.'[22] There are echoes here of Harrington as well as of Hume, but also of Rapin. Like Hume, too, Guizot invoked the influence of puritanism. The 'Anglican Church', which had emerged in the sixteenth century, was by the very nature of its royal origins yoked to 'the cause of civil despotism'. Conversely the 'nonconformists', in their bid for further reforms, found themselves at loggerheads with the monarchy and thus were 'compelled ... to assert the liberties of the citizen'. Again the pioneer cited in this connexion was Peter Wentworth: increasingly religion 'emancipated men's minds from thraldom and inspired them with a boldness previously unknown'.[23]

Guizot envisaged that his *Histoire* when completed would span the years 1625 to 1688. By 1827 he had reached the execution of Charles I in 1649, but a quarter of a century was to elapse before any further volumes appeared. This was largely because of his increasingly active political career, which culminated with him serving as chief minister during the later stages of the July Monarchy in France. With the abdication of Louis Philippe, however, in 1848, Guizot was driven from office and shortly thereafter resumed his career as a historian,[24] the first fruit of which was his *Discours* on why the English Revolution had succeeded. Written very much with the 1848 European revolutions in mind, Guizot elaborated his argument of the 1820s that underlying the political and religious issues at stake in Tudor and Stuart England was 'a social question'. During the sixteenth century 'great changes had taken place in the relative strength of the different classes of society, without an analogous change having been effected in the government'. The ensuing civil war was to be explained partly, therefore, by frustrated political ambition, and it divided the nation along broadly social lines: 'nobles' and their followers versus 'burgesses and people', albeit 'many country gentlemen, and several of the most considerable of the nobility, appeared at the head of the popular party'. At the same time Guizot was now especially concerned to contrast as well as compare the English and French experiences. Whereas the English Revolution had resulted in a settlement which had endured, France since the 1790s, and Europe more generally, had been wracked by continuing upheavals. How then to explain the difference? According to Guizot, it was the eventual triumph of moderation which guaranteed success – with the emergence of a constitutional monarchy in England based on widespread public support.[25] This was also the message of his friend and admirer Macaulay, the first two volumes of whose own *History of England* were published in 1849. Macaulay too suggested that the English Civil War had involved an element of class conflict.[26]

At first sight surprisingly, this analysis – especially as offered by Guizot – had much in common with the notion of an English bourgeois revolution which Marx and Engels were beginning to advance at this very period. Politically speaking, of course, Marx and Engels were at daggers drawn with Guizot, whom they singled out in their *Manifesto* of 1848 as one of those currently seeking to 'exorcise' the 'spectre of communism'. Marx also wrote a very disparaging review of Guizot's *Discours* for the *Neue Rheinische Zeitung*.[27] But in private he struck a rather different note, acknowledging in 1852 his debt to 'bourgeois' authors such as Guizot who 'had described the historical development' of the 'struggle between the classes'. Marx saw his own contribution as showing that the 'existence of classes' was 'bound up with certain historical phases in the development of production' and that the 'class struggle necessarily leads to the dictatorship of the proletariat' – followed, ultimately, by the transition to a 'classless society'.[28]

Neither Marx nor Engels ever provided more than brief sketches of how they envisaged developments in early modern England. Of these, probably the fullest is an outline of the English Revolution published by Engels as late as 1892. Despite baldly stating at the outset that 'the middle class of the towns brought it on and the yeomanry of the country districts fought it out', he went on to argue that the English 'aristocracy' had become increasingly bourgeoisified during the sixteenth century thanks to a combination of sheep-farming and land transfers. Partly as a result, by the end of the seventeenth century a 'compromise' had been reached between 'the rising middle class and the ex-feudal landowners'. The 'political spoils of "pelf and place" were left to the great land-owning families, provided the economic interests of the financial, manufacturing and commercial middle classes were sufficiently attended to'. Engels also provided his own formulation of the thesis, later developed by Max Weber, concerning the relationship between Calvinism and capitalism:

> Calvin's creed was one fit for the boldest of the bourgeoisie of his time. His predestination doctrine was the religious expression of the fact that in the commercial world of competition success or failure does not depend upon a man's activity or cleverness, but upon circumstances uncontrollable by him. It is not of him that willeth or of him that runneth, but of the mercy of unknown superior economic powers.[29]

It was thanks mainly to Guizot, however, that Victorian readers were familiarised with the notion of an English Revolution as having occurred in the middle of the seventeenth century, his *Histoire* made available in three separate translations between 1838 and 1854.[30] Yet the preferred description in Anglophone circles remained 'Great Rebellion'. This was how the period was 'known to respectability', as Engels put it, 'revolution' being on the whole still reserved for the 'comparatively puny event' of 1688.[31] Widespread use of 'Great Rebellion' in fact dated from the accession of James II in 1685, when the words – highlighted by use of capital letters – were incorporated into the revised service of thanksgiving for the restoration of the Stuart monarchy. This version comprised part of the Prayer Book until 1859, when a decision was taken to omit such commemorations.[32] Originating in the context of Tory and high-church reaction, the idea of a Great Rebellion also came to be employed after the French Revolution as a way of denying any kind of equivalence between the two phenomena.[33]

Even Gardiner seems to have taken up the concept of an English Revolution only under the influence of the approaching centenary of the French Revolution. Prior to this his favoured sobriquet was 'Puritan Revolution', by which he meant an explosive combination of religious and political ideas. Nevertheless by 1889 Gardiner was using the two terms synonymously: 'Revolutions, no less than smaller political changes, are to be accounted for as steps in the historical development of nations.' They occur when 'the path of political progress' has become blocked. It was the 'essence' of the French Revolution 'that there should cease to be privileged orders', whereas the key concern in the 'English Revolution' was 'that the authority of the king should be restricted'. As regards the latter, the 'central facts are to be traced in the legislation of the first months of the Long Parliament'.[34] In both cases, according to Gardiner, what followed arose from the need to secure the original revolutionary ends. He and his Whig successors, however, like Hallam before them, largely eschewed social explanations of the English civil war. Instead they emphasised constitutional developments and above all the role of the English parliament, which Gardiner described as 'the noblest monument ever reared by mortal man'. Puritanism, by comparison, was an intellectual 'backwater', alien to 'the master current of the age' – as represented by the likes of Hooker, Bacon and Shakespeare, and linked somewhat accidentally with political opposition due to the provocative actions of Archbishop Laud.[35] At the theoretical level, therefore, Gardiner had little to say that was obviously new. His forté lay in an unrivalled command of the original sources, on the basis of which he produced an immensely detailed political narrative which has broadly stood the test of time.

But the missing social dimension in Gardiner was to an extent compensated for by the emergence, from the late nineteenth century, of economic history as a distinct subject. Many of the practitioners of the new specialism, interested as they were in the changing role of the state, associated the triumph of *laissez-faire* attitudes with the defeat of Charles I in the 1640s. English governments until then, so they thought, had hampered the operation of market forces and could in a sense be regarded as anti-capitalist.[36] Of particular importance in the present context, however, is R. H. Tawney, who in a remarkable series of publications between 1912 and 1941 developed what amounts to a neo-Harringtonian interpretation as to why England experienced an upheaval in the middle of the seventeenth century. Under the Tudors a body of capitalist landowners had emerged, often themselves purchasers of ex-monastic property and for whom profit was the overriding concern. Commercialism now increasingly rode roughshod over traditional social relations, one facet of this being the enclosure of former common fields and the consequent suffering of the peasantry. The crown while seeking to buttress the old order was in the event to be transformed along with it, a victim of the changing 'balance' of economic power.[37]

This was the theme pursued by Tawney in *The agrarian problem in the sixteenth century*. During the 1920s, in *Religion and the rise of capitalism*, he turned to consider the ethos or ideology informing the changes which he had earlier analysed. Influenced to some extent by Weber, Tawney argued that although the ' "capitalist spirit" is as old as history . . . it found in certain aspects of later puritanism a tonic which braced its energies and fortified its already vigorous temper'. In the event, therefore, puritanism proved the ally of economic individualism and of those social forces which came to challenge the Stuart monarchy.[38] Tawney concluded his investigation with a lecture and an article, both published in 1941. The lecture, entitled 'Harrington's interpretation of his age', provided a kind of coda to the whole enterprise. In the event, however, it was the article 'The rise of the gentry, 1558–1640' which became a *cause célèbre* because of the attempt to demonstrate statistically that a shift in the balance of landed property, from nobility to gentry, had occurred during this period .[39]

Thus over some thirty years Tawney elaborated a highly ambitious explanation of the English civil war in terms of antecedent socio-economic change. One consequence is that Christopher Hill was being less original than he claimed when, in 1940, he first mounted his challenge to the 'orthodox' interpretation of mid-seventeenth century events. Rather than a struggle for liberty, 'the state power protecting an old order that was essentially feudal was violently overthrown, power passed into the hands of a new class, and so the freer development of capitalism was made possible'.[40] Although Tawney, in contrast to Hill, was no Marxist, there are definite similarities between their two accounts. On the other hand Hill did revive the term 'English Revolution', which had effectively lapsed since the death of Gardiner in 1902. But, mainly due to the Second World War, reaction to Tawney – and by extension to Hill – was delayed until the mid-1950s. During the interim, however, an ally had appeared in the person of Lawrence Stone, then at the outset of his career, whose conclusions concerning the declining fortunes of the Elizabethan nobility appeared to reinforce the view that the gentry were rising at their expense.[41]

Clearly this is not the place to rehearse the intricacies of the resulting gentry controversy, including the attempt to turn Tawney's original proposition on its head. Suffice it to say that serious methodological problems were exposed in the work of both Tawney and Stone, notably at the hands of J. P. Cooper and Hugh Trevor-Roper, the net effect of which was to refute the claim that in the century or so prior to 1640 a significant transfer of land had occurred from nobility to gentry.[42] Harringtonian ideas, so it seemed, had finally been put to the test and found wanting. The resulting sense of disillusionment was to provide the seedbed for subsequent revisionist historiography. Associated particularly with the work of Conrad Russell in the 1970s, the roots in fact date back considerably earlier. Thus the original begetter of revisionism was the American historian J. H. Hexter, who in his 1961 collection of historical essays first began to spell out the broader implications of the gentry controversy and its collapse into statistical disarray. In a Foreword recommending the book, Peter Laslett compared the English civil war to a road accident, concluding: 'it does not follow that the more dramatic and important the crash and its consequences, the more profound the causes'.[43]

Hexter clearly regarded the work of Tawney as ultimately Marxist inspired and as such fundamentally misconceived. Yet somewhat paradoxically, and in marked contrast to later revisionists, he retained a decidedly Whiggish view of English politics in the seventeenth century as involving a struggle for liberty. Moreover while engaged in exposing the follies of the rival advocates of rising or declining gentry fortunes, Hexter also advanced his own alternative 'framework for social history'. This centred on the changing role over time of the English nobility. During the early-modern period, so he argued, the magnates 'lost their vocation for commanding retinues of armed squires' but 'had not yet found their vocation for commanding solid phalanxes of borough members sitting in parliament'. Military retaining became largely a thing of the past and, with the associated demise of good lordship, a temporary 'power vacuum' was created into which 'poured the country gentry'. Hence the leadership of the Long Parliament in the early 1640s by John Pym, who 'was not a great territorial magnate but a substantial squire'. At the same time Laslett, in his Foreword to Hexter's essays, made the further and equally important point that out of time of parliament political activity still carried on at the county level and was becoming increasingly *issue* orientated by the death of Elizabeth. One facet of this change was a much better educated gentry.[44]

Perhaps wisely, Hill kept his distance from the gentry controversy and as a result remained comparatively unscathed by it. There is also the obvious fact that most of his massive oeuvre appeared subsequently. In these writings Hill elaborated with great erudition on the Marxist model which he had originally outlined in his 1940 essay. Although there was a conscious attempt to modify the terminology, the basic argument remained unaltered, as is apparent from his 1961 book *The century of revolution, 1603–1714*. This was followed in 1967 by *Reformation to industrial revolution*. Some of the most perceptive criticism of these general treatments came from economic historians, especially Charles Wilson.[45] Hexter too exercised his barbed wit at the expense of a 1974 collection of Hill's essays entitled *Change and continuity in seventeenth-century England*; according to Hexter, the author was guilty of a combination of 'source-mining' and 'lumping', and he poked fun at an admission made elsewhere by Hill that he had 'picked out evidence which seemed to support my case'. Yet the gravamen of the complaint remains that Hill too readily accepted that material base determines intellectual superstructure. Much the same point, of course, has been made apropos those who assumed that the changing fortunes of the gentry translated into clear-cut political attitudes, whereas in reality matters were more complicated. We should not conclude from this, however, that such connexions can simply be ruled out.[46]

Despite the priority claim of Hexter, Russell is today rightly remembered as the principal founding father of civil war revisionism, because of his having rejected Whig along with Marxist accounts and their allegedly shared belief in 'inevitable historical progress'. The point of departure for Russell was, however, the same – namely, the negative conclusions of the gentry controversy. Nevertheless when he claimed, in 1973, that 'social change explanations . . . must be regarded as having broken down' it would have been more strictly accurate to say that a particular version of the thesis originally propounded by Harrington had been disproved.[47] The gentry had not risen at the expense of the nobility. But meanwhile, albeit little remarked by political historians, a new consensus was already emerging to the effect that the gentry were the prime beneficiaries of the sales of church and crown lands after the Reformation. Thus an alteration in the balance of property *had* occurred after all, to the detriment of the monarchy and in favour of the gentry.[48] More recent research by medieval historians also tends to confirm the relative eclipse of the magnates, as postulated by Hexter, from the late fifteenth century onwards.[49] In addition there has been a great deal of work on the expansion of higher education, much of it done by Stone himself.[50] All this helped produce an environment conducive to change, since the gentry provided most of the members of the House of Commons as well as running the county administration.[51]

According to Russell, however, parliament was an institution in decline by the early seventeenth century, manifestly failing in the purposes for which the crown had traditionally summoned it – especially with regard to the making of laws and the granting of taxation; furthermore the increasing incidence of political conflict in the Commons at this time was a sign of weakness not strength. Indeed, Russell went so far as to write of a growing 'functional breakdown', in which the irresponsible antics of members of the Commons threatened the very survival of parliament.[52] In making these particular claims Russell had to some extent been anticipated by the Tudor historian Geoffrey Elton, who enjoyed making polemical forays outside his main area of specialism, and others were soon to jump on the bandwagon.[53] More generally, it is significant that Russell identified historiographically with Clarendon and his 'story of mistaken decisions and missed opportunities' as serving to explain the civil war.[54]

Political historians working within a broadly Gardinerian tradition became the main target of revisionism as it developed during the 1970s. One past master in particular, however, tended to be singled out. He was the American Wallace Notestein, whose lecture of 1924 'The winning of the initiative by the House of Commons' was in many ways the parliamentary counterpart of Tawney's article on the gentry. In that lecture Notestein sought to show how, under the early Stuarts, a 'new leadership' emerged in the Commons and 'gained the real initiative in legislation'. From the last years of Elizabeth the power of privy councillors had begun to erode. Control passed instead to men independent of the government, the spokesmen of the latter being forced on to the defensive. The key to these developments, so Notestein thought, was 'the rapid growth of new procedure'. He particularly emphasised the role of the committee of the whole house, which emerged in about 1607 and by the early 1620s had evolved into four standing committees. The most formidable of these was that concerned with 'grievances'.[55] But whereas Notestein ascribed great constitutional significance to the growth of the committee system, revisionsits have subsequently reinterpreted this in much more neutral terms, essentialy as a function of greater administrative efficiency. Notestein has also been censured for talking in the binary terms of 'government' and 'opposition'.[56] What, however, neither Notestein nor his critics appear to have noticed is that Charles I, or whoever drafted the royal declaration issued after the dissolution of parliament in 1629, had already rehearsed the central argument of the 'winning of the initiative' by the Commons:

> We are not ignorant how much that house hath of late years endeavoured to extend their privileges, by setting up general committees for religion, for courts of justice, for trade, and the like; a course never heard of until late: so as, where in former times the knights and burgesses were wont to communicate to the house such business as they brought from their countries; now there are so many chairs erected, to make inquiry upon all sorts of men, where complaints of all sorts are entertained, to the unsufferable disturbance and scandal of justice and government, which, having been tolerated awhile by our father and ourself, hath daily grown to more and more height; insomuch that young lawyers sitting there take upon them to decry the opinions of the judges; and some have not doubted to maintain that the resolutions of that house must bind the judges, a thing never heard of in ages past: but in this last assembly of parliament they have taken on them much more than ever before.

This declaration went on to speak of those in the Commons whose 'drift was to break, by this means, through all respects and ligaments of government, and to erect an universal over-swaying power to themselves'. Nevertheless a distinction was drawn between 'turbulent and ill-affected spirits' and 'wise and moderate men'.[57] Some twenty years earlier Lord Chancellor Ellesmere can be found commenting on the beginnings of the process to which the 1629 declaration refers, and in almost equally alarmist terms: the 'popular state ever since the beginning of his majesty's gracious and sweet government hath grown big and audacious, and in every session of parliament swelled more and more'. Ellesmere proceeded to illustrate this proposition from the five parliamentary sessions between 1604 and 1610, including an episode in 1607 which contributed to the emergence of the committee of the whole house. Analysing the fourth session in 1610, he also referred to 'some' who 'did single them from others, and kept secret and privy conventicles and conferences, wherein they devised and set down special plots, for the carrying of business in the house according to their own humour and drifts'.[58] While making all allowances for exaggeration, there thus remains a prima facie case for the rise of opposition in early Stuart parliaments and one which revisionists have never adequately addressed.

Such opposition was linked with puritanism, by both contemporaries and later commentators. At the same time a distinction has traditionally been drawn between puritans according to whether they were of the church or the state variety, but more helpful, especially when dealing with the laity, is to regard these as two sides of the same coin.[59] Although revisionists have been dismissive of puritanism as a political phenomenon, in line with their general denial of ideological differences in this period, there are again grounds for thinking them mistaken.[60] Most obviously, of course, the persecution of puritans tended to put them on a collision course with the government, and it is striking that the rusty sword of Magna Carta was refurbished, during the 1590s, in the course of a growing dispute over the legality of proceedings by the Court of High Commission against nonconformist clergy. The specific issue at stake was the use of the inquisitorial *ex officio* oath, and one of those leading the attack was the puritan lawyer James Morice. What, he asked, when raising the matter in the parliament of 1593, has become of 'the Greate Charter of England . . . wherein is conteyned that no freeman shall be apprehended, imprisoned, distreyned, impeached, disseised, or putt from his freehold or franchize, but by the lawe of the lande', and 'which lawe utterlye forbiddeth the imposing of an oathe uppon him that is accused of anye crime or matter of disgrace'? The reference here is to the celebrated clause 39 of Magna Carta, which was now in process of being adapted to the needs of a new age.[61]

Another puritan lawyer, Nicholas Fuller, was to become notorious for arguing the same case as Morice during the early years of James I's reign. Fuller also cited Magna Carta (clauses 39 and 41) when denying the legality of the novel royal revenue-raising devices of monopolies and impositions, while combining this with an appeal to the 'law of God'.[62] Peter Wentworth, too, as early as 1587, had repeatedly invoked God in his bid greatly to extend the bounds of freedom of speech in parliament.[63] Moreover, in the 1620s a similar combination of secular and religious arguments can be found emanating from puritan opponents of the forced loan levied by Charles I. Here the writings of Thomas Scott of Canterbury are particularly illuminating. Responding to Isaac Bargrave, dean of Canterbury, who had described loan-refusers as 'men whose purity consists in parity, whose conscience in disobedience', Scott elaborated on the theme of the 'conscientious puritan' who is obliged to hold out against 'tyranicall and lawlesse commaunds'.[64] Morice, Fuller, Wentworth and Scott were linked by a shared moral imperative whereby conscience reinforced their interpretation of the law of the land. Furthermore they all emphasised the limited or mixed nature of the English monarchy, in contrast to the absolutist claims now increasingly advanced by government spokesmen.[65] Accordingly, it is no accident that puritans were prominent in the opposition both to the forced loan in the 1620s and ship money in the 1630s – when Magna Carta was again deployed against the crown (clauses 39 and 12).[66]

The attacks of Morice and Fuller on the *ex officio* oath were, however, to be taken considerably further by the great common lawyer Sir Edward Coke, who became the chief scourge of High Commission under James I.[67] Shortly after being appointed a judge in 1606 Coke also delivered a sweeping indictment of the ills of society. The published version of this charge, delivered at the Norwich assizes, is subtitled 'A discoverie of the abuses and corruptions of officers'. After a lengthy tirade against Catholics, Coke touched lightly on the subject of puritanism: the 'Brownings', i.e. Brownists, who 'can indure no bishops' and 'the last sort of recusants' who 'do with too much violence contend against some ceremonies used in the church'. He then proceeded to list 'those growing enormities', the 'ungovernd height' of which 'is already to such imperfection grown as that the justice of this kingdome's government receiveth scandall by their meanes'. These 'enormities' included 'the multiplicity of ecclesiastical courts', the 'abuses done by purveyors' – that is suppliers of the royal court – and monopolists. Some of the last mentioned 'hinder and annoy the whole publicke weale' for their 'owne privat benefit'.[68] Coke, however, is perhaps best remembered as an exponent of the 'ancient constitution', whereby the powers of the crown were limited by law. During the 1620s Coke emerged as one of the most formidable parliamentary critics of the Government, and shortly before he died his papers were seized by the authorities, who appear to have been especially worried about an exposition by him of Magna Carta. This manuscript, in which Coke did indeed argue that monopolies and impositions were both in breach of the great charter, remained unpublished until the meeting of the Long Parliament, which as part of a great mass of reforming legislation proceeded to abolish High Commission.[69]

While it is true, as revisionists stress, that failure to suppress a rebellion in Scotland forced Charles to summon an English parliament in 1640, there also existed comparable long-term problems in both kingdoms.[70] In 1590 Queen Elizabeth had written to James VI that 'there is risen, both in your realm and in mine, a sect of perilous consequence, such as would have no kings but a presbytery'. Despite James's imprisoning and exiling of the Scottish presbyterian leadership after his accession to the English throne, as well as suppressing the general assembly, subsequent developments in Scotland under Charles I have about them a real sense of nemesis, especially when in 1638 episcopacy was abolished by a revived assembly.[71] A related development in 1640 is the elimination, at the hands of the Scottish parliament, of the lords of the articles – a mechanism which had been used hitherto by the crown to muzzle debate. Also in 1640 this same parliament passed a triennial act, anticipating an equivalent English measure of the following year and designed in both cases to secure frequent meetings. Moreover the early modern period generally in Scotland has been described in terms of a transition 'from lordship to patronage' as regards the changing role of the nobility. Part of this process saw the emergence of the lairds as a political force in their own right, marked by their recognition in 1587 as a separate estate in parliament.[72] (The Scottish lairds were roughly equivalent to the English gentry.) Although Charles had fairly comprehensively alienated the Scottish nobility by the 1630s, and hence their leading role in the rebellion, it has been suggested that this disguised a previous erosion of traditional 'feudal' relations, with many of the nobility themselves later gravitating back to supporting the monarchy during the 1640s.[73]

On the other hand Russell was undoubtedly correct to emphasise the deepening financial malaise of the English Government in the early seventeenth century. At a time when the revenue needs of the state were expanding, yields from both ordinary and extraordinary sources of income were contracting. Against a background of price inflation, crown lands were increasingly being sold for short-term profit, and the value of the occasional taxes voted by parliament was being eroded by chronic under-assessment. Only the customs revenue remained buoyant, but attempts to increase it were already running into parliamentary difficulties by 1610. While it proved possible to limp along in peacetime, the onset of foreign wars served to highlight the underlying problem: 'the war with Spain in 1588 therefore fell on a financial and administrative system which was already creaking at the seams.' The situation in the 1620s, when England became involved in the Thirty Years' War, proved even more dire. Russell himself clearly envisaged the position of the Government as a deteriorating one, commenting that at some point in the future 'royal finances were bound to collapse' and thus precipitate a 'crisis'.[74] Although he did not explicitly make the point, arguably one is witnessing in the fifty years or so prior to the civil war the birth-pangs of what has come to be called the fiscal–military state. Greatly increased and, above all, regular taxation was required to meet the escalating costs of warfare – especially the funding of armies and navies. If parliament was to end up footing the bill then, in Russell's words, this 'was bound to disturb the balance of power'.[75]

Although a good case can be made for tracing the origins of the English Revolution to the 1620s, by the end of which decade, in the words of the contemporary historian Thomas Fuller, 'two parties are plainly to be discovered',[76] an even better one exists for going back to the 1590s. I have already commented on the puritan resurrection of Magna Carta at this time. It was also in the final years of Elizabeth's reign that renewal of warfare on a large scale both exposed the weakness of crown finances and encouraged the exploitation of the royal prerogative for fiscal purposes. One particularly controversial aspect of this latter approach was the granting of industrial monopolies, leading to a 'minor constitutional crisis' when parliament met in 1601 and marked by heated debates in the Commons with which historians have long been familiar.[77] Much less well known, however, is the growing chorus of complaint over the previous fifteen years, from as far afield as Yorkshire and Cornwall, and involving a broad band of public opinion. Originally intended to foster new industries and regulate old ones, from the 1580s patents of monopoly increasingly began to develop into essentially money-making schemes – all the more objectionable because the profits went mainly to the patentees, who either forced existing producers to pay a fee to remain in business or deprived them of their livelihood. It also meant that consumers had to pay higher prices for a sometimes inferior product. The attraction from the point of view of the monarchy was that such monopolies could be used to reward courtiers and the like, thus meeting part of the cost of government by what was in effect a tax on consumption.[78] Fiscally speaking monopolies are the ancestor of the excise, although levied by virtue of the royal prerogative as opposed to parliamentary grant; they also raised a number of important issues, not least the question of their legitimacy.

An early example of how the nature of monopolies was changing is afforded by the case of Thomas Wilkes, clerk of the privy council, who in 1585 was granted a patent for making and selling 'white salt' at King's Lynn and Boston; the patent was extended in 1586 to include Hull. Outcry was almost immediate, the towns-men being supported by the local justices of the peace. Opponents argued that salt was 'of use so generall and of such necessitie that it is not apte for a monop-olie'. The granting of such a patent was 'a manifest publication to the subjecte that all other thinges whatsoever' were liable, and might also breed a 'generall suspicion' that Elizabeth planned to 'extend her prerogative . . . further than ever heretofore'.[79] By the early 1590s, however, the pace of change was clearly quick-ening. In 1592 Henry Warner received a patent for 'salting, drying and packing fish' in the counties of Devon and Cornwall. The same year an agitation was mounted against it at the Cornwall assizes, by gentlemen, merchants, fishermen and others 'in greate nombers'. In a letter to Lord Treasurer Burghley, the jus-tices described the grant as 'repugnant to the liberties of hir majesties lawes' and added that 'we finde the people's mynde so greatlie moved with theise restraints and impositions as wee greatlie feare the same may turne to some matters of higher consequence'. The complainants themselves were less restrained, describing Warner's patent as a 'miserable servitude' and 'more intollerable, the qualitie of this country considered, then to prohibit us the savinge of our corne at harvest'.[80]

Yet the eye of the rapidly developing storm became the patent for searching and sealing of leather, also granted in 1592. The recipient was Edward Darcy, a groom of the Privy Chamber. In this case the protesters had the backing of the mayor and corporation of London. Writing to Burghley, in January 1593, the then lord mayor characterised Darcy's grant as being 'to the great grief and discontentment of this whole citie and, I doubt [not], this whole realm, and the impoverishing of many of hir majesties subjects'. By the following March Darcy had literally come to blows with one of the aldermen, Sir George Barne. (Darcy allegedly punched Barne in the face, drawing blood, as well as addressing him in the derogatory form of 'thou'.) Meanwhile the aggrieved leather-sellers had to be dissuaded from directly lobbying the royal court.[81] Nevertheless a petiton from some of them complained of the 'intollerable taxe and rate [which] the said Mr Darcye goeth about to obtaine', and claimed that it fell mainly on 'poore personnes'. The petitioners went on to ask 'whether the same taxe be meete, necessarie or convenient to be laide upon the people, not being graunted by parliament nor warrantable by lawe?' Darcy in turn accused his opponents of inciting a 'tumultious exclamation, as it were in manner of a rebellion', while at the same time he sought to mobilise the glovers and leather-dressers against the leather-sellers. The latter, however, stood firm and four of their leading members were imprisoned. From prison they appealed to Burghley, asking that Darcy's patent be tried by 'the lawes of the lande', which are 'the surest anchore holde by which the greateste subjecte in the realme doth enjoy all he hath'.[82] Moreover by 1595 the leather-sellers can be found making common cause with all those affected by monopolies. They itemised six other patents, including that of Richard Drake – another groom of the Privy Chamber – for making aqua vitae and vinegar, and reported a 'fear in the poore people that the lyke patents may bee granted for all other commodities'.[83]

The deadlock was broken only in early 1596 by a promise to revoke the leather patent, in return for a £4,000 'fine'. Two years later, in 1598, the detested Darcy received what appears to have been compensation in the form of a patent for the manufacture and sale of playing-cards, over which battle was rapidly rejoined with the corporation of London. It also transpires that the puritan lawyer Nicholas Fuller represented both the leather-sellers and makers of playing-cards in their respective disputes with Darcy.[84] While questions had been raised in parliament about the salt patent as early as 1589, it was not until 1597 that MPs took up the general issue of monopolies. One of the four recorded speakers was Nathaniel Bacon, member for King's Lynn which was directly affected by the salt patent. Bacon was in addition a committed puritan, as was Sir Francis Hastings, who also spoke.[85] Fobbed off with promises of redress, nothing had been done by the time the last parliament of the reign met in 1601, when the torrent of mounting opposition burst its banks. Puritans again played an important part, notably in the person of Sir Robert Wroth. But a posse of Middle Temple lawyers, of no clearly defined protestant persuasion, almost certainly collaborated in forcing the government into a remarkable *volte face*. They spoke of the 'beggerye and bondage to the subjecte' at the hands of 'bloodsuckers of the commonwealth', and Francis Moore went so far as to say that 'there is noe acte' of the queen 'that hath bene or is more derogatorye to her owne majestie and more odious to the subjecte, or more dangerous to the commonwealth, then the grauntinge of these monopolyes'.[86] According to the parliamentary diarist Hayward Townshend, it was during these same debates that Sir Walter Raleigh 'blusht' at the mention of the patent for playing-cards, which if true suggests that in this instance at least Darcy was fronting for a much more important courtier.[87] Although many members wished to proceed by way of legislation, the compromise actually reached was a royal proclamation cancelling some ten existing patents of monopoly, among them those originally granted to Wilkes and Warner, and opening the way to challenging the rest at common law. This last led in 1603 to Thomas Allen, a London haberdasher, winning a case against Darcy who had prosecuted him for infringing the playing-card monopoly. As well as Fuller being one of the lawyers acting for Allen, the corporation of London undertook to pay his costs.[88]

Yet the issue did not go away, not least because monopolies remained an attractive option for the impecunious early Stuarts. Damped down as an issue in the first half of the reign of James I, they flared up again in 1621 when the leading monopolist Sir Giles Mompesson was put on trial and found guilty – using a revived form of parliamentary judicature. A number of monopolies were also cancelled at this date, by royal proclamation, followed in 1624 with a statute against monopolies.[89] Crown lawyers, however, were able to exploit a legal loophole in this legislation, with the result that during the 1630s monopolies were issued on a large scale to corporate bodies rather than individuals. Retribution came in 1640 when, within days of the meeting of the Long Parliament, an attack was launched against the 'frogs of Egypt', as Sir John Culpeper memorably dubbed the hated monopolists. MPs known to have been involved in such schemes were expelled

16

from the Commons and a general investigation launched.[90] Within three years, however, erstwhile royal grants of monopoly were in process of being transmuted into the parliamentary excise, as part of the tax revolution born out of the exigencies of civil war.[91] Patents of monopoly are in many ways symptomatic of the problems of prerogative finance in an age of inflation.[92] The situation cried out for reform but in the meantime produced successive constitutional crises: monopolies in 1601 and 1621, impositions in 1614, the forced loan in 1628 and ship money in 1640. Furthermore, the perennial grievances over monopolies may well help to explain the different social make-up, which contemporaries claimed to discern, of the two sides in the civil war, since it was the manufacturing and trading sectors that were most directly affected.

At this point, however, we do well to recall some words of Russell to the effect that religious passions as well as financial grievances were involved in the outbreak of the English civil war. What particularly he had in mind was the 'rise of Arminianism' and the divisive policies associated with Archbishop Laud. But such an eventuality was increasingly likely from the 1590s onward, when a group of anti-Calvinists first clearly emerged.[93] Nor is it the case that puritanism had been destroyed by the end of Elizabeth's reign, as Russell and others have tended to assume. Rather it was a question of regrouping, after the failure of a particular experiment in clandestine ecclesiastical organisation – the so-called 'classical movement'.[94] While puritan clergy remained liable to prosecution by the church courts, their gentry patrons were virtually untouchable. Thus the Elizabethan *fin de siècle* witnessed an intensification of what may be called seigneurial puritanism, which allowed the wider movement not only to survive but to grow, courtesy of lay support.[95] Moreover Russell provided, albeit unintentionally, a prime example of this mechanism at work – namely the setting up of a trust fund in 1630, by Richard Knightley of Fawsley in Northamptonshire, on behalf of the veteran puritan minister John Dod. An executor of the leading Elizabethan presbyterian Thomas Cartwright and himself deprived for nonconformity in 1607, Dod remained a very influential figure in 'godly' circles. The list of trustees is a remarkable roll-call of the puritan great and good: Viscount Saye and Sele, Sir Nathaniel Rich, John Hampden, John Crew, John Pym and Christopher Sherland; Edward Bagshaw and Sir Arthur Hesilrige were added on the deaths of Rich and Sherland. All these men, along with Knightley, served in parliament, and four – Saye and Sele, Hampden, Pym and Hesilrige – came to play major political roles in the 1640s.[96]

As already remarked, however, there is an artificiality in separating out puritanism as a religious phenomenon narrowly defined. Almost by definition, lay puritans were committed to reform of the state as well as the church. Furthermore we now know that such a twin-track agenda, most likely formulated by puritan supporters of the late earl of Essex, was in existence by the end of Elizabeth's reign. The two long lists in tandem of 'commonwealth' and 'churche' grievances, as presented to James I in 1603, were headed respectively by 'monopolies' and 'subscription' – the latter required of the clergy to the Prayer

Book and the articles of religion. An initially favourable reception by the new king led to high hopes of the parliament which met the following year. Yet by June 1604 reform appeared to have stalled and the resulting sense of acute frustration is reflected in the Apology drawn up by a seventy-or-more-strong Commons committee.[97] The Apology is a fascinating document, not least due to what it has to say about the nature and function of the House of Commons. Referring to the 'many millions of people' there 'representatively present', the authors concluded that

> the voyce of the people in thinges of their knowledge is said to bee as the voyce of God. And if your majestie shall vouchsafe at your best pleasure and leasure to enter into gracious consideration of our petitions for ease of these burthens, under which your whole people have of longe tyme mourned, hopeing for releife by your majestie, then may you bee assured to bee possessor of their harts for ever, and if of their harts then of all they can doe or have.[98]

Employment of the concept *vox populi vox dei* by the authors of the Apology bears witness to the widening sphere of politics at this time, nourished in part by the religious wars of the later sixteenth century and the domestic burdens which they entailed. Calls were also now beginning to emerge for annual parliaments, and by the 1620s there were moves by the House of Commons itself to widen the borough franchise in disputed elections.[99] Thus there is an important pre-history to the situation in the 1640s, graphically described by Michael Braddick in chapter 2 of the present volume, when so much was thrown into the political melting-pot. Moreover, as Richard Cust argues in chapter 3, the appeal to public opinion on the eve of the Short Parliament of 1640 can be seen as the culmination of a trend at least as old as the Warwick election contest of 1586, and the 'patriot' stance then adopted by the radical puritan Job Throckmorton. Cust discerns at work here a mix of 'classical republicanism and godly Calvinism', increasingly at odds with what was perceived by many as a corrupt royal court. The obverse of this was the accusation of 'popularity' levelled against critics of the government, as for example during the parliamentary debates about monopolies in 1601. Drawing here partly on forthcoming work by Peter Lake, Cust traces back the origins of the so-called 'public sphere' to this period.[100]

While Braddick and other contributors to this volume rightly emphasise the extraordinary religious diversity spawned by the collapse of traditional controls during the 1640s, Anthony Milton cautions against too readily assuming that communities prior to the civil war were united in the worship of their local parish church. Not only the varieties of puritanism but Roman Catholicism, as well as religious indifference, set people apart. Nor did a homogeneous 'Anglicanism' serve to define the rest. In this connection Milton, in chapter 4, applies the Dutch sociological model of *verzuiling*, or 'pillarisation', according to which each religious denomination formed 'its own political, social and cultural community'.[101] Conversely Andy Wood also demonstrates (chapter 5) that in this same pre-war period those formally excluded from the political process, by considerations of class and even more of gender, were nevertheless able to find a voice of sorts. He cites numerous cases of plebeian women, but also men, who attacked the female rulers Mary I and Elizabeth I as 'whores'. Nor were male rulers, for example Henry VIII, exempt from sexual slander. In at least some of these cases, however, religious hostility would seem to have been the trigger. The pattern continued after the Restoration, with attacks on Charles II, among others – 'the deployment by subjects of gendered language against their rulers' inverting 'established political hierarchies'.[102]

The prologue must not, however, be allowed to steal the play. For the epicentre of the English Revolution is indeed located in the two decades between 1640 and 1660. As Braddick argues, the 'sustained public argument', and indeed the 'legitimation crisis', to which the civil war and its aftermath gave rise, had a profound impact on the nature of politics. Developing this theme in chapter 6, John Walter demonstrates how in the early 1640s 'political division' opened up 'new political space', as print, rumour and rival governmental directives collided, and 'deference no longer sufficed to mobilise popular support'. At the same time a tradition of popular politics already existed, medieval in origin but reinforced by the experience of the Reformation. On the eve of the civil war this manifested itself especially in widespread unofficial iconoclasm, directed mainly at Laudian innovations and ironically often sparked by the loyalty oaths imposed from Westminster. Walter is at pains to stress, however, that despite often highly alarmist contemporary reporting the targets remained delimited and did not fundamentally threaten the existing social order, with earlier notions of protest continuing to inform crowd actions. But, to echo Anthony Milton, the religious genie was now well and truly out of the bottle, and one facet of this was a great upsurge in petitioning.[103] The resulting situation in London and the provinces is further explored by Ann Hughes and Dan Beaver (chapters 7 and 8). London in particular rapidly developed into a 'religious marketplace', fed by pulpit and press, and with its competing publics impinging on both parliament and the city government. Moreover, radicalism in religion spilled over into radicalism in politics, the Leveller movement being an obvious case in point – emerging as it did from a separatist milieu.[104] Religious strife itself, however, also provided a form of political education. Existing fault lines now widened greatly, abetted by the demise of the ecclesiastical courts, and as the 1640s yielded to the 1650s so a new denominationalism developed which tended to fracture the parish community still further.

Meanwhile, at the national level, the saying 'no bishop, no king', earlier popularised by James VI and I, was apparently borne out by events, as both episcopacy and monarchy disappeared within a few years of each other. The brutal fact of regicide also served to drive home the unprecedented nature of events. Remarkably, however, the royalists at their darkest hour, in 1649, proceeded to stake out a claim on the future with the publication of *Eikon basilike*, the purported political testament of the, by then dead, Charles I. Despite the political gymnastics performed by the king in his lifetime and the continuing dissension in the royal camp, analysed here in fascinating detail by Sean Kelsey (chapter 9), the book encapsulates the church and king ideology which was to become the hallmark of the Tory party after the Restoration. At the same time *Eikon basilike* lays the blame for the civil war and the subsequent abolition of the monarchy squarely on the shoulders of those 'demagogues and patrones of tumults', who had pandered to the 'madnesse of the people' from the beginning of 'this black parliament'.[105] The experience of the Interregnum served, if anything, to reinforce such views. Thus, come the Restoration, Edward Hyde, then earl of Clarendon, took up this refrain in his opening speech as chancellor to the Cavalier Parliament of 1661. Looking back on recent years, when 'all ages, sexes and degrees, all professions and trades' had taken upon themselves to be 'reformers', he concluded that 'the confounding [of] the Commons of England, which is a noble representative, with the common people of England was the first ingredient into that accursed dose, which intoxicated the brains of men with that imagination of a commonwealth'.[106]

Yet notwithstanding such sentiments, as expressed by Clarendon, repeated attempts during the early 1660s to repeal *en bloc* all the legislation to which Charles I had agreed in 1641 met with failure. Hence in the main was saved what S. R. Gardiner, with good reason, regarded as a key component of the English Revolution.[107] But that such disagreement was possible, even at the start of the reign, helps to explain the subsequent rise of party politics discussed by Mark Knights, who argues, in chapter 10, for a transformation of the 'public sphere' arising from the 'mid-century crisis'. As a result 'the people' became established, in effect, as a court of appeal, or umpire. Whatever their initial misgivings, this was a new fact of political life, which Tories as well as Whigs were forced to accept. The increasing frequency of elections from 1679 onwards and a relatively free press, along with the emerging role of parliament as guarantor of the fiscal–military state, all contributed to this development. Only in 1716, with the passing of the Septennial Act, was the resulting 'rage of party' to some extent reduced. Underlying much of this political conflict, of course, was the legacy of religious division bequeathed by the English Revolution, further discussed, in chapters 8 and 11, by Dan Beaver and Justin Champion – the 'church of law' versus the 'church of conscience'. Moreover while Tories proved very reluctant to accept the implications of the 1689 Toleration Act, Whigs in the person of Benjamin Hoadly now sought fundamentally to recast the relations of church and state by invoking Christ's claim: 'My Kingdom is not of this world.' The upshot, however, from the 1720s onwards was an ecclesiological 'compromise between privilege and voluntary persuasion'.[108]

In a recent book, Mark Knights has suggested that the England of the later Stuarts 'saw the culmination of trends' which 'had been evolving over the long seventeenth century (1580–1720)', and that within that time frame the 'period from 1675 needs to be seen as the second stage of a seventeenth-century revolution'.[109] A similar periodisation is employed also in the present volume. More recently still David Cressy, in a masterly study of England on the eve of civil war, has underscored just how *revolutionary* were the years 1640–42 – as well as those that followed.[110] Undoubtedly the longer term developments discernible at work earlier speeded up dramatically at this time, producing in the process a qualitatively different political culture.

Notes

1 For help and advice in writing this introduction, I would particularly like to thank Richard Cust, Angus Gowland, Peter Lake, Simon Hornblower, Simon Renton and Paul Seaver.

2 See p. 7 above.

3 For Marx and Engels, and their nineteenth-century contemporaries, see pp. 4–7 above.

4 C. Russell, *Unrevolutionary England, 1603–1642* (London, 1990).

5 R. Cust and A. Hughes (eds), *Conflict in early Stuart England: studies in religion and politics 1603–1642* (Harlow, 1989); cf. also R. Cust and A. Hughes (eds), *The English civil war* (London, 1997). Although closely associated with the beginnings of revisionism, the present writer has long entertained doubts about many of the claims made in its name.

6 T. May, *The history of the parliament of England: which began november the third, mdcxl, with a short and necessary view of some precedent years* (1647), i. 6, 14–20, 115–19, ii. 21–6; J. Harrington, *The commonwealth of Oceana* and *A system of politics*, ed. J. G. A. Pocock (Cambridge, 1992), 11–13, 54–6; E. Hyde, earl of Clarendon, *The history of the rebellion and civil wars in England*, ed. W. D. A. Macray, 6 vols (Oxford, 1888), i. 1–4, 241–50.

7 A helpful historiographical introduction is R. C. Richardson, *The debate on the English revolution revisited*, 3rd edn (Manchester, 1998).

8 D. Underdown, *Pride's purge: politics in the puritan revolution* (Oxford, 1971), 259–60; J. G. A. Pocock, *The ancient constitution and the feudal law: a study of English historical thought in the seventeenth century*, 2nd edn (Cambridge, 1987). The inscription on the first great seal of the English republic does, however, read 'in the first year of freedom, by God's blessing restored': S. Kelsey, *Inventing a republic: the political culture of the English commonwealth, 1649–1653* (Manchester, 1997), 94. One way of defending such a proposition was to claim, as John Dodderidge had at the beginning of the seventeenth century, that parliaments in England predated the monarchy: P. Croft, 'Sir John Dodderidge, King James and the antiquity of parliament', *Parliaments, Estates and Representative Institutions*, 12 (1992), 95–107. Contemporaries can also be found arguing for the divine origins of republicanism: Harrington, *Oceana*, 25–8.

9 An example of the subsequent recycling of this material in the royalist cause is P. Heylyn, *Aerius redivivus: or the history of the presbyterians* (Oxford, 1670).

10 L. Stone, *Social change and revolution in England, 1540–1640* (1965), 164, 166–7.

11 D. Forbes, *Hume's philosophical politics* (Cambridge, 1975), 233–323; D. Hume, *Political essays*, ed. K. Haakonssen (Cambridge, 1994), 18, 95, 208–9, 248–9; D. Hume, *The history of England, from the invasion of Julius Caesar to the revolution in 1688*, Liberty Fund edn, 6 vols (Indianapolis, IN, 1983 [1778]), iii. 80–2, iv. 354–70, v. 124–9, 131, 134–7, 223–4, 575; May, *The history of the parliament of England*, i. 2–3, 6, 8, 11–12.

12 P. de Rapin-Thoyras, *The history of England*, trans. N. Tindall, 2 vols (1732), i. 152–6, 275, 340 n. 2, ii. 796–800 ; H. R. Trevor Roper, 'A Huguenot historian: Paul Rapin', in I. Scouloudi (ed.), *Huguenots in Britain and their French background, 1550–1800* (Basingstoke, 1987), 3–19.

13 Hume, *Political essays*, 209; Hume, *History*, ii. 56, iv. 355.

14 Hume, *History*, iii. 76–7, iv. 381–5, v. 170.

15 *Ibid.*, iii. 80, iv. 143, 178–0, 286, 402, v. 140, 160.

16 *Ibid.*, v. 387.

17 The main rival of Hume was the republican Catherine Macaulay, who also provided a recognisably Harringtonian interpretation of the English civil war: C. Macaulay, *The history of England, from the accession of James I to that of the Brunswick line*, 8 vols (1763–83), v. 380–91.

18 D. Johnson, *Guizot: aspects of French history, 1787–1874* (London, 1963), 2.

19 J. W. Burrow, *A liberal descent: Victorian historians and the English past* (Cambridge, 1981), 33.

20 H. Hallam, *The constitutional history of England, from the accession of Henry VII to the death of George II*, 2 vols (1827), i. 2, 287. Hallam also devoted considerable space to Peter Wentworth: *ibid.*, i. 275–8.

21 F. Guizot, *History of Charles I and the English revolution*, trans A. R. Scoble (1854), i, pp. xi, xxi.

22 *Ibid.*, i., pp. xix–xx, 125–6, 131–3; C. H. Firth, *The history of the House of Lords during the English civil war* (London, 1910), 31.

23 Guizot, *History*, 135–8, 383–9.

24 Johnson, *Guizot*, 321.

25 Guizot, *History*, i. 1, 11–13, 102–13.

26 T. B. Macaulay, *The history of England, from the accession of James II*, ed. C. H. Firth, 5 vols (1913–15), i. 90–1, 460 n. 2, iii. 1304–12.

27 K. Marx and F. Engels, *The communist manifesto*, ed. G. Stedman Jones (London, 2002), 218; *Karl Marx Frederick Engels: collected works*, 50 vols (1975–2001), 10. 251–6 (hereafter, *MECW*).

28 *MECW*, 39. 60–5.

29 *Ibid.*, 27. 291–3

30 The translators were L. H. R. Coutier (1838), W. Hazlitt (1846), and A. R. Scobel (1854–6).

31 *MECW*, 27. 292.

32 *A form of prayer, with thanksgiving to Almighty God for having put an end to THE GREAT REBELLION* (1685): BL 3407.c.43; G. Cuming, *A history of Anglican liturgy* (London, 1969), 196. A myth has grown up that the originator of this term was Edward Hyde, earl of Clarendon, as author of a work allegedly entitled *The history of the great rebellion*: C. Hill, *The English Revolution 1640*, 3rd edn (1955), 8; E. Hyde, *The history of the great rebellion*, ed. R. Lockyer (1967); C. Russell (ed.), *The origins of the English civil war* (London, 1973), 3; Cust and Hughes, *Conflict in early Stuart England*, 15. Clarendon's book was, of course, *The history of the rebellion*.

33 Modern instances include C. V. Wedgwood, *The great rebellion: the king's peace, 1637–1641* (London, 1955), A. M. Everitt, *The community of Kent and the great rebellion, 1640–60* (Leicester, 1966), and I. Roots, *The great rebellion, 1642–1660* (London, 1966).

34 S. R. Gardiner, *The first two Stuarts and the puritan revolution, 1603–1660* (London, 1874); S. R. Gardiner (ed.), *The constitutional documents of the puritan revolution, 1625–1660*, 3rd edn (Oxford, 1906 [1889]), ix–xi.

35 S. R. Gardiner, *History of England from the accession of James I to the outbreak of the civil war, 1603–1642*, 10 vols (London, 1900), i. 2; and *Cromwell's place in history* (London, 1897), 3–7.

36 G. Unwin, 'The aims of economic history', in N. B. Harte (ed.), *The study of economic history* (London, 1971), 43–5; for this interpretation in full bloom, see E. Lipson, *The economic history of England*, 3 vols (London, 1915–31).

37 R. H. Tawney, *The agrarian problem of the sixteenth century* (London, 1912), 38–9 and generally.

38 R. H. Tawney, *Religion and the rise of capitalism*, 2nd edn (London, 1929 [1926]), 226–7 and generally.

39 R. H. Tawney, 'Harrington's interpretation of his age', in L. Sutherland (ed.), *Studies in history* (Oxford, 1966), 238–61; and 'The rise of the gentry, 1558–1640', *Economic History Review*, 11 (1941), 1–38.

40 Hill, *English Revolution 1640*, 6.

41 L. Stone, 'The anatomy of the Elizabethan aristocracy', *Economic History Review*, 18 (1948), 1–53.

42 J. P. Cooper, 'The counting of manors', *Economic History Review*, 2nd series, 8 (1956), 377–89; H. R. Trevor Roper, 'The Elizabethan aristocracy: an anatomy anatomized', *Economic History Review*, 2nd series, 3 (1951), 279–98, and *The gentry, 1540–1640* (*Economic History Review* Supplement, no. 1, 1953).

43 J. H. Hexter, *Reappraisals in history* (London, 1961), xiv.

44 *Ibid.*, xvii–xix, 14–25, 140–9; on Pym now see the authoritative treatment by Conrad Russell in the *ODNB*.

45 *Historical Journal*, 5 (1962), 80–92.

46 J. H. Hexter, *On historians* (London, 1979), 227–51; D. Brunton and D. Pennington, *Members of the long parliament* (Cambridge, 1954).

47 Russell, *The origins of the English civil war*, 4–8.

48 F. M. L. Thompson, 'The social distribution of landed property since the sixteenth century', *Economic History Review*, 2nd series, 19 (1966), 505–17; J. P. Cooper, 'The social distribution of land and men in England, 1436–1700', *Economic History Review*, 2nd series, 20 (1967), 419–40; G. E. Mingay, *The gentry* (Harlow, 1976), 57–61; C. G. A. Clay, *Economic expansion and social change: England, 1500–1700*, 2 vols (Cambridge, 1984), i. 143.

49 P. Cos, 'Bastard feudalism revisited', *Past and Present*, 125 (1989), 27–64, and 'The formation of the English gentry', *Past and Present*, 147 (1995), 38–64.

50 L. Stone (ed.), *The university in society* (Princeton, NJ, 1974).

51 For a valuable overview, see F. Heal and C. Holmes, *The gentry in England and Wales 1500–1700* (Basingstoke, 1994).

52 Russell, *Unrevolutionary England*, 31–57.

53 G. R. Elton, *Studies in Tudor and Stuart politics and government*, 3 vols (Cambridge, 1974–92), ii. 155–89; K. Sharpe, *Faction and parliament* (Oxford, 1978).

54 Russell, *The origins of the English civil war*, 3–4.

55 W. Notestein, 'The winning of the initiative by the House of Commons', in Sutherland (ed.), *Studies in history*, 145–203.

56 S. Lambert, 'Procedure in the House of Commons in the early Stuart period', *English Historical Review*, 95 (1980), 753–81; Russell, *Unrevolutionary England*, 33–4; Sharpe, *Faction and parliament*, 1–2.

57 Gardiner, *Constitutional documents*, 83–4, 93–5.

58 E. R. Foster (ed.), *Proceedings in parliament, 1610*, 2 vols (New Haven, CT, 1966), i. 276, 278–9; W. Notestein, *The House of Commons, 1604–1610* (New Haven, CT, 1971), 460–1.

59 In this connexion historians often cite *A discourse concerning puritans* (1641) by Henry Parker, but it is not clear that Parker wanted to deny the link between politics and religion: C. Hill, *Society and puritanism in pre-revolutionary England* (London, 1964), 20–1.

60 C. Russell, *Parliaments and English politics, 1621–1629* (Oxford, 1979), 25–32; G. Burgess, *The politics of the ancient constitution: an introduction to English political thought, 1603–1642* (Basingstoke, 1992), 170 and generally.

61 T. Hartley (ed.), *Proceedings in the parliaments of Elizabeth I*, 3 vols (Leicester, 1981–95), iii. 32, 34, 37–8; P. W. Hasler (ed.), *The history of parliament: the House of Commons, 1558–1603*, 3 vols (1981), iii. 99; W. S. McKechnie, *Magna Carta* (Glasgow, 1905), 436; J. Guy (ed.), *The reign of Elizabeth I: court and culture in the last decade* (Cambridge, 1995), 132, 136–8; F. Thompson, *Magna Carta: its role in the making of the English constitution* (Minnesota, MN, 1948), 197–230.

62 R. G. Usher, *The rise and fall of the high commission* (Oxford, 1913, repr. 1968), 170–9; *The English reports*, 74 (1907), 1135, 1137–8; Foster, *Proceedings in parliament, 1610*, ii. 153, 159–162; McKechnie, *Magna Carta*, 436, 464; *ODNB*, entry for: Fuller, Nicholas (d. 1620). Already by 1610, however, there is evidence of a backlash against Magna Carta, by those seeking to bolster the powers of the monarchy: Foster, *Proceedings in parliament, 1610*, ii. 190.

63 Hartley, *Proceedings in the parliaments of Elizabeth I*, ii. 320–1.

64 R. Cust, *The forced loan and English politics, 1626–1628* (Oxford, 1987), 66–7, 176–9. I am indebted to Richard Cust for advice concerning Scott.

65 Guy, *The reign of Elizabeth I*, 11–12, 127–49; P. Lake, *Anglicans and puritans? Presbyterianism and English conformist thought from Whitgift to Hooker* (London, 1988), 135–9.

66 Cust, *Forced loan*, 170–2, 220–1; J. P. Kenyon (ed.), *The Stuart constitution*, 2nd edn (Cambridge, 1986), 69–70; A. P. Newton, *The colonizing activities of the English puritans* (New Haven, CT, 1914); T. B. Howell (ed.), *A complete collection of state trials* (1816), 982–3, 1130; McKechnie, *Magna Carta*, 274, 436.

67 Usher, *Rise and fall of the high commission*, 180–221.

68 *The selected writings of Sir Edward Coke*, ed. S. Sheppard, 3 vols (Indianapolis, IN, 2003), ii. 523–54.

69 Pocock, *Ancient constitution*, 30–69; J. P. Sommerville, *Royalists and patriots: politics and ideology in England 1603–1642* (Harlow, 1999), 81–104; S. D. White, *Sir Edward Coke and 'the grievances of the commonwealth', 1621–1628* (Chapel Hill, NC, 1979); Sheppard (ed.) *Coke*, ii. 851–2, 876; *The journal of Sir Simonds D'Ewes*, ed. W. Notestein (New Haven, CT, 1923), 108–10, 118, 174, 330, 358. The relationship of Coke to puritanism was complex, but his most recent biographer, Allen Boyer, comes close to portraying him as a fellow traveller: *ODNB*, entry for: Coke, Sir Edward.

70 Russell, *Unrevolutionary England*, 231–51; J. Morrill, *The nature of the English revolution* (Harlow, 1993), 91–117.

71 C. Cross, *The royal supremacy in the Elizabethan church* (London, 1969), 51–2; A. MacDonald, *The Jacobean kirk, 1567–1625* (Aldershot, 1998); J. Goodare, *State and society in early-modern Scotland* (Oxford, 1999), 172–213; A. MacInnes, *Charles I and the making of the covenanting movement, 1625–1648* (Edinburgh, 1991), 186–9.

72 D. Stevenson, *The Scottish revolution, 1637–44: the triumph of the Covenanters* (Newton Abbot, 1973), 194; R. Mitchison, *Lordship to patronage; Scotland, 1603–1745* (London, 1983); J. Goodare, 'The admission of the lairds to the Scottish parliament', *English Historical Review*, 116 (2001), 1103–33.

73 J. Goodare, 'The nobility and the absolutist state in Scotland, 1584–1638', *History*, 78 (1993), 161–2; K. Brown, 'Aristocratic finances and the origins of the Scottish revolution', *English Historical Review*, 54 (1989), 46–87.

74 Russell, *Origins of the English civil war*, 31, 97; see also Russell, *Unrevolutionary England*, 47.

75 J. Brewer, *The sinews of power: war, money and the English state, 1688–1783* (London, 1989), 1–24; M. J. Braddick, *The nerves of state: taxation and the financing of the English state, 1558–1714* (Manchester, 1996), 1–20; Russell, *Origins of the English civil war*, 31.

76 T. Fuller (ed.), *Ephemeris parliamentaria* (1654), sig. 4.

77 J. Guy, *Tudor England* (Oxford, 1988, pbk 1990), 398–403; J. E. Neale, *Elizabeth I and her parliaments, 1584–1601* (London, 1957), 376–93.

78 W. H. Price, *The English patents of monopoly* (Boston, MA, 1906), 1–24 ; J. Thirsk, *Economic policy and projects: the development of a consumer society in early modern England* (Oxford, 1978), 51–105; G. Unwin, *The gilds and companies of London*, 4th edn (London, 1963), 257–8, 293–328.

79 *CPR, 1584–5*, 56; *CPR, 1585–6*, 59; BL, Lansdowne MS 47, fo. 190, MS 50, fo. 41.

80 *CSPD, 1591–4*, 187; BL, Lansdowne MS 74, fos 8, 16v.

81 CLRO, *Remembrancia*, i. nos 632, 651; BL, Lansdowne MS 73, fo. 55.

82 BL, Lansdowne MS 74, fos 118, 134v, 137.

83 CLRO, *Remembrancia*, ii. no. 84.

84 I. Archer, 'The London lobbies in the later sixteenth century', *Historical Journal*, 31 (1988), 31–4; CLRO, *Remembrancia*, ii. no. 142.

85 S. D'Ewes (ed.), *The journals of all the parliaments during the reign of Queen Elizabeth* (1682), 554; Hasler, *House of Commons*, i. 385, iii. 621; *ODNB*, entry for: Hastings, Sir Francis. The other two speakers were Francis Moore and Robert Wingfield.

86 Hartley, *Proceedings in the parliaments of Elizabeth I*, iii. 374–7, 380–1, 388–90, 392, 396–9; Hasler, *House of Commons*, iii. 660. The four Middle Temple lawyers were Laurence Hyde, Richard Martin, Henry Montagu and Francis Moore.

87 Hartley, *Proceedings in the parliaments of Elizabeth I*, iii. 374. Darcy was apparently also a 'kinsman' of Raleigh, and 'fellow-tenant' of Durham House in London: *The letters of Sir Walter Raleigh*, ed. A. Latham and J. Youings (Exeter, 1999), 246 n. 5.

88 P. L. Hughes and J. F. Larkin (eds), *Tudor royal proclamations*, 3 vols (London, 1964–69), iii. 235–8; D. S. Davies, 'Further light on the case of monopolies', *Law Quarterly Review*, 48 (1932), 394–414.

89 Price, *Patents of monopoly*, 25–34; R. Zaller, *The parliament of 1621* (Berkeley, CA, 1971); *Commons debates, 1621*, ed. W. Notestein, F. H. Relf and H. Simpson, 7 vols (New Haven, CT, 1935), vii. 311–564 ; C. Tite, *Impeachment and parliamentary judicature in early Stuart England* (London, 1974), 86–110; J. F. Larkin and P. L. Hughes (eds), *Stuart royal proclamations*, 2 vols (Oxford, 1973–83), i. 513–14.

90 Price, *Patents of monopoly*, 35–46; *Journal of Sir Simonds D'Ewes*, 19–20; J. Rushworth, *Historical collections*, 8 vols (1721), iii. 1338.

91 C. H. Firth and R. S. Rait (eds), *Acts and ordinances of the interregnum, 1642–1660*, 3 vols (London, 1911), i. 277, 365.

92 My hope is, on another occasion, to investigate further the political implications of monopolies.

93 Russell, *Origins of the English civil war*, 116; H. C. Porter, *Reformation and reaction in Tudor Cambridge* (Cambridge, 1958), 344–90; N. Tyacke, *Anti-Calvinists: the rise of English Arminianism, c. 1590–1640* (Oxford, 1987, pbk 1990), 29–37.

94 N. Tyacke, *Aspects of English protestantism, c. 1530–1700* (Manchester, 2001), 111–31.

95 This is not, of course, to deny the importance of municipal corporations in fostering puritanism, although such bodies were more vulnerable to government pressure.

96 Russell, *Unrevolutionary England*, 207, n. 10; Tyacke, *Aspects of English protestantism*, 20, 66–7.

97 N. Tyacke, 'Puritan politicians and King James VI and I, 1587–1604', in T. Cogswell, R. Cust and P. Lake (eds), *Politics, religion and popularity in early Stuart Britain: essays in honour of Conrad Russell* (Cambridge, 2002), 36–44; Elton, *Studies in Tudor and Stuart politics and government*, ii. 172.

98 HMC, *Salisbury*, xxiii. 152.

99 P. Croft, 'The debate on annual parliaments in the early seventeenth century', *Parliaments, Estates and Representative Institutions*, 16 (1996), 163–74; D. Hirst, *The representative of the people? Voters and voting under the early Stuarts* (Cambridge, 1975), 44–89, 195–212.

100 See pp. 51, 56 below.

101 See p. 64 below.

102 See p. 90 below.

103 See pp. 27–8, 95, 103 below.

104 J. F. McGregor and B. Reay (eds), *Radical religion in the English revolution* (Oxford, 1984), 65–90; M. Tolmie, *The triumph of the saints: the separate churches of London, 1616–1649* (Cambridge, 1977), 144–72.

105 *Eikon basilike* (1648), 17–25, 247.

106 Kenyon, *Stuart constitution*, 348.

107 P. Seaward, *The Cavalier parliament and the reconstruction of the old regime, 1661–1667* (Cambridge, 1989), 23, 133–4; see above.

108 See 141–3, 169–71, 195 below.

109 M. Knights, *Representation and misrepresentation in later Stuart Britain: partisanship and political culture* (Oxford, 2005), 9 and dust jacket.

110 D. Cressy, *England on edge: crisis and revolution, 1640–1642* (Oxford, 2006).

2

The English Revolution and its legacies[1]

THE 2004 NEALE LECTURE

Michael J. Braddick

It is a familiar thought that the civil war was really a process of armed negotiation and that this negotiation took place in a larger public context than was usual
for seventeenth-century political life. The sustained public argument to which this
gave rise is revealing of some of the central elements of English political culture; that is, the vocabulary of images, metaphors, rituals, assumptions and
performances through which political life was understood, together with the
grammar which governed the use of that vocabulary. But this book is concerned
also with the transformative effect of the crisis of the 1640s. Political cultures, like
languages, are not static and the rules are not usually consciously invoked. We
learn our native grammar through use, and in using our language we change it: new
grammatical conventions become recognised and new vocabularies develop in order
to comprehend and communicate new realities.[2] By making manifest contradictions between common-sense assumptions, and between forms of argument that
had previously seemed unproblematical, the polemical battles of the 1640s led to
innovative uses of standard forms of argument – and to innovative arguments.
This had real implications for the ways that contemporaries understood, and therefore created, their political world. In this chapter I offer a brief exploration of
these issues, considering how the experience of civil war and revolution might
be seen as revealing of contemporary political culture; and, secondly, of how we
might set about examining the transformative effects of this crisis.[3]

The study of this political culture, and of its transformation, offers rich possibilities for a more integrative approach to the history of the English Revolution.
It also offers new possibilities for accounts of its legacies because the processes
which led to the public revelation of that political culture led also to its transformation. Of course, there is much more to this political culture than print, and
a fuller study of the issues would explore the resonance of these discourses
in other areas: for example, in the demonstrative actions of soldiers, crowds and
iconoclasts.[4] But even a cursory review of the debate in print reveals attempts
to render complex events comprehensible in terms of existing political forms
and to find new legitimations for extraordinary circumstances by shifting the

grammar or vocabulary of political culture. This pressure to find new forms of expression reflected the deeper problem that lay behind the polemic: how to establish the truth of any particular proposition. This crisis of authority had profound implications for the legitimation of all sorts of social and political arrangements; it constituted, in other words, a legitimation crisis.

Working on the three generations prior to the war, Lake and Questier have re-read murder pamphlets, sermons, plays and last dying speeches as a series of performances, archetypes and narratives, accessible to a wide cross-section of contemporary society, through which polemical battles could be fought out.[5] In this sense they are drawing attention to the ways in which common cultural assumptions, values and performances could be deployed for the purposes of political polemic. What was true of Elizabethan and Jacobean England was certainly true of England in the 1640s, with its luxuriant print culture, armies, the widely reported crowd actions and, for example, very public political executions.

If Lake and Questier draw our attention to the deployment of these cultural resources for polemical purposes, their work is complemented for the 1640s by a growing number of studies of how polemic could be deployed for local purposes. Hughes's work stands as the acme of a particular form of post-revisionism in relationship to 'localism' the pursuit of local goals and the defence of local interests was not, necessarily, without ideological purpose or significance; neither was it separate from national politics.[6] National issues were experienced as local controversies; local controversies acquired meaning in the light of national debate. This strand of writing can now be placed in a much wider social context. Studies by Walter and Wood demonstrate how the national conflict, and national polemical battles, could acquire a considerable local resonance, and, in particular, how they could resonate with groups outside those traditionally considered to constitute the political nation.[7] The resonance of national politics is evident not simply in representations, therefore, but in actions; and where the armies came from is no longer as puzzling a question as it may once have been.[8] That peasants could live through the 1640s in bucolic innocence until they bumbled on to the field of battle, unaware that there was a war on, is unthinkable – the material costs of the wars in taxes, lives and property were so great that they must have attracted the attention of even the most thick-skinned contemporaries.

If we concentrate on the issue of representation, however, it becomes immediately clear that the ephemeral print of the 1640s provides an opportunity to observe quite closely the deployment of standard tropes, or narrative forms, for current polemical purposes. The literature of monstrosity, for example, spoke of the ills of the body politic; that of *gangraena* spoke to an equally prominent line of polemic about the significance of religious sectarianism. These concerns nested closely with patriarchal anxieties – ecstatic prophecy was of no less concern than the threat of mob rule. The dangers of uppity women and unbridled spirits were constantly represented in inversionary terms. Providentialism, another staple element of contemporary thought, provided the means to make sense of civil and religious babel.

Anti-popery, already an elastic term, was made to embrace ever-wider areas of religious practice, both Catholic and protestant.

The print and well-documented performances of the 1640s do not just provide a window on to the experience of the war and revolution, however: they were parts of the process itself. Ephemeral publications were time-sensitive – their impact depended not on their generic form or the effectiveness of their execution, but on the skill with which they deployed or subverted generic conventions for current political purposes. The need to represent political positions to a wider audience was, of course, a source of anxiety in itself, and the king's answer to the petition accompanying the Grand Remonstrance expresses some unease at the necessity of discussing the *arcana imperii* before a print audience.[9] At the same time, however, the royalists also played this game. In captivity, in 1647, Charles turned once more to the cure of scrofula and, later in the year, apparently approved plans for a new royal palace constructed on a particularly grand scale.[10] With his eyes on the larger prize, and despite the apparent bleakness of his bargaining position, Charles had a clear sense of the performative requirements of a refurbished regality.

The ritual and symbolic language of political polemic was widely understood and, we can presume, widely available. We are very familiar with religious iconoclasm and increasingly aware of the precision with which iconoclastic acts were calculated.[11] Less familiar, but no less important, are the forms of secular iconoclasm which created such good copy for the writers of ephemeral polemic. Recent work by Beaver has recovered the cultural context of attacks on deer parks, which can be understood as quite precise attacks on the claims of particular individuals to genteel status or local authority.[12] Thomas Edwards reported that after the battle of Naseby social inferiors had become bold, denying the gestures of respect that they owed to their superiors.[13] Whatever the truth of the claim, its power to shock (surely Edwards's purpose) reveals how small gestures might signify big politics. Certainly the refusal of hat honour by Quakers and others made a point clearly understood by contemporaries. These transgressions of the rituals and representation of authority and hierarchy surely affected the way in which vulgar invasions of country houses were interpreted. We are accustomed to reading houses as expressions of authority, the disposition of internal space and access to it as a carefully choreographed statement about order and obedience. Lurid tales of invasions by the vulgar built on the symbolic value of these transgressions.[14]

Many authors during the 1640s sought to understand their condition in a historical frame. Very commonly this was a Christian history, leading towards a defined apocalyptic end which may, or may not, be redemptive. Within this Christian framework it was possible to discern movement towards that end, or signs of God's pleasure or displeasure with the course of human affairs. Rival histories of this kind lay close to the heart of the crisis opened up by the Prayer Book rebellion in Scotland. For example, when parliament met it did not display the kind of unconditional loyalty that might have been expected in the face of rebellion and invasion. Instead Charles was confronted by disagreement over what, in this Christian history, his English Church represented, how it related to that in Scotland, and what the future held for the true religion. His opponents argued that rather than leading his Scottish subjects towards a condition of greater purity he was opening the gates to a reintroduction of popery or, at least, allowing them to be opened. This interpretation of the ecclesiastical policies of the 1630s became yoked to a larger fear about the future of protestantism, which was apparently under threat across Europe. Hopes that the English Church could be saved, on the other hand, became identified with hopes for the salvation of the true religion across the whole of Europe. Commitment to reform was therefore intimately connected to fear for the future, informed by the experience of the recent past; and that vision was most clearly articulated in theories about a popish plot to subvert protestantism everywhere.[15]

The rhetoric of anti-popery was pervasive in this crisis because it was a means by which to establish the identity and boundaries of protestantism. According to its adherents, the English protestant church had been recovered rather than founded: Reformation politics was driven not by a desire to establish a new church but by the urgent need to purify an old one. Unfortunately there was no unambiguous agreement about what a restored church would look like it, but it was clear to many protestants that the principal enemy of that restoration was the bishop of Rome. Polemic about the nature of the true church, or of its opponents, was therefore often couched in terms of opposition to popery, an almost unobjectionable sentiment. The language of popery, by the same token, was used to mark the boundaries of acceptable belief and practice.[16] However, in this as in so many arguments, the anti-christ was in the detail: exactly which elements of inherited practice and belief were legitimate within a properly reformed church? Not only were views of the church inherently historicised, therefore, but that history was frequently glossed in terms of an apocalyptic battle with the many agencies of popery.

Popery was not simply an external threat, therefore, but might also originate in the weakness and fallibility of fellow protestants, even a king and particularly an archbishop. Nonetheless, scare-mongering about the machinations of Jesuits and other agents of international popery was very prominent in the public discourse of 1640–42, and clearly had local resonance.[17] It was met by an alternative conspiracy theory, that those promoting further protestant reform were populists intent on the subversion of the Anglican Church and of the crown. Pulled between these two conspiracy theories, both equally frightening, many were no doubt immobilised. Activists, on the other hand, escalated the rhetorical stakes to the point where a war became possible.[18] The claim that social, political and religious authority were necessarily bound together in the maintenance of political order was profoundly shaken in the 1640s, as individuals sought to identify their dissent from convention with only one of those three areas. In particular, the destructiveness of this crisis for convention lay in the explicit separation and relative prioritisation of religious and political duties.

These rival histories were stated with increasing stridency and increasingly openly. This dissonance, and the political rupture that it reflected, had profound implications for some important elements of public discourse in early Stuart England. Influential Erastian visions of the relationship between church and state, and commonly invoked organicist metaphors for the relationship between social, political and religious order, were undermined. Since those forms of argument were widely circulated by the institutions of church and state, this dissonance had immediate local significance. For example, in Holt, Cheshire, in 1638 a godly householder named Alexander Powell turned away a beggar from his house, saying: 'No sirrah you shall have no Almes here for shortly you wilbe prest to war, and then you will fight ag[ains]t us.' Soldiers were about to be pressed in the northwest to fight against the Scots, and when the press was used it was exactly such men who were vulnerable: it was not unlikely that this man was on the verge of being pressed into service against the Covenanters. Powell seems, then, to have been asserting the importance of a religious affiliation with the Scots over obligations to his ungodly but vulnerable neighbours.[19] Events made the balancing of potentially conflicting obligations increasingly difficult, and the separation of spheres of political discussion unsustainable. Local affairs – communal relations, administrative commitments – could certainly be represented and understood within a much larger framework.

Another important component of the crisis was the failure to find politically acceptable means by which to raise money and men. Parliaments had not delivered in the 1620s; the royal prerogative had been perhaps more functionally effective during the 1630s, but at a very significant political cost.[20] That cost too was paid in the first year of the Long Parliament. Attacks on the prerogative swept away courts held responsible for threats to liberty and property, in a remarkable transformation of the state, which was never reversed. An unintended consequence of those victories, however, was the collapse of censorship, and it was never really successfully reimposed, despite the best efforts of subsequent regimes. The immediate consequence of this was a transformation of the English publishing industry, manifest in an explosion in the number of titles being produced from a rapidly increasing number of presses. This represented a substantial challenge to contemporary notions of political propriety: secrecy was seen as essential to good government in Stuart England and Charles I had been keen to preserve the *arcana imperii* from the public gaze. Now, however reluctantly, he was forced to publicise his views, in a snow-storm of declarations and counter-declarations relating to his arguments with the Covenanters and with his English parliament.

In those conditions, unfamiliar to say the least, political actors laid claim to existing legitimations to justify their actions, but they did so in ways that became controversial, incomprehensible or straightforwardly incredible. Resistance to Charles's policies, for example, was couched in terms of loyalty to the monarch, even when that entailed raising an army through parliament but without the king's consent. Opponents claimed that they were protecting Charles from his evil advisers, from himself – or, eventually, protecting the office from its present incumbent. Treason was reinterpreted creatively to embrace advising the king wrongly, surrendering a city to the royal army (an unsuccessful prosecution that one) and, eventually, to kill the king himself. Political battles were fought out on the scaffolds, where these novel claims were asserted and resisted. 'Strained readings' is a polite term for the often bizarre, incomprehensible or incredible uses to which standard terms were put.

Unsurprisingly this was a great age of satire but there was also a very evident desire to uncover the truth. Private letters were often published in order to reveal underlying truths; cabinets were opened, plots discovered and *true* news was repeatedly broadcast.[21] A desire to penetrate the underlying purposes of actors, or the fundamental meaning of their actions, was ubiquitous. So, too, was the desire to know what really was going on. John Castle, newsletter writer to the earl of Bridgewater in 1640 and 1641, was scrupulous about identifying and weighing sources, advertising particular reports as 'likely to be true', distinguishing between rumour, report and news in complex ways. Nonetheless, Bridgewater was unsure what to believe, and on 4 August 1640, for example, he wrote to Castle that although 'the various reportes of the Newes of this Time be such that noe great Creditt be to be geven to the Rumours spread abroade' he would make use of them, 'though I doe not purpose to make them all to be parte of my creed'.[22]

The birth of the newsbook seems to have accentuated rather than alleviated this uncertainty about truth-telling. The services of a man like Castle may have cost around £20 per annum for, perhaps, three letters every two weeks.[23] A little over a year later one penny bought 5,000 words of news each week; if the market had provided them Bridgewater could have had 4,800 titles (more than 90 each week) for his £20, but he may have felt that he knew less as a result. More important than the potential banquet that this provided for Bridgewater, readers who could not possibly have enjoyed the services of a newsletter-writer could, for less than one-ninetieth of the price, have a weekly newsletter which was fuller and not necessarily less well informed than a professional letter-writer of the 1630s. But which was one to believe? Newspapers proclaimed from the bookstalls their bona fides: *The kingdomes weekly intelligencer: sent abroad to prevent misinformation*; *Mercurius civicus: Londons intelligencer as truth impartially related from thence to the kingdome to prevent mis-information*; *The moderate: impartially communicating martial affaires to the kingdom*; or the *Mercurius anti-mercurius*, which claimed to be '*communicating all humours, conditions, forgeries and lies of mydas eared newsmongers*'.

Contemporary chronicling was unashamedly polemical, and its politics were often quite complex. For example, Josiah Ricraft's account *England's champions*, written towards the end of hostilities, reviewed the military history of parliament's campaigns from a shamelessly partisan angle. His purpose was to promote the reputation of those within the parliamentary coalition who were, in his view, faithful to the Solemn League and Covenant. His account therefore rested on a clear view of which programme of political and religious reform God had favoured by delivering victories in battle. In seeking to establish his political and religious case

Ricraft wrote a military history in which the heroes were Leslie, Manchester and Essex; 18 senior commanders were celebrated individually, a further 27 given an important supporting role. Oliver Cromwell does not merit individual treatment and he appears in the chronology of parliament's military history only for his victory at Stamford and his seizure of Basing House in 1645. According to Ricraft the truth about the second battle of Newbury, so controversial among members of the parliamentary coalition, was simple: Manchester, 'this noble Generall utterly routed [the royalists]'.[24]

Actions in the present were located with reference to the larger historical canvass, and this often implied a predictive claim. Contemporary commentators frequently placed English history in the context of developments in Europe as a whole; indeed the lessons of history were often those relating to the whole Christian community, and many newsbooks carried European news. The newsbooks also pilloried strained readings of the standard terms of contemporary political discourse. Bruno Ryves, for example, reporting on the actions of parliamentarian soldiers, crowds and religious radicals, juxtaposed their behaviour with their claim to be acting to preserve religion and liberty. Political conflict in the 1640s was, in that sense, a battle over key words: treason, honour, allegiance, reformation, custom, popery, law. Elsewhere in Europe, an active response to this indeterminacy of meaning was to seek a new and transparent language that did not occlude people's access to key ideas. In Spinoza this was a disdain for the 'language of men', in Descartes an aspiration for a mathematical philosophy and in Hobbes a careful definition of terms. Many reformers were attracted to the study of Chinese and Arabic: Chinese was attractive as a pictographic language, which communicated ideas, not sounds, and which was comprehensible to those whose spoken languages were quite different; Arabic, while not pictographic, was also a written language shared by people whose spoken languages were quite different. Ricraft, in fact, may have shared this interest.[25]

One of the texts published by Ryves in 1647 was the *Micro-chronicon*, a narrative of the battles of the civil war akin to that published by Ricraft. In this case, however, the text originated with George Wharton, on whose earlier publication Ryves's version clearly rested. Wharton is better known, however, as the royalist astrologer, a man who saw in these events the consequences of the secondary causes of God's will. The 1640s was in fact the first golden age of English astrology and Wharton was the main opposition to the decade's publishing sensation, William Lilly. The search for signs, in the natural world, of God's purpose took many other forms. Prophecies were recounted with relish and may have affected events: Castle informed Bridgewater in 1640 that Scottish soldiers invading northern England were heartened and confident of victory because of a Latin prophecy of Merlin that had been translated into Scots and was circulating among them.[26]

There was also a minor boom in monster and prodigy pamphlets. Almost everyone could agree that events in the natural world might be read as signs of God's attitude towards human affairs. Numerous providentialist texts sought to attribute human and natural events directly to the will of God, as a means both of lending meaning to the present and of providing a guide to action in the future. These stories were told about individuals and kingdoms – the misfortunes of others may be made to serve as a guide to action for those who came after them – and they made a connection between the local, the national and the cosmic. The language of providence, and of monstrosity and wonders, was ubiquitous and certainly extended far beyond the pamphlets specifically reporting such wonders. But if God's judgements were evident, the identity of the culprit and the nature of the sin were far less so, and in reporting the signs of God's will in this world there was a double problem: to establish the truth of the phenomena and then to come uncontested interpretations of their meaning.

This was as true of reports of battles as it was of reports of giant toad fish like the one caught at Woolwich and displayed at Glove Alley, London, in 1642. Its appearance was attested by many witnesses, among them gentlemen, and that it meant something was attested by classical sources, including Pliny and Josephus, as well as more contemporary examples: large fish coming ashore had meant, throughout history, trouble for reigning monarchs. 'These unnaturall accidents[,] though dumbe, do notwithstanding speake the supernaturall intentions and purposes of the Divine powers, chiefly when they meete just at that time when distractions, jars, and distempers are a foote in a Common-weale or Kingcome [sic].' Again: 'It is further observed by those that professe skill in Prognostication, that of how much the monster is of feature or fashion, hatefull and odious, so much it portends danger the more dreadfull and universall.' The second part of the pamphlet was an ostensibly factual report of military developments in England and abroad. It was printed for Natthaniel Butter, better known to posterity as one of the founding fathers of the English press: a newspaper pioneer.[27] News was partisan, and reports of human and natural events were of equal value in coming to terms with the times.

But this literature, too, was open to satire. Earlier in 1642 a marine monster was reported to have appeared to six sailors near the mouth of the Thames. The monster 'was very terrible; having broad fiery eyes, haire blacke and curled, his brest armed with shining skales, so that by the reflection of the Sunne they became so blinde and dazled, that hee might have taken or slaine every man of them, he having a musket in one hand, and a large paper in the other, which seemed to them a Petition'. Able to travel at miraculous speeds the monster moved away from the sailors to observe the French fleet on its way to Catalonia, returning within minutes with news of it. In discussion with the amazed sailors the monster emphasised to them the dangers faced by the kingdom, a clear warning about the consequences of divisions. Appended was a report of a minor victory in Ireland, a providence of God and an encouragement to the protestants. The six sailors were named, and the story was said to have been taken down by a gentleman – a contemporary code for the reliability of the testimony. The names of the witnesses, however, suggest a satirical intent.[28]

That human and natural events bore meaning was uncontested; how to decipher that meaning was much more controversial because the particular readings were hotly contested. In fact there were conventional means by which authors sought to establish the authenticity of their accounts and the trustworthiness of their readings: reliable testimony, detailed observation, cataloguing, classifying, vindications and animadversions. At this distance in time, however, it is difficult not to feel that they protested too much: England's print culture was full of certainties, but there was a premium on fundamental truths.

Perhaps the most profound element of this crisis of authority was the collapse of spiritual authority. The appeal to scripture for quite contrary purposes is easy to document. The injunction in Psalm 105.15, for example, 'Touch not mine anointed and do my prophets no harm', became unstable in its meaning. The royalists claimed, on the basis of long practice, that the king was God's anointed, and that this clearly ruled out the possibility of legitimate resistance. Prynne argued that the anointed were all God's chosen ones, and that the injunction was directed at kings – more than a counter-blast, since it in fact indicted Charles of already having breached the injunction.[29] A veritable babel of conflicting inter-pretations emerged, which was intimately connected to the debate about church government, since religious sects claimed spiritual warrant for their practices from either scripture or personal revelation, with varying degrees of independence or control. On the other hand, religious pluralism was denounced in terms of well-established idioms – as a disease or a rupture in the divine order – but exactly which forms of belief were pathogens, or threatened the organic moral order? There seemed to be no agreement as to how to answer this question. Those who took on these questions seemed to Milton, and presumably to others, to be 'in wandering mazes lost'. Many polemicists, rather than reasoning high 'Of providence, foreknowledge, will and fate, /Fixed fate, free will, foreknowledge absolute',[30] simply cut to the chase: the boundaries of acceptable belief could surely be established on the basis of the behavioural consequences of a prophet's teaching, rather than on the basis of scripture or authority. If there was a definitive text here it was Matthew 7.20: 'by their fruits shall ye know them'. False prophets led the flock to sin.[31] In some cases this led those so accused to deny the reality of sin, but this was probably a minority view, held only for a short time. Antinomianism seems to have been, for those who genuinely embraced it, a youthful enthusiasm rather than a lifetime commitment. But the terrible truth was that this emphasis on fruits conceded the real problem – explicit reference to scripture, tradition or authority could not settle these disputes, and there was no agreement about what could.

Another response to the sectarian scare was taxonomical, and these taxo-nomies were also, frequently, historical in content, equating current errors with others in Christian history.[32] This process of numbering and taxonomising both captured the escalating threat and promised, by labelling and counting, to contain it. Ephraim Pagitt's *Heresiography* of 1645 promised a *Description of the heretickes and sectaries of these latter times*: numbering and historicising at the same time. Thomas Edwards's more famous work in this genre combined cataloguing with denunciation in terms of established organic metaphors: *Gangraena* was an examination of the monstrous and diseased in the body politic. It rested on 'credible report' to verify the claims about behaviour and belief, in order to confirm the imperative need to re-establish religious and political order.[33]

Political cultures are probably best understood as 'common-sense systems'. Certainly, early Stuart political culture was not a coherent philosophical system but, rather, 'a relatively organised body of considered thought' consisting of heterogeneous, unsystematic, 'down-to-earth, colloquial wisdom', something more than 'mere matter-of-fact apprehension of reality', but something less than a fully coherent, consciously articulated worldview.[34] The crisis during the 1640s made plain some of the contradictions and lack of clarity in this system: for example, between law, custom, providence, prerogative, scripture and reason as sources of authority. Public debate during the 1640s had exposed fundamental elements of political culture to sustained critical observation; and that public debate was far less socially bounded than was considered decent prior to 1640. This, in itself, had dangerous implications.

The crisis was remarkable not for the novelty of these problems, but for the depth and extent of their public discussion, the urgency with which they imposed themselves and the radicalism of some responses to them. An earlier historiography gave great prominence to this radicalism, for example in accounts of the Levellers, Diggers and Ranters, or of the fillip given to English Baconianism by intellectual activity during the 1640s. This almost certainly exaggerated the significance of such radical thinking, if significance is measured in quantitative terms: it seems likely that most people were not radicals or Baconians. On the other hand, the convention of taking the story only as far as 1660 implicitly accepts that the essence of the Revolution lay in the institutional measures taken after the regicide: with the failure of kingless constitutions this Revolution can be said to have failed. However, the splintering of English protestantism and the widening of the public sphere had profound implications for authority in the most general sense. It is not possible to trace the effects of this comprehensively, not least because they changed with successive reinventions of the crisis and because they extended across the globe.[35] But we can begin the more limited task of tracing the legacies of this crisis in England during the second half of the seventeenth century in the history of two kinds of political order: the state and the parish community.

There is an institutional story to be told about the effects of political crisis on the development of the state: of functional failure, political crisis and institutional recovery. Prior to 1640 the English state, more or less capable of keeping a lid on social conflict to the satisfaction of elite expectations, was not equal to the more challenging task of establishing religious uniformity and was chronically unable to muster the financial and military resources to defend its territory. Its collapse in the face of the Covenanter movement set loose a political crisis that led to the disintegration of monarchical power and civil war. In the course of fighting the war new military and financial institutions were established which were of lasting significance to the capacity of the state. But this new Leviathan rested on unprecedented organisational complexities and called into being specialised, differentiated offices, tenure of which depended to a greater extent on expertise than on lineage. While the regulation of social order in the localities continued to rest on the shoulders of the county, borough and village elites, their control of the financial and military institutions of the state was loosened. After 1660 the desire to establish protestant uniformity, or conformity, within a national church was acutely felt by those who were shocked by the experience of sectarianism during the civil war and the Interregnum. That impulse, however, was gradually defeated by the resilience of dissent, and the religious practices prescribed by the 'confessional state' took their place amid a penumbra of forms of licensed dissent.[36]

Behind this story of institutional change lies another, deeper story of the successful legitimation of political action. The failures of the early Stuart state were not simply a matter of structural weakness if by that we intend to suggest that they were not political. Acts of state were acts of persuasion, attempts to secure practical ends through appeal to larger legitimating ideas – politics was in that sense part of the functioning of the state and, therefore, of its construction.[37] We might go even further and suggest that it was in part through the contested actions of the state that political culture was expressed and changed.

Although the discursive repertoire of political actors had changed, some forms of legitimation persisted, because they worked; others developed which seemed to offer more persuasive reasons to obey particular practical commands. Forms of patriarchy continued to provide compelling explanations of the basis of relations between rich and poor, old and young, men and women. In other areas new legitimations took root. For example, it is now a familiar thought that the material costs of the fighting drove the roots of political argument deep: the middling sort of Warwickshire, seeking to mobilise for war, or to resist the costs of that mobilisation, laid claim to the languages of necessity that are seen by historians of political thought as component parts of the modern state.[38] As a currency of legitimation their value lay in their capacity to persuade. They became crucial to the legitimation of the new institutions of the fiscal–military state, increasingly replacing a now devalued idiom of service.

The political thinkers of the new canon did not start with the golden chain and religious decency. Hobbes, like Locke, sought certainty not in divine truth but in a counter-factual, a thought-experiment about the state of nature and the natural state of man. In a sense their accounts of politics were based on arguments about the individual rather than about the good society, and the problem of political life was to reconcile the interests of these individual people. Harrington, on Jonathan Scott's reading, was also concerned to establish order from competing individuals and many other less secular thinkers seem to have accepted that this was a central problem. Cheney Culpeper's hopes for the godly society, for example, lay in setting all consciences free from human constraint – if all men followed God's will for them then the millennium, by definition, would have arrived. In this view it was human authority in religious matters, rather than its opposite, that caused conflict. In fact, it may be that the politics of the

Restoration period was dominated not so much by Lockean thought as by the politics of priestcraft – if there was an individualism rampant, it centred on the conscience, not the will.[39] Nonetheless, the creation of order from the cacophony of competing individual interests seems to have been a very pressing problem for many post-Restoration thinkers. Other influential discourses survived, of course, but some in rather different forms. For example, the resilience of anti-popery seems to have rested on its extraordinary flexibility, allowing for the denunciation not just of Catholics but of many protestants too. Despite the many continuities, however, apologists for regality and episcopacy confronted greater challenges of persuasion than their early Stuart forebears. Contestation of their claims was more explicit and more public, and that made the hopes of restoring the world of Hooker look remote. A world of coffee houses and sects, and of partisan polemic, offered new sources of legitimacy and solidarity, not easily reconciled with early Stuart Aristotelianism and Erastianism.

In this story of state formation the 1640s occupies a crucial place because of the reconstitution of the legitimacy of the state and of the ways in which that legitimacy was asserted; and because of the growth of sectarianism and the implications that had for the national church. At an overarching level, that relates to the effects of the rapidly expanded public sphere of the 1640s and the splintering of English protestantism. In these senses the energies unleashed in the 1640s provided the dynamic for a long revolution, encompassing the exclusion crisis and the 'Glorious Revolution'; it is certainly difficult, for reasons made plain by Jonathan Scott, to envisage the latter without the former.[40]

We can also be sure that these things were felt at parish level. This suggests a second way of reading these legacies – through an examination of the transformation of community, the changing political culture of the parish. It is easy to make a case for the restoration of normality after 1660. The famous image of the Tichborne dole, which has become a regular feature of accounts of early modern patriarchalism, is a later seventeenth-century image, but the ideals which it communicates seem as applicable a century earlier.[41] In Rotherham, on 25 September 1664, Lionel Copley, a former moderate parliamentarian, made a graphic demonstration that the world had been turned right side up. He beat Richard Firth, put a bridle in his mouth and rode on his back for half an hour, kicking him to make him move; this was obviously a response to the Leveller claim that no man should be born with a saddle on his back, with others booted and spurred to ride astride him.[42] John Locke, often a hero of modernisation narratives, was wedded to, and indeed advanced, a patriarchalism recognisable to his great grandfather's generation. A social history primarily interested in material inequality, and its implications for social relations, places little emphasis on the transformative effects of the Revolution. There was material change, and winners and losers, but there was no long-term disjunction in the development of social structure. Indeed, the heat had gone out of the politics of subsistence and Restoration governments seem to have been more anxious about religious dissent than poverty and its consequences.

Anxiety about dissent suggests that other equally fundamental dimensions of social life may have been affected more radically, however. Prior to 1640 the ritual and symbolic repertoire around which communities had formed was centred on the church, which gave physical expression both to the community of Christian believers and to the status hierarchy from which it was harmoniously established. Of course, and as Beaver has shown, these things were contested in Elizabethan and early Stuart England, but the bitterness of conflict over the ritual cycle and the symbolic repertoire of community seems to have been much increased thereafter.[43] The splintered and contested local ritual and symbolic systems were supplemented, but not replaced, by the conscious construction in print of solidarity, the boundaries of respectability or of truth. During the 1640s partisan and sectarian solidarities were consciously fostered in communities of print and certainties were presented using its authority. Although the intensity of the polemics of the 1640s was not quickly to be matched, the possibility of extra-local partisan community, and the extra-local authority of printed communication, offered new sources of social solidarity and new resources for the making of social order which were of lasting significance.[44]

Tracing legacies in these ways is less determinative than the more traditional concern with institutional change, narrowly construed. Moreover, this approach to political culture and its discontents necessarily draws our attention to processes best understood in terms of continuous modulation rather than revolutionary and irreversible ruptures. The 1640s represents a particularly intense period of crisis, and one ripe with alternative and competing possibilities, but the English Revolution was not transformative of all aspects of political life, and the changes that it reflected and prompted were not determining for the subsequent epoch.

Despite these complexities, examination of the process of state formation and the politics of community clearly do offer means to explore some of the legacies of the English Revolution. The widening sphere of political discussion, the perceived widening of political participation and growth of sects combined to corrode still further organic views of the body politic and the social body of the unified Christian community. Challenges to these influential ideas created space for new forms of legitimacy and new political metaphors for a world grown more public and more plural. Of course, it is not clear how far these anxieties, so evident in print, reflected local realities or resonated in local disputes, although there are plenty of signs that they did. But we can begin to explore what had changed, and what contemporaries made of that change, by exploring the politics of the parish, the development of the public sphere and the consequences of religious division.

Notes

1 This is the text of the Neale lecture delivered in February 2004, intended as an introduction to the colloquium of the same title which followed. Much of the research for this paper I undertook while a Chase Securities Fellow at the Huntington Library. Earlier versions were delivered in the Centre for English Local History at the University of

Leicester, the European University Institute Florence and the early modern Britain seminar at Oxford University, and as my inaugural lecture in the University of Sheffield. I am grateful for the many helpful comments I received on those occasions and at the Neale Colloquium, and also to Karen Harvey and Sean Kelsey for discussing this material with me.

2 For fuller discussion of this approach to the study of political culture see M. J. Braddick, 'State formation and political culture in Elizabethan and Stuart England: microhistories and macro-historical change', in R. G. Asch and D. Freist (eds), *Staatsbildung als kultereller prozess* (Köln, 2005), 69–90.

3 An understanding of the political and military calculations of leading politicians clearly requires a British (and European context), but the effects of the war on English, Irish or Scottish political culture are separate historical questions, answered from a different body of source materials. For fuller discussion of the themes laid out in this chapter see M. J. Braddick, *God's fury, England's fire: England during the civil wars* (Manchester, forthcoming).

4 For this notion of 'resonance', see D. Wahrman, *The making of the modern self* (New Haven, CT, 2004), pp. xv–xvi; for the cultural and political significance of cheap print in the 1640s see J. Raymond, *Pamphlets and pamphleteering in early modern Britain* (Cambridge, 2003), and J. Peacey, *Politicians and pamphleteers* (Aldershot, 2004).

5 P. Lake and M. Questier, *The antichrist's lewd hat: protestants, papists and players in post-reformation England* (New Haven, CT, 2002).

6 A. Hughes, 'Militancy and localism: Warwickshire politics and Westminster politics, 1643–1647', *Transactions of the Royal Historical Society*, 5th series, 31 (1981), 51–68; and *Politics, society and civil war in Warwickshire, 1620–1660* (Cambridge, 1987).

7 J. Walter, *Understanding popular violence in the English revolution* (Cambridge, 1999); A. Wood, *The politics of social conflict: the Peak Country, 1550–1770* (Cambridge, 1999), ch. 12.

8 For influential studies of popular allegiance see D. Underdown, *Revel, riot and rebellion: popular politics and culture in England 1603–1660* (Oxford, 1985), and M. Stoyle, *Loyalty and locality: popular allegiances in Devon during the English civil war* (Exeter, 1994). For a critique of Underdown see J. Morrill, 'The ecology of allegiance in the English civil wars', reprinted in Morrill, *The nature of the English revolution* (Harlow, 1993), 224–41.

9 Reprinted in *The constitutional documents of the puritan revolution 1625–1660*, ed. S. R. Gardiner, 3rd edn (Oxford, 1906), 233–6, esp. 233–4; Peacey suggests that the royalists were in general more reluctant to resort to print: *Politicians and pamphleteers*, esp. 307–8.

10 Discussed in Braddick, *God's fury*.

11 J. Walter, 'Confessional politics in pre-civil war Essex: prayer books, profanations and petitions', *Historical Journal*, 44 (2001), 677–701; ' "Abolishing superstition with sedition"? The politics of popular iconoclasm in England 1640–1642', *Past and Present*, 183 (2004), 79–123; and 'Popular iconoclasm and the politics of the parish in eastern England, 1640–1642', *Historical Journal*, 47 (2004), 261–90.

12 D. Beaver, 'The great deer massacre: animals, honour and communication in early modern England', *Journal of British Studies*, 38 (1999), 187–216; and ' "Bragging and daring words": honour, property and the symbolism of the hunt in Stowe, 1590–1642', in M. J. Braddick and J. Walter (eds), *Negotiating power in early modern society* (Cambridge, 2001), 149–65, 278–86.

13 T. Edwards, *Gangraena*, 3 vols (1646), ii. 127.

14 For a discussion of *Mercurius rusticus* in these terms see Braddick, *God's fury*.

15 For the importance of fear of a popish plot see A. Fletcher, *The outbreak of the English civil war* (1981), especially the Conclusion, and C. Hibbard, *Charles I and the popish plot* (Chapel Hill, NC, 1983).

16 The classic statement is P. Lake, 'Antipopery: the structure of a prejudice', in R. Cust and A. Hughes (eds), *Conflict in early Stuart England* (Harlow, 1989), 72–106.

17 R. Clifton, 'Fear of popery', in C. Russell (ed.), *The origins of the English civil war* (London, 1973), 144–67, 262, 271–4; and 'The popular fear of Catholics during the English revolution', *Past and Present*, 51 (1971), 23–55.

18 Fletcher, *Outbreak of the English civil war*.

19 Quoted from A. Wood, *Riot, rebellion and popular politics in early modern England* (Basingstoke, 2002), 127 (although I have differed in my reading of this incident). For impressment in 1638 see M. C. Fissel, *The bishops' wars* (Cambridge, 1994), 10–14 and, more generally, ch. 6.

20 M. J. Braddick, *State formation in early modern England* (Cambridge, 2000), ch. 6.

21 Raymond, *Pamphlets and pamphleteering*, esp. 214–5; for a discussion of true news see Braddick, *God's fury*.

22 Huntington Library, San Marino, California (hereafter HEH), EL 7848.

23 Fees varied, as did the services offered or requested, but £20 was the annual charge made by John Pory to Viscount Scudamore: I. Atherton, 'The itch grown a disease: manuscript transmission of news in the seventeenth century', in J. Raymond (ed.), *News, newspapers and society in early modern Britain* (London, 1999), 39–65, at 41. Bridgewater paid £20 to Castle, although it is not clear what period of service this 'token' was intended to cover: see HEH, EL 7808, EL 7809. For a concise discussion of the growing literature on the widening market for news see I. Atherton, 'The press and popular political opinion', in B. Coward (ed.), *A companion to Stuart Britain* (Oxford, 2003), 88–110.

24 J. Ricraft, *A survey of England's champions and truth's faithful patriots* (1646). For Ricraft see also Peacey, *Politicians and pamphleteers*, 109, 166, 320 and n. 58.

25 J. Ricraft, *The peculier characters of the orientall languages* (1645?). On programmes of language reform both as means of reducing public discussion to order and, more positively, to increase knowledge see S. Achinstein, 'The politics of Babel in the English Revolution', reprinted in J. Holstun (ed.), *Pamphlet wars* (1992), 14–44. I discuss Ryves at greater length in *God's fury*.

26 HEH, EL 7859.

27 *A relation of a terrible monster* (1642); for the reporting of wonders in newsbooks see J. Raymond (ed.), *Making the news* (Moreton-in-Marsh, 1993), ch. 4.

28 I am grateful to Anthony Milton for pointing this out to me. The sailors are: Nicholas Treadcrow, Josias Otter, Humfrey Hearnshaw, Alexander Waterrat, Sim Seamaule and Tim Bywater: J. Hare, *The marine mercury* (1642). The *English short title catalogue* (*ESTC*) identifies Hare as the author of later tracts critical of the lingering effects of the Norman conquest on the rights and liberties of Englishmen.

29 W. Prynne, *A vindication of psalme 105.15* (1642).

30 J. Milton, *Paradise lost*, bk ii, ll. 559–61, quoted from *John Milton*, ed. S. Orgel and J. Goldberg (Oxford, 1991), 355–618, at 389.

31 This is one reading of central arguments in J. C. Davis, *Fear, myth and history* (Cambridge, 1986).

32 See, for example, J. Taylor, *A cluster of coxcombs* (1642); *The divisions of the Church of England* (1642); *A discovery of 29 sects* (1641); *Religions lotterie or the churches amazement* (1642).

33 E. Pagitt, *Heresiography* (1645). See, for comparison, the subtitle of *Gangraena* by Edwards: *A catologue and discovery of many of the errors, heresies and blasphemies and pernicious practices of the sectaries of this time*; for *Gangraena* see A. Hughes, *Gangraena and the struggle for the English revolution* (Oxford, 2004).

34 C. Geertz, 'Common sense as a cultural system', in C. Geertz, *Local knowledge: further essays in interpretive anthropology* (New York, 2000), 73–93, at 75.

35 For a fascinating account of the successive re-inventions of the memory of the Interregnum see B. Worden, *Roundhead reputations* (Harmondsworth, 2001).

36 This is a summary of central arguments in Braddick's *State formation*.

37 *Ibid.*, esp. 20–43; see also Braddick, 'State formation and political culture'.

38 A. Hughes, 'Parliamentary tyranny? Indemnity proceedings and the impact of the civil war: a case study from Warwickshire', *Midland History*, 11 (1986), 49–78.

39 J. Scott, 'The rapture of motion: James Harrington's republicanism', in N. T. Phillipson and Q. Skinner (eds), *Political discourse in early modern Britain* (Cambridge, 1993), 139–63; M. J. Braddick and M. Greengrass (eds), 'The letters of Sir Cheney Culpepper, 1641–1657', in *Camden Miscellany*, 33 (Camden Society, 5th series, 7, 1996), 105–402, esp. 137–44; J. Champion, 'Political thinking between restoration and Hanoverian succession', in Coward, *Companion*, 474–91.

40 J. Scott, *England's troubles* (Cambridge, 2000). This is also a context in which to place M. Knights, *Politics and opinion in crisis, 1678–81* (Cambridge, 1994). I am grateful to Steve Pincus for the idea of a 'long revolution'.

41 The image is reproduced in J. Walter, 'The commons and their mental worlds', in J. Morrill (ed.), *The Oxford illustrated history of Tudor and Stuart Britain* (Oxford, 1996), 191–218, at 200.

42 A. J. Hopper, 'The Farnley Wood plot and the memory of the civil wars in Yorkshire', *Historical Journal*, 45 (2002), 281–303, at 302.

43 Beaver, *Parish communities*.

44 This is one set of contexts into which to place the career of Edmund Hickeringill: J. Champion and L. McNulty, 'Making orthodoxy in late restoration England: the trials of Edmund Hickeringill, 1662–1710', in Braddick and Walter (eds), *Negotiating power*, 227–48, 302–5.

3

'Patriots' and 'popular' spirits: narratives of conflict in early Stuart politics

Richard Cust

Elections

The parliamentary elections in the spring of 1640 formed a moment of high drama in the politics of early Stuart England. Up and down the country freeholders and townsmen were given an opportunity to pass judgement on the Personal Rule and elect MPs who could express their grievances and assuage their anxieties. In the most 'open' elections that had ever taken place, years of pent up frustration were released in a great outpouring of dispute and recrimination. Campaigning began almost as soon as the parliament was announced on 6 December 1639 and, in some cases, persisted well after the elections themselves, most of which took place in March 1640. Derek Hirst has calculated that 62 out of 241 parliamentary constituencies were contested – compared to between 20 and 40 in each of the elections of the 1620s – and because most of these contests were in counties or large borough seats the involvement of electors was maximised.[1] Wherever there was a contest – and in many cases where there was not – there were appeals to voters and efforts to shape political opinion.

In the battle for the hearts and minds of the electors every available form of communication was utilised, with the exception of the print. There was a feverish correspondence among the local gentry, as potential candidates appealed to backers and weighed up the strength of their support. Manuscript newsletters were full of comment on the mood of the electorate and the prospects of particular individuals. This deterred some would-be MPs and encouraged others. In Essex, Gloucestershire and Northamptonshire, local ministers got in on the act, often preaching 'out of their parishes' to rally support for (mainly) puritan candidates. Gossip, rumour and hearsay abounded, playing a vital role in the processes by which electors determined the qualities they were looking for in their MPs and the validity of candidates' claims to possess those qualities. In Northamptonshire the rumour was spread in 'markets, sessions and other publique places' that deputy lieutenants would be questioned in the coming parliament for raising coat and conduct money and levying troops for the Scots war. This was said to have destroyed the prospects of one of the local contestants.[2] The hostility to anyone connected with the 1630s regime was manifest in the little jingle which circulated in Lincolnshire:

> Choose noe shipp sheriffe, nor Court Athyst
> Noe fen drayner, nor Church papist.[3]

Sir Edward Dering believed that his chances had been undermined in Kent by a series of contradictory rumours which accused him, on the one hand, of being 'a courtier', 'another Buckingham' and of having 'set up the first altar in Dover castle', and, on the other, of opposing the deputy lieutenants and the secretary of state, Sir Henry Vane, and of refusing 'to go up to the rails at communion'.[4]

The intensity of discussion was matched by the intensity of the electioneering. Meetings were held, speeches were made and deals were struck. At the Kent assizes on 26 February, over two weeks prior to the election, a group of senior gentry met to engage in the well-tried procedure of agreeing their choice of candidates in advance, to avoid a contest. However, discussions broke down on the animosity felt towards Vane as 'a courtier', and this led to a bitter contest as two new candidates stepped into the arena.[5] In Cheshire, Essex and Northamptonshire groups of court-based peers mobilised their influence in what appears to have been a co-ordinated campaign to ensure the return of MPs sympathetic to the regime.[6] There were allegations of a similar campaign being mounted by oppositionist peers and puritan supporters of the Scots, although the evidence for this is much less clear.[7] Bribery, coercion and intimidation were often the order of the day. It was alleged that in Essex one of these oppositionist peers, the earl of Warwick, used his powers as lord lieutenant to threaten voters with being charged for extra arms. In Abingdon, Sir George Stonehouse was said to have won round 'the Commons' with the time-honoured promises of 'bacon, beefe and bagge pudding'. In Northamptonshire, Sir Christopher Hatton sent his agent to canvass the views of local gentry and opinion formers, then decided to withdraw from the county contest in favour of a safer seat at Higham Ferrers. Dering in Kent even undertook an opinion poll drawing on his contacts among the gentry and clergy to identify 485 freeholders who promised him their vote.[8]

At the elections themselves carefully worked out techniques for avoiding public conflict and minimising dissension often broke down, and proceedings sometimes came to resemble the half-ordered chaos of the carnival or the food riot. At Northampton the county election unfolded over three days (19–21 March), with thousands of freeholders thronging the town and attempts to resolve the contest by the traditional methods of the 'view' or the 'shout' having to give way to the polling of individual voters. The three court-based peers who supported Thomas Elmes rode up and down on horseback calling to the crowds to join his company; and Elmes's puritan opponent, Sir Gilbert Pickering, retaliated by allowing himself to be 'horsed' around the town on the shoulders of his supporters. Throughout the first day Pickering's allies kept up a constant shout of 'Wee'le have noe deputy lieutenants! Take heed of deputy lieutenants! Noe deputy lieutenants!' To add to the confusion the sheriff kept changing the venue of the poll, ostensibly because of the size of the crowds, but, according to Elmes, so that Pickering's supporters could get to the front of the queue.[9] Comparable scenes were reported at the elections for Essex and Gloucestershire.[10] The borough election at Salisbury was a more decorous affair which took place in the Common Assembly under the supervision of mayor and aldermen. But proceedings were interrupted when Maurice Aylerugg, one of the aldermen, broke into the reading of the writ to question the credentials of the corporation's candidate and town recorder, Robert Hyde. He insisted that since 'their religion and liberties were at the stake . . . it would concerne them to choose such men as were well affected in religion and towards the commonwealth', which ruled out Hyde who was a known opponent of puritans and an advocate of ship money. There then ensued some bitter exchanges as Hyde protested that his honour was being impugned and another alderman weighed in in support of Aylerugg by arguing that 'it was noe newes to have the Recorder of a towne rejected, for the Recorder of London was refused, & so was the Recorder of Excester . . .'. Order was eventually restored, Hyde was elected and the two aldermen were disciplined; but not before townsmen had been treated to another example of the power of these elections to stir up dissension and polarise opinion.[11]

The elections of the spring of 1640 – and, indeed, the autumn of the same year – were a prime example of 'the politics of the public sphere' which Peter Lake and others see as developing in the late Tudor and early Stuart period.[12] The political arena was being opened up and a variety of 'publics' were being addressed, invoked, appealed to and performed in front of in order to mobilise support for particular candidates and shape the complexion of the coming parliament. Topics such as ship money, the powers of the lieutenancy, Laudian policy in the church and, even, the Scottish war which, on one reading, could be seen as part of the *arcana imperii* – the preserve of the king and his advisers – were becoming the subject matter of sermons, newsletters, speeches at the hustings, and everyday rumour and gossip. Opinions which a few weeks earlier might have landed an individual with an appearance before the privy council or a spell in prison were now – under the umbrella of a 'free' parliament and the freeholders' right to liberty of voice – openly discussed and debated.

Two aspects of this particular instance of the politics of the public sphere were unusual. First, there was the fact that most of the debate and discussion was taking place outside the metropolitan context, away from the opinion-formers and men of business operating around the court and parliament who were the initiators of this style of politics. Here it was the provincial elites and middling sorts and, indeed, anybody who became involved in the debate or bothered to turn out on election day (which much of the comment suggests included the 'rude, vulgar sort' who were not qualified as freeholders) who were mainly involved. Second, there was the fact that it happened without resort to the print. Instead a far reaching and potentially momentous public debate was conducted using the manuscript news media, the pulpit, gossip, rumour and face-to-face exchange. It is important, however, not to exaggerate the novelty of what was taking place. There is plenty of evidence that sophisticated mechanisms for promoting public debate had been developing at a provincial level since at least the 1580s and, in some respects, much earlier.[13] Perhaps the most striking feature of this whole process is not the mechanisms of communication, or the variety of audiences being engaged, but the legitimating narratives used by the participants. Looking at how those involved made their pitches for support, sifted the qualifications of the candidates paraded before them and understood what the whole process was about, helps to address important questions about the nature of public opinion and the defining features of early Stuart political culture.

Two principal narratives emerged from the debate accompanying the election. The first was about *patriots*. Aspiring MPs were represented, and represented themselves, as 'fathers of the country' and 'good commonwealthmen' who would apply their restorative powers to curing the nation's ills. The qualities required of these 'patriots' were most often defined negatively. In Kent, according to Sir Roger Twysden, 'the common people had been so bytten with shippe money they were very averse from a courtyer'. In Leicestershire, it was said,

> the contry in generall take the same excepcons against Sir Henry Skipwith which in Derbyshire they doe against Sir John Harpur, which is that he is a courtier and hath bin sheriffe and collected the shipp money and that he lives out of the contrey; and these thinges are privately urged by his opposers to the freeholders & worke much to his disadvantage even with his neerest neighbours.[14]

Comments like these, together with the rhymes and rumours circulating in counties such as Lincolnshire and Northamptonshire, indicate that most electors were determined not to return candidates who were associated with the court, who had served the regime in the 1630s, or who could be regarded as papists or Arminians. What they were seeking were their polar opposites: staunch Calvinists who were opposed to the policies of the Personal Rule and whose allegiance was firmly rooted in the 'country'.

When he heard the news that there was to be a parliament, the puritan steward of Northampton Robert Woodford recorded in his diary a fervent prayer that the 'country and corporations' would 'make choyce of gracious and able men'.[15] What he meant by 'gracious and able men' – as is clear from other diary entries – was those who were godly opponents of Arminianism, particularly the altar policy, those who opposed ship money and other illegal local levies, like the forest fines, and those who were prepared to root out the 'evil counsellors' at court. Thus, when he was approached to give his support to Sir Christopher Hatton, a few weeks later, he refused to do so. Although Hatton had been a generous patron to him in his business as an attorney, he had close links with the royal court and was a supporter of the Arminians. Instead Woodford backed Pickering, the opponent of papists and deputy lieutenants.[16] His belief in the power of 'gracious and able men' to cure the nation's ills was widely shared, and those involved in electioneering did everything possible to persuade electors that they fell into this category. In their Cheshire campaign, Sir George Booth and Sir Richard Wilbraham sought to gloss over the fact that they had served as deputy lieutenants by styling themselves 'the patriots'. Their hope seems to have been that they could draw on the immense prestige of their close friend and political ally Sir Richard Grosvenor who during the 1620s had acquired a reputation as the archetypal 'father of the country', standing out against papists, Arminians, monopolists, projectors and Buckingham.[17] But they failed. In a bitter and confused contest, their candidates (probably their own sons) lost out to Sir Thomas Aston who was able to obscure his own court connections by adopting the leading local puritan Sir William Brereton as his running-mate.[18] In Kent, Twysden, who was acting as Vane's campaign manager, attempted to repackage his candidate in a similar fashion. The argument he used to win support was that Vane was 'a man truly devoted to God and hys countrye's good, and that had perswaded the king to this course', i.e. the summoning of the parliament.[19] Once more the ploy failed to work; but Twysden's strenuous efforts again demonstrate the positive force carried by the image of the 'patriot'.

An important part of the narrative about patriots related to the process of election itself. It was widely presumed that the right sort of candidate would emerge only if the freeholders were allowed to make an open and unfettered choice. This was a point which Brereton emphasised in his pitch for support in Cheshire:

> I could much wish . . . that every man might come so free to the election as that they might be under no manner of engagement, but might bee at liberty to give their voyces as they see cause; so might there bee a faire and free election, sutable to the nature of a parliament . . . seeing that we trust our estates, libertyes, posterityes and religion with them that are elected, and are concluded by whatsoever they doe.[20]

Brereton was deploying a familiar discourse which Grosvenor had expounded before the Cheshire freeholders over two decades earlier in an address prior to the 1624 county election. Drawing on the language of civic humanism, Sir Richard explained that the main safeguard against corruption within the political system was 'active citizenship': the willingness of ordinary freeholders to participate in elections and make an open and informed choice. It was this which guaranteed the integrity and effectiveness of a parliament. 'Freedome of voyce', he proclaimed, 'is your inheritance, and one of the greatest prerogatives of the subjecte which ought by all means to bee kept inviolate and cannot bee taken from you by anie commaund whatsoever.'[21] The 'patriots' narrative, then, presented a vision of how the 'voice' of the people could be channelled through a freely elected parliament to remedy the grievances of the 'commonwealth'. 'Fathers of the country' acted as the human links between the will of the electors and the counselling and legislative functions of parliament. It was up to them to ensure that there would be no repetition of the Personal Rule.

There was, however, a second, very different, reading of events which represented the activities of anti-court MPs and a large, unconstrained electorate as sources of threat and danger. According to this narrative, the elections had been hijacked by 'popular spirits', agents of faction and puritanism, who were working with the rebel Scots to return a House of Commons which would destroy royal authority. Rumours of such a campaign spread far and wide. Sir Thomas Aston, writing from the court four days after the announcement of the parliament, promised a potential supporter that he would 'endeavour a quyet election without trouble', but warned that it was 'feared the puritan faction will universally through the kingdom struggle for a party'.[22] From Gloucester, John Allibond wrote to his Laudian friend Peter Heylyn in March 1640, voicing the concern 'that there is a kind of cunning underhand canvass . . . the greater part of this kingdom over' which involved puritan ministers with Scots connections. 'If it be true, we are like to have a brave lower house of it . . . that if their hearts were known affect nothing more than to hold the king's nose to the grindstone and ruin the church'.[23] Thomas Elmes's supporters in Northamptonshire took this rumour as the starting point for a description of Pickering's election as a full blown 'popular' conspiracy. His 'agents' were ambitious, self-seeking and conniving, hatching 'the consultation and plot' in London 'the very next day after the king's resolucon to cale a parlyment'. Their methods were those of the classic populist demagogue, hoodwinking the people and whipping up alarm with lies, smears and false rumours. Pickering's behaviour on election day was of a piece with this, especially 'his triumphant riding upon their shoulders from the castle yard to the town & soe round about the market place under the lords' windows in a kind of affront to them'. Throughout the campaign his supporters conducted themselves in such 'a tumultuous manner as did ill beseem the demeanour of men bred up in a civill commonwealth, especially such as make profession of the most syncear practice of the gospell'.[24] This account contained many of the standard ingredients of narratives of 'popular' conspiracy: ambitious demagogues plotting with external forces to serve their own ends; a gullible multitude whipped up into a state of unreason and disorder; affronts to social superiors; even an element of puritan hypocrisy – and underpinning the whole account a sense of the danger to order, security and royal authority.

Similarly structured narratives appeared elsewhere. In Kent, Sir Edward Dering explained his defeat at the hands of Sir Roger Twysden largely as the work of 'the obscure and peevish sort that are separatists, or lovers of separation [who] did make it their cause to have a child of theirs in the house'.[25] Allibond in Gloucestershire stressed the chaos and damage where electoral arrangements were overturned by a populist puritan lobby. And Henry Neville, the defeated candidate in Essex, described how on election day the earl of Warwick played to the gallery and stirred up 'the multitude' to the point at which some freeholders threatened that 'if Nevill had the day they would tear the gentlemen to pieces'.[26] Neville and his principal supporter Lord Maynard, however, added an extra ingredient to their accounts by insisting that many of the problems stemmed from the open and unregulated nature of the elections. They were 'popular assemblies' in which, as Maynard famously put it, 'fellowes without shirts challenge as good a voice as myself'. Freeholders from the puritan towns were also able to vote twice, in both the borough and the county, which meant they enjoyed more of a say in the elections 'than the greatest lord in England hath'. This was a recipe for the chaos witnessed at Chelmsford. Neville therefore proposed that the franchise be altered so that the county qualification became a £20 rather than a 40 shilling freehold. Such a measure, he predicted, 'were a great quiet to the state' and 'then gentlemen would be looked upon', i.e. treated with proper respect.[27]

Neville's proposal highlighted the direct conflict between the 'popular' and the 'patriot' narratives of the election: they presented diametrically opposed visions of how the political process should operate, and each fed off fears of the other. The openness and independence which, on one account, was the best guarantee of a 'free' and effective parliament, on another constituted its greatest danger. Without the exercise of authoritarian constraints, the electorate threatened to return to parliament a party of puritan zealots who would conspire with the Scots to destroy royal power. The significance of this clash of narratives will be discussed in due course. For the moment, suffice it to say that both were well established and resonated widely.

As the reactions of the electors demonstrated, the 'patriot' narrative spoke to the hopes and expectations of the greater part of the political nation in 1640. The 'popular' reading had a shallower resonance and was, understandably, most developed in the 'royalist' circles of the court;[28] however, it was not confined to them. Aston's remarks were addressed to William Whitmore, a south Cheshire esquire; Allibond was writing from the precincts of Gloucester cathedral where he held a living; and Maynard's comments were directed to Sir Thomas Barrington, one of the victorious puritan candidates in Essex. The spring election of 1640 provides the clearest instance of these narratives being deployed in an electoral context; but it is by no means the only one. Throughout the early seventeenth century one can find instances of the same frameworks and sets of assumptions being used to make sense of what was going on in elections.[29] Indeed one can discern some of the same features in an election held over fifty years earlier, at Warwick in October 1586.[30] By the standards of the day this was an example of unusually precocious electioneering; but it offers an important insight into the way in which 'the politics of the public sphere' was starting to have an impact locally.

The candidate who brought about the contest was Job Throckmorton who was seeking to unseat John Fisher, the town clerk and Warwick's representative in the three previous parliaments. Throckmorton was one of the prototypes of the 'patriots' and 'fathers of the country': a skilled and aggressive exponent of the new style of politics, once elected to the 1586–87 parliament he spoke out with considerable effect in support of the execution of Mary Queen of Scots and the adoption of Cope's 'Bill and Book'. He was also the probable author of the Marprelate tracts, which deployed the new methods of political pamphleteering to deliver a scurrilous and highly damaging exposé of the hypocrisy and corruption of bishops. Whether Throckmorton received support for his actions from more senior figures within the protestant establishment is unclear. (The suspicion is that he did.) But in public he presented himself as an outsider, the simple, 'honest', mouthpiece of the 'country'. This stance was skilfully worked into his speech supporting the Bill and Book, which began as a defence of parliament's right to freedom of speech, but quickly turned into an attack on councillors who failed to discharge their duty of counselling the queen on the dangers she faced. 'It is wondered at above', he acknowledged, that 'symple men of the countrey should be so forward'; but, equally, he insisted, 'it doth amate[sic] us in the countrey that wise men of the courte should be so backeward . . . Is it a fault in a pryvate man to be to busye, and can it be excused in a councellor to be to sleepy[?]'[31] Throckmorton was to bring some of the same perspectives to his earlier campaign at Warwick.

His first move was to mobilise his puritan contacts. He received backing from Sir John Harrington and Sir Fulke Greville, two of the principal godly gentlemen in Warwickshire, and also – one presumes – from his friend Thomas Cartwright who had recently been installed as preacher at the Lord Leycester hospital. It is possible also that 'Busie Richard Brooke', who organised support among the 'Commons' of the town, was a puritan.[32] However, if religion played a role in gathering support, it was not the principal theme of his campaign. His main tactic was to exploit the divisions between the principal burgesses and 'the Commons' of Warwick, primarily over town revenues and municipal elections. He presented himself as the candidate who backed openness, participation, and the disinterested service of town and country. To justify his tactic of appealing to 'the Commons' he insisted that he 'would not have the matter [of the election] huddled upp in a corner as the most of your matters be amongst yourselfs . . .'. It must be 'all in public'. He also brought pressure to ensure that if there was an election the time and venue were announced two days in advance, and threatened that if 'the Commons' were denied the opportunity to participate he would appeal to parliament. Finally, to allay doubts among the principal burgesses he took an oath that in the coming parliament he would devote himself 'to the best of my power, witte and skill . . . to work for the good government and benefitting of the same borough, liberties, franchises and the people of the same'.[33] Throckmorton, then, was drawing heavily on the notions of openness and participation which were inherent in the 'monarchical republicanism' of Elizabethan England; and he was coupling these with a rhetoric of faithful service to town and commonwealth.[34]

Fisher countered by resorting to the narrative of 'popularity'. Throckmorton, he claimed, had mounted a blatantly popular campaign, making 'very great labor' towards 'those that be ready to runn headlong into any looseness', 'much assisted by Busie Richard Brooke & his complices'. His 'practizers' had engaged in treating and dirty tricks involving the sheriff, and there were hints that this was all part of a broader puritan conspiracy. It was suggested to Throckmorton that he had no 'desire to be a burgesse of the towne, but for the parliament, where, peradventure, some freends of yours may have some causes in handeling'. The result of all this irresponsible and underhand plotting was only what was to be expected. According to Fisher it led to 'perillous division and disencon emongs the townesmen' and the 'froward and unreasonable behaviour of the worst sort of inhabitants'.[35]

The Warwick election may have lacked the broader ideological dimension of 1640. There was no reference – as far as we can tell from the account in Fisher's 'Black Book' – to popery, or illegal taxes or the corrupting influence of the court. The issues talked about were mainly local ones. But this discussion was taking place within a framework which was still recognisable in 1640: in terms of narratives which set public- minded 'patriots' against those members of the establishment who would have politics 'huddled upp in a corner', and openness and participation against the disorder and disruption of the popular 'multitude'. This tells us something important about the ways in which contemporaries structured their attitudes and assumptions not just about elections, but about politics more generally. Before discussing what this is, it is necessary to look more closely at the construction and composition of these narratives.

'Patriots'

The 'patriots' narrative was made up of various themes and ideals inherent in contemporary notions of classical republicanism and godly Calvinism. It was this same mix which had produced the new-style politics of the public sphere. The 'classical republican' strand drew much of its strength from the powerful influence exerted on the minds of Elizabethan and early Stuart Englishmen by the writings of Cicero, especially his *De officiis* which was almost a textbook for the governing classes. The principal message of this work was that man's highest earthly duty and aspiration was the active service of his *respublica* (literally, 'public thing', but commonly translated in the sixteenth century as 'commonwealth' or 'country'). For contemporaries this was generally taken to mean that true honour and nobility could best be achieved by service in office – as royal counsellor, local magistrate or member of parliament.[36] The principles which were expected to guide such service were often summed up in the contrast between 'public' and 'private' which, in the political vocabulary of the day, stood for fundamentally opposed approaches to government and magistracy. 'Private' signified that which was selfish, corrupt, even tyrannical, and was equated with vices such as covetousness, ambition, pride and anger. 'Public' was its antithesis, a concept which embraced the common good of 'the country' and the duty of every good citizen to serve it unselfishly. The magistrate who displayed those qualities would earn the accolade of 'honest' – again a key word in the contemporary political lexicon (as it was for Cicero, for whom *vir honestus* described the man who possessed the four cardinal virtues, wisdom, justice, temperance and fortitude, and also the man who was worthy of honour). And the 'honest' man was crucial to safeguarding the common weal, since it was his readiness to stand up and be counted, and to set an example to others which provided the surest means of preventing corruption and tyranny. Such an individual earned the right to be called *pater patriae*, which translated as 'father of the country', 'good commonwealthman' or 'patriot'.

Many of the same themes were highlighted in Calvinist readings of scripture. Calvinist ministers of the late sixteenth and early seventeenth century were generally well versed in the language and concepts of civic humanism, and sermons about magisterial office were full of references to honesty, the four cardinal virtues and putting the 'public' before the 'private'. However, that rhetoric was overlaid with a language based on scripture which gave their vision of public service its own distinctive character. They saw magistracy as a godly vocation. Magistrates, like princes, were little gods, called on by the Almighty to fulfil the divine purposes of promoting justice and order, and fighting sin. If they failed to do this then the nation was liable to face God's providential wrath. For the godly Calvinist, the 'patriot' was not simply a virtuous bulwark against corruption and tyranny; he was also the spearhead of a godly crusade.

But against whom were the patriot's efforts to be directed? At the local level the enemy was straightforward enough. It was those 'vices' castigated by the humanists, such as 'greed', 'pride', 'covetousness' and 'idleness', or those 'sins' against which Calvinist preachers inveighed. At a national level, however, the target was often less clear. Most Calvinists could agree that the main enemy was 'popery' – and 'popery' could do duty as the symbol for a whole multitude of vices, corruptions and threats to the commonweal. But beyond this there were the more elusive forces of *privacie* which encapsulated all manner of other evils. By the latter part of Elizabeth's reign many of these threats were becoming associated with the royal court.

The changing image of the royal court and those who inhabited it at this time is a topic badly in need of investigation; but it would appear that in the early part of Elizabeth's reign it enjoyed an unusually positive reputation.[37] Traditional depictions of the court as a source of vice and iniquity had been tempered by the reception of an Italian humanist literature which stressed the superior wisdom and sophistication of cities and courts when compared with the country. By the middle of Elizabeth's reign the courtier–counsellor was well on the way to being established as the model of the wise and virtuous 'public man', with Roger Ascham's famous portrayal of Lord Burghley (taking time out from the affairs of state to discuss round his dinner table the education of youth) as a seminal image.[38]

The big change in the image of the court appears to have taken place in the 1580s and 1590s. Works of Catholic polemic, such as *The treatise of treasons* (1572) and *Leicester's commonwealth* (1584), which depicted the likes of Burghley as 'Machiavel Catilines' may well have had an impact here; for a protestant audience, however, the work which probably had the greatest effect was John Stubbes's *Discoverie of a gaping gulf*. Published in 1579 as part of the campaign of opposition to the 'Anjou match', this set out to explain that, in spite of the obvious dangers in the queen marrying a foreign Catholic, the whole project had got off the ground because of the existence of evil counsellors at court. 'Flatterers' and 'politics', whose natural home was the court of France – 'where Machiavelli is their New Testament and atheism is their religion' – were plotting to serve their 'private' ends and threatening to destroy English protestantism. In such circumstances, the clearest remedy, Stubbes implied, was the willingness of 'Christian commonwealthsmen', like himself, to speak out and alert the queen to the dangers of what was going on. The *Gaping gulf* was widely circulated, and the fuss made about its suppression ensured that the whole episode had a profound impact on the psyche of the political nation.[39] From that point onwards, the image of the outsider, willing to speak out where the compromises and corruptions of the court prevented professional councillors from doing so, appears to have become an established part of the political lexicon. Throckmorton appears to have been keying in to just this image with his reference to the 'simple men of the country' in 1587.

As the image of the court deteriorated further in the 1590s (with the vicious, and well publicised, infighting between Essex and Cecil factions and the vogue for Tacitist readings of the nature of court politics) and under James (with the sale of offices and honours, the series of court scandals culminating in the Overbury murder and the trial of Somerset, and the revelations about the activities of the earl of Northampton and Spanish pensions being paid to leading councillors), the need for an antidote to its corrupting influence became more and more obvious.[40] Contemporaries found this in the purifying influence of 'the country'. As the court's reputation declined, that of 'the country' became purer and more pristine, and the imagery associated with it came to be appropriated by those with more overtly political agendas. For the godly 'the country' was taken to represent a vision of a reformed nation, such as might exist if popery and sinfulness were overcome and England remodelled along Calvinist lines. For those with a more secular outlook, it tended to mean a commonwealth freed from projectors, evil counsellors and threats to liberty. By the 1620s, if not before, 'court' and 'country' were widely perceived as representing two ideological poles: while the court stood for corruption, privacy and popery, the country was its direct antithesis, its image that of a healthy, balanced and purified common weal.[41]

The main onus for bringing the influence of the country to bear on the court fell on parliament which had responsibility both as a counsellor (opening the monarch's eyes to the dangers faced by the kingdom and his subjects) and as a lawmaker (legislating against specific abuses). If it was to fulfil those roles adequately, a good deal depended on the quality of the individuals chosen to represent the country. It was essential that the House of Commons be filled with men who were wise, virtuous, godly and 'honest'; and this could only happen if the freeholders took their responsibilities seriously, engaged fully with the system for electing MPs and exercised their 'freedom of voyce'.

The view of the electoral process put forward by Brereton, Grosvenor and many others encapsulated the main features of the 'patriot' narrative. It envisaged an integrated political system in which the localities were linked to the centre through the representative functions of parliament, and in which informed and active citizens at the local level had the power to shape events in the national arena. Holding that system together, and enabling it to function effectively, were the 'patriots' themselves, men distinguished for their godliness, determination and commitment to 'country' values. It was they who transmitted information backwards and forwards, who used their rhetorical skills to persuade and influence others and who, as 'parliament men', had the contacts and opportunities to effect reform. These were the men in whom the majority of the political nation invested their hopes in the spring of 1640.

'Popular spirits'

The 'popular spirits' narrative was not invented in the sixteenth century; its origins can be traced back to ancient Greece and Rome, the histories of which contain numerous examples of the dangers of democracy and the threat posed by ambitious demagogues. These were picked up by political commentators in the sixteenth century who identified the 'many-headed monster' of the popular 'multitude' as one of the paramount threats to order and stability.[42] The person who started the trend of applying such models to contemporary politics was John Whitgift. As Peter Lake has demonstrated, the case Whitgift made against Thomas Cartwright in the Admonition Controversy of the early 1570s drew together themes and arguments which were to re-used repeatedly in the late sixteenth and early seventeenth centuries.[43] He attacked Cartwright's vision of a presbyterian church based on democratic principles and 'active godly citizenship', as dangerously popular both in style and form. The presbyterian movement was fronted by arrogant and ambitious young clerics who played to the crowd in whipping up opposition to bishops and magistrates. In a characteristic display of hypocrisy and self-advertisement they presented themselves as more virtuous and more zealous than the ordinary ministers by denouncing the church and its ceremonies to a fickle and novelty-addicted populace. At the same time he depicted Cartwright's emphasis on presbyterian self-government as a threatening mix of quasi-republicanism and popular liberty. It allowed a dangerous amount of power to a people who were 'ignorant, unlearned and unapt to govern' and was basically a means of bringing the church and, ultimately the state, under the sway of ambitious demagogues. In a passage headed 'Elections by the multitude are for the most part disordered', Whitgift anticipated several of the diatribes of 1640. He warned of the hazards of allowing too much freedom and participation to the people.

> The disorder of such popular elections hath been such, the contentions moved in them so great, the ambition of the persons standing in election so notorious, the partial affection of the people inclining to their kinsfolks, friends or landlords etc. so untolerable, to be short the lack of judgement and discretion in many of them so apparent that that manner of electing upon great considerations hath been altered in divers places and desired to be altered in others by all those that are wise and discreet and that wish for peace and good government.[44]

Whitgift, then, was establishing a template for later analysis of the effects of popularity.

His arguments were restated with greater vigour in the response to the Marprelate tracts and the presbyterian classical movement during the late 1580s and early 1590s. Richard Bancroft took the lead in a series of polemical works which portrayed the presbyterians as populist firebrands. Again he highlighted the perils of allowing 'the multitude' to participate in church government, but this time added a chilling account of how such a policy had been exported from Calvin's Geneva to France, Scotland and now, through the classical movement, to England. Once established it would promote resistance theory and principles of consent which had the potential not only to sweep away bishops in the church, but also destroy monarchy and nobility. Sovereign power would reside with 'the multitude' and the world would be 'set all upon liberty.' The effect of this campaign was to brand the puritans as being as much of a danger to the state as were the papists. Both were foreign inspired, wedded to resistance theory and populist in their means of attracting support. They presented equivalent threats to the established order and government. From then on the puritans could readily be labelled as subversive and anti-monarchical.[45]

The narrative assembled by Whitgift and Bancroft was given added force by the recent trends in the politics of the public sphere. The standard response of those on the receiving end of the new-style politics was to denounce their opponents as dangerously populist. By exposing the secrets of the *arcana imperii*, encouraging the populace to consider questions and form judgements which it was beyond them to make, and by feeding their fickle desire for novelty, they were opening up a dangerous and uncontrollable Pandora's box. The fact that those doing the denouncing often resorted to precisely the same methods for getting their message across seems to have been of limited concern. It was taken as read that to be an effective political operator this was what one now had to do. A fascinating commentary on this development is provided by Francis Bacon, in a letter of advice to the earl of Essex after his triumphant return from Cadiz in 1596. Essex was being depicted in some quarters as an example of the most dangerous type of ambitious demagogue, a military leader, lionised by the people, whose arrogant determination to secure his due appeared to be plunging the court into political strife.[46] Bacon was acutely conscious of the dangers of this image, particularly insofar as it might have become lodged in the mind of Elizabeth. He therefore advised his patron to do all in his power to 'quench it' by taking 'all occasions to the queen to speak against popularity and popular courses vehemently and to tax it in all others'. To ensure that Essex's words carried conviction, he offered the intriguing advice that in the next parliament he should set himself up as a spokesman who favoured supply for the wars. Such an action, Bacon assured him, would allay any suspicion that the earl was seeking to cultivate a popular following: 'if her Majesty object popularity to you at any time, I would say to her a Parliament will show'. Having said all this, however, Bacon also acknowledged that the earl's 'popular reputation' was one of his greatest political assets. He should go on cultivating it 'because it is a thing good in itself, being obtained as your Lordship obtained it, that is *bonis artibus*; and besides well governed is one of the best flowers of your greatness both present and to come'. The thing to remember always was that 'it would be handled tenderly'.[47] Bacon's advice constituted a recognition that politicians were now operating in a world in which creating a public image, communicating with the people and developing a popular following had become key elements in the struggle for power. But such matters had to be handled with extreme delicacy if one was to secure the benefits without leaving oneself open to the potentially dangerous charge of popularity. This was, arguably, one of the areas where Essex failed the test of a good politician; but there were plenty of others who played the game with great skill and effectiveness.

By the 1590s the ingredients of the early Stuart 'popularity' narrative were all in place, except one. That was the element which explicitly linked 'popularity' to the activities of oppositionist MPs in the House of Commons. As we have seen, Fisher hinted at this in the Warwick election of 1586; but the first national politician to make the connection on a regular basis was Robert Cecil. During the monopolies debate of 1601 he alleged that the chief critics of the government 'have desired to be popular without the house for speaking against monopolies', and also complained that 'parliament business' was being 'talked of' in the streets, where there were those saying: '"God prosper those that further the overthrow of these monopolies. God send the prerogative touch not liberty."' During the parliament of 1604–10, he used similar language to label those who complained about purveyance, describing John Hare, the leading agitator in the Commons as 'a tribune of the people', and throughout this assembly he and others decribed oppositionist MPs as 'the populars' or 'the popular party'.[48] The person who did most to familiarise Englishmen with this vocabulary as it applied to MPs, however, was James I.

In the *Basilicon doron*, written while he was still in Scotland in the 1590s, James had picked up on the Bancroftian language of popular conspiracy in the church, representing Scottish presbyterians in similar terms to their English counterparts.[49] Once in England he extended this analysis to encompass 'free speakers' in parliament. Exasperated by the failure of the Great Contract of 1610 he himself complained that elements in the Commons had 'perilled and annoyed our health, wounded our reputation, emboldened an ill-natured people, encroached upon many of our privileges and plagued our purse with their delays'. He developed this theme in a speech in Star Chamber in 1616 which castigated oppositionist MPs as those who 'cannot be content with the present forme of gouvernment, but must have a kind of libertie in the people ... and in every cause that concernes prerogative give a snatch against monarchie, through their puritanicall itching after popularitie'. And in the second session of the 1621 parliament, when the Commons attempted to petition him about the marriage of his son to the Spanish *infanta*, he responded furiously, blaming the whole episode on 'fiery and popular spirits' debating 'publicly of ... matters far above their reach or capacity, tending to our high dishonour and trenching upon our prerogative royal'.[50] James, then, was adding new ingredients to the narrative. Freedom of speech, which in other contexts was seen as intrinsic to parliament's ability to carry out its coun-selling role effectively, was now seen as being hijacked by individuals who regarded themselves as 'patriots' but were, in reality, populist demagogues. What, at first sight, might appear to be a vindication of the subject's liberties and the rule of law emerged, on closer examination, as a dangerous challenge to the prerogative and monarchical authority. The king's denunciations provided a template – in much the same way as Whitgift and Bancroft had done – for apply-ing the 'popularity' narrative to parliamentary politics. The vocabulary, the assumptions, the explanations about how the threat would play out in a parlia-mentary context were all adopted by privy councillors wary of a summons of parliament, courtiers seeking to ingratiate themselves with king or favourite and, of course, by his own son.

James's assaults on 'popular spirits' also demonstrated how the 'popularity' nar-rative was increasingly used to underpin authoritarian readings of the power of monarchy. By promoting a conspiracy theory which could be used to label the activities of almost anyone who appeared to challenge royal authority as dangerous and subversive it could bolster and legitimise increasingly aggressive assertions of that authority. That was how the narrative was being used from the 1590s onwards. Peter Lake, John Guy and others have demonstrated that it was a key element in the reaction which took place against the quasi-democratic politics of Elizabeth's 'monarchical republic'. The openness, participation and involvement of the public that were, in many respects, the hallmarks of the politics practised by Lord Burghley and his allies were retyped – initially by Whitgift, Bancroft and critics of resistance theory, and later by James, Charles and a whole cohort of apologists for divine right – as dangerous, subversive and potentially destructive of order and hierarchy.[51] This led to the emergence of a significantly limited vision of the state in which the involvement of the aristocratic and democratic elements was reduced and the power of the divinely ordained monarch, and his natural allies the *iure divino* bishops, were presented as the principal guarantors of order. Active citizenship, the liberty of the freeholders and the connecting and facil-itating role of the patriots were played down and there was a renewed emphasis on keeping the *arcana imperii* hidden from public view. The role of parliament in balancing the state and avoiding the corruptions of power was minimised in the face of an uncompromising message that the giving of counsel and the redressing of grievances were to be regulated by the monarch. Of course, this reac-tion did not go unchallenged, and it was out of this that many of the electoral clashes of 1640 – and indeed the conflicts of the early Stuart period more gen-erally – derived their origins.

Narratives of conflict

Recent work on narrative and political identity has brought home the extent to which both perceptions and actions in politics are structured by stories. Narrative it has been said, is 'co-terminous with the cognitive process, part of the human condition in which knowing occurs through telling, knowledge through narrative'. Applied to political action, this means that narrative is central to agents' thought processes, shaping the ways in which they make sense of what is going on, but also how they envisage their own role in this, their hopes and fears, aspirations and expectations. Hence, it has been argued that 'stories guide action . . . people construct identities by locating themselves or being located within a repertoire of emplotted stories . . . experience is constituted through narratives'.[52]

Stories about 'patriots' and 'popular' spirits are no exception. It was through these narratives that a wide range of contemporaries made sense of what was happening in the world of politics and visualised how events were likely to play out. Stories provide a sense of purpose and direction since they imply movement towards an ending. In the case of the 'patriot' narrative, it imbued contemporaries with a sense of empowerment, since they appeared to be moving towards the relatively optimistic goals of reform and stability. In the 'popular' narrative, of course, it was movement in the direction of something altogether darker and more alarming. The stories investigated here were relatively flexible and open-ended, and that was one of their great strengths. It meant that they could be applied to a whole variety of political contexts. With the 'patriot' narrative, those contexts could cover everything from parliamentary elections and puritan reform agendas to specific episodes such as the opposition to the Spanish Match or resistance to the forced loan. The 'popularity' narrative was applied equally widely, again to explain opposition to the Spanish Match and the forced loan, but also to account for challenges to the prerogative in parliament, puritan agitation in the church and the Prayer Book rebellion in Scotland. They could also be appropriated by, and applied to, a wide range of political actors. Twysden believed that the courtier Sir Henry Vane could be convincingly represented as a 'patriot', and Henry Neville that the earl of Warwick, the premier peer in Essex, could be cast as a 'popular spirit'. This did not always work, of course, because there were limits to the flexibility and manipulability of the narratives – as Vane discovered in Kent and Booth and Wilbraham in Cheshire. But what seems clear is that over a period stretching from at least the 1580s to the 1640s these two narratives played an important role in structuring political attitudes and responses.

Early Stuart historians are familiar with the 'popular' and 'popish' conspiracy theories which enabled contemporaries to explain conflict and disruption and find appropriate means of dealing with them.[53] However, it is now clear also that many of the stories and categories and assumptions which structured the politics of the 1640s, and thereafter, can be traced back to the rise of a new-style 'politics of the public sphere' in Elizabeth's reign. Bound up with this was the emergence of a fundamental, almost binary, opposition between two visions of politics. One saw security and stability as depending on openness, involvement and the participation of a well-informed public of active, godly citizens; the other saw such involvement as itself destabilising, and therefore sought to close down politics and restrict it to a hierarchical elite presided over by the monarch. That was to be an enduring divide through the Revolution and well beyond.[54]

Notes

1 D. Hirst, *The representative of the people? Voters and voting under the early Stuarts* (Cambridge, 1975), 150–3, 216–22; J. K. Gruenfelder, 'The election to the short parliament, 1640', in H. S. Reinmuth (ed.), *Early Stuart studies* (Minneapolis, MN, 1970), 180–230. Depending on one's definition of 'contest' this total can almost certainly be added to. There is, for example, evidence of bitterly fought contests in both Derbyshire and Leicestershire which Hirst missed: Derbyshire Record Office, Gell of Hopton Papers, D258/34/5/4, a poll book for the Derbyshire election to the short parliament which was contested by Sir John Curzon, Sir John Harpur and John Manners Esq. (I am grateful to David Scott for providing me with details of this); HEH, Hastings MSS, HA Corre. 16/5557. For a different approach to the electoral politics of early Stuart England, see M. A. Kishlansky, *Parliamentary selection* (Cambridge, 1986).

2 TNA, SP 16/449/48; 448/79; Bedfordshire Record Office (BRO), St John (Bletso) MSS, no. 1369; Bodleian Library, Oxford, Bankes MSS, 44/13, 65/62.

3 C. Holmes, *Seventeenth-century Lincolnshire* (Lincoln, 1980), 138.

4 F. W. Jessup, 'The Kentish election of March 1640', *Archaeologia Cantiana*, 84 (1971), 2–4.

5 L. B. Larking (ed.), *Proceedings principally in the county of Kent* (Camden Society, 80, 1862), 5–8.

6 University College of North Wales, Bangor (UCNW), Mostyn MSS, 9082, nos 17–19 (I am grateful to Simon Healey for these sources); J. Walter, *Understanding popular violence in the English revolution* (Cambridge, 1999), 116–20; BRO, St John (Bletso) MSS, no. 1369; Bodleian Library, Bankes MSS, 44/13, 65/62.

7 BRO, St John (Bletso) MSS, no. 1369; TNA, SP 16/448/79.

8 TNA, SP 16/449/48; *The diary of Bulstrode Whitelocke 1605–1675*, ed. R. Spalding (Records of Social and Economic History, new series, 13, Oxford, 1990), 119–20; New College, Oxford, MS 9052, Diary of Robert Woodford, pp. 456–7; J. Peacey, 'Tactical organisation in a contested election: Sir Edward Dering and the spring election at Kent, 1640', in C. R. Kyle (ed.), *Parliament, politics and elections, 1604–1648*, Camden Society, 5th series, 17 (London, 2001), 237–72.

9 BRO, St John (Bletso) MSS, no. 1369; New College, Oxford, MS 9502, pp. 456–8.

10 TNA, SP 16/449/48 and 16/448/79.

11 P. Slack, 'An election to the short parliament', *Bulletin of the Institute of Historical Research*, 46 (1973), 108–14.

12 For the Elizabethan and early Stuart 'politics of the public sphere', see P. Lake and M. Questier, 'Puritans, papists and the "public sphere" in early modern England: the Edmund Campion affair in context, *Journal of Modern History*, 72 (2000), 586–627; K. Fincham and P. Lake, 'Popularity, prelacy and puritanism in the 1630s: Joseph Hall explains himself', *English Historical Review*, 111 (1996), 856–81; and the various contributions to the volume edited by P. Lake and S. Pincus, *The politics of the public sphere in early modern England* (Manchester University Press, forthcoming).

13 For the 1580s, see 49–51 above; for earlier manifestations, see Hirst, *Representative of the people*, 166–7; and E. Shagan, 'Protector Somerset and the 1549 rebellions: new sources and new perspectives, *English Historical Review*, 114 (1999), 34–66.

14 Larking (ed.), *Proceedings principally in the county of Kent*, 6; HEH, Hastings MSS, HA Corre. 16/5557.

15 New College, Oxford, MS 9502, pp. 456–8.

16 A. J. Fielding, 'Opposition to the personal rule of Charles I: the diary of Robert Woodford, 1637–1641', *Historical Journal*, 31 (1988), 778–86.

17 TNA, SP 16/448/43 and 16/449/14; R. Cust and P. Lake, 'Sir Richard Grosvenor and the rhetoric of magistracy', *Bulletin of the Institute of Historical Research*, 54 (1981), 40–53.

18 J. S. Morrill, *Cheshire 1630–1660* (Oxford, 1974), 32–4; P. Lake, 'Puritans, popularity and petitions: local politics in national context, Cheshire 1641', in T. Cogswell, R. Cust and P. Lake (eds), *Politics, religion and popularity* (Cambridge, 1992), 260–1.

19 Larking (ed.), *Proceedings principally in the county of Kent*, 6.

20 UCNW, Mostyn MSS, 9082, no. 21.

21 *The papers of Sir Richard Grosvenor, 1st Bart (1585–1645)*, ed. R. Cust (Lancashire and Cheshire Record Society, 134, 1996), 1–7.

22 UCNW, Mostyn MSS, 9082, no. 19.

23 TNA, SP 16/448/79.

24 BRO, St John (Bletso) MSS, no. 1369.

25 Jessup, 'Kentish election of March 1640', 3.

26 TNA, SP16/448/79; 16/449/48.

27 TNA, SP 16/449/48; Walter, *Understanding popular violence*, 116–19. Neville reckoned that his calculation allowed for the process of inflation since the franchise had been devised in the fifteenth century.

28 See also Lord Keeper Finch's remarks to the assize judges in February 1640, which may have been made with the elections in mind: 'there are some that affect popularity, diving into the people's hearts with kisses, offerings and fawnings. This becomes no subordinate magistrate. It is your part, my lords, to break the insolencies of such – before it approach too near the royal throne': J. Rushworth, *Historical collections of private passages of state, weighty matters of law, remarkable proceedings of five parliaments*, 7 vols (1659–1701), iii. 986. The accounts both by Elmes's supporters and by Neville were addressed to the privy council in an attempt to get the elections re-run and were, presumably, couched in terms which the authors thought would find favour at court.

29 R. Cust, 'Politics and the electorate in the 1620s, in R. Cust and A. Hughes (eds), *Conflict in early Stuart England* (Harlow, 1989), 134–67.

30 *The black book of Warwick*, ed. T. Kemp (Warwick, 1898), 385–97; J. E. Neale, *The Elizabethan House of Commons*, pbk edn (London, 1976), 240–4; Hirst, *Representative of the people*, 210–11; P. W. Hasler (ed.), *The history of parliament: the House of Commons 1558–1603*, 3 vols (London, 1981), i. 263–4.

31 Hasler, *History of the House of Commons*, iii. 492–4; P. Collinson, 'Puritans, men of business and Elizabethan parliaments', in his *Elizabethans* (London and New York, 2003), 69–70; T. E. Hartley (ed.), *Proceedings in the parliaments of Elizabeth I*, 3 vols (Leicester, 1981–1995), ii. 311–12. For more on Throckmorton and the Warwick election of 1586, see my article 'The "public man" in late Tudor and early Stuart England', in Lake and Pincus (eds), *The politics of the public sphere*.

32 *Black book of Warwick*, 389–90; A. F. Scott Pearson, *Thomas Cartwright and Elizabethan puritanism* (Cambridge, 1925), 290–304; Neale, *Elizabethan House of Commons*, 242–3.

33 *Black book of Warwick*, 393–6; Hirst, *Representative of the people*, 210–11.

34 For the political culture of 'monarchical republicanism', see Patrick Collinson's essays '*De republica Anglorum:* or history with the politics put back', and 'The monarchical republic of Queen Elizabeth I', in *Elizabethans*, 1–57.

35 *Black book of Warwick*, 389–94, 397. For John Fisher, see Hasler, *History of the House of Commons*, ii. 122–3.

36 M. Peltonen, *Classical humanism and republicanism in English political thought 1570–1640* (Cambridge, 1995); for a fuller discussion of the themes outlined in this section, see my article 'The "public man" in late Tudor and early Stuart England'.

37 The research currently being done by Mary Partridge promises to open up the whole subject.

38 R. Ascham, *The schoolmaster* (1570), ed. L. V. Ryan (Ithaca, NY, 1967), 5–12; R. M. Smuts, *Culture and power in England 1585–1685* (Basingstoke, 1999), 32–40.

39 For discussion of these works, see Lake, 'The politics of "popularity" and the public sphere', forthcoming in Lake and Pincus, *The politics of the public sphere*.

40 Smuts, *Culture and power in England*, 38–9, 66–70, 76–82; A. Bellany, *The politics of court scandal in early modern England: news culture* (Cambridge, 2002).

41 R. Cust and A. Hughes, 'Introduction: after revisionism', in *Conflict in early Stuart England*, 19–21; for the traditional view of the 'court' and 'country' divide which gives insufficient weight to the malleability of these images, see P. Zagorin, *The court and the country* (London, 1969), 33–9.

42 The themes outlined in this section are discussed more fully in my article 'Charles I and popularity', in Cogswell, Cust and Lake (eds), *Politics, religion and popularity*, 235–58.

43 For what follows, see Peter Lake's forthcoming article 'John Whitgift and the invention of popularity', in D. Hoak and J. F. McDiarmid (eds), *The monarchical republic*.

44 *The works of John Whitgift*, ed. J. Ayre, 3 vols (Cambridge, 1851–53), i. 372–3.

45 P. Lake, *Anglicans and puritans? Presbyterianism and English conformist thought from Whitgift to Hooker* (London, 1988), 11–30, 130–1.

46 Smuts, *Culture and power in England*, 66–70.

47 *The letters and life of Francis Bacon*, ed. J. Spedding, 7 vols (1861–74), ii. 40–5.

48 Hirst, *Representative of the people*, 178; D. H.Willson, *Privy councillors in the House of Commons 1604–1629* (Minneapolis, MN, 1940), 123.

49 *Basilicon doron*, in *King James VI and I: political writings*, ed. J. P. Sommerville (Cambridge, 1994), 25–7.

50 HMC, *Salisbury*, xxi. 266; *King James VI and I: political writings*, 23, 222; J. R. Tanner (ed.), *Constitutional documents of the reign of James I, 1603–1625* (Cambridge, 1960), 279.

51 Lake, 'John Whitgift'; J. Guy, 'The Elizabethan establishment and the ecclesiastical polity', in J. Guy (ed.), *The reign of Elizabeth I: court and culture in the last decade* (Cambridge, 1995), 126–49.

52 P. Joyce, *Democratic subjects: the self and the social in nineteenth-century England* (Cambridge, 1994), 153–61.

53 P. Lake, 'Anti-popery: the structure of a prejudice', in Cust and Hughes (eds), *Conflict in early Stuart England*, 72–106.

54 See, for example, the way in which the narrative of 'popular tumults' in the elections of 1640 was picked up in *Eikon basilike* and thus became embedded in later royalist accounts of the origins of the English civil war: *Eikon basilike*, ed. P. A. Knachel (Ithaca, NY, 1966), 4, 168; see also chapter 10, in this volume, by Mark Knights.

4

Religion and community in pre-civil war England

Anthony Milton

'We hold that seing there is not any man of the Church of England, but the same man is also a member of the Commonwealth nor any man a member of the Commonwealth which is not also of the Church of England . . . no person appertayning to the one can be denied to be also of the other'.[1] So wrote Richard Hooker, the late Elizabethan ideologue (some would say the creator) of Anglicanism. Those words are familiar to historians, as is the sentiment that they express. Pre-civil war England was, historians are used to thinking, a country where church and commonwealth were considered to be merely two different aspects of the same society – the same constituency viewed from two different angles. Church and commonwealth were coterminous, and this meant that, on the parish level, the social community *was* the religious community.

It is that assumption which was fundamentally challenged by the seismic interruption that was the English civil war and the Interregnum. The destruction of ecclesiastical discipline and the removal of persistent censorship created an outpouring of radical religious ideas, and also of new forms of religious organisation. The failure to replace the episcopalian church with an effective presbyterian system, and the removal of penalties for non-attendance at church, meant that the inclusive parish community, where the religious community duplicated the civil community, was dead. The experience of religious diversity, the breaking of a religious unity expressed in collective attendance at weekly religious services, fundamentally changed how the role of religion in the commonwealth was understood. Contemporaries' profound attachment to the idea of religious unity as the cement of the social order, and to the notion that church and commonwealth were mutually supporting and mutually inclusive, was forced to give way to the practical reality of religious pluralism. The Restoration would of course seek to restore the old religious unity and mutuality of church and commonwealth, but the genie was now out of the bottle, and religious peace could never again be secured. Dissent was effectively established, and by the 1690s the kingdom had given up on the idea of religious uniformity altogether. That is one of the legacies of the English Revolution.

Or so we are often told. The implication, of course, is that the religious unity of the parish was so ingrained that it was only through confrontation with the reality of religious pluralism engendered by the 1640s that it would cease to be central to the experience of the English people. And the same bonds of religious unity would even continue in a time of confessional diversity in the shape of parishioners' reluctance to report on and prosecute their sectarian neighbours.[2]

In this chapter I look again at this notion of the inclusive pre-civil war parochial religious community. Obviously, the model of the English Revolution outlined above presupposes the existence of this inclusive community in the prewar years. And even those social historians who are anxious to analyse the divisions among the social groups that make up the pre-civil war parish have tended to take the parish *religious* community as given. However else they might have been divided, all parishioners met up in the parish church each week, where they could play out all the more fully their rituals of inclusion and exclusion, hierarchy and deference.[3] But was there really universal participation in a unified parish religious community in this period? First, it is worth reminding ourselves of just how far the ideal of religious community was potentially undercut in practice, even in the pre-civil war period. But rather than simply provide a checklist of religious difference, it is also important to explore how ideas of social community and religious community relate – how far those who were divided by religion still acted together as members of local society (and were perceived as such by their neighbours). Did communal bonds still unite those of different faiths? Or was religious diversity attended by social distancing? Was it, in other words, a case of 'who can't pray with me, can't love me'?[4] And even if the focus is turned to those who prayed together, can it really be assumed that they constituted a single religious community?

It seems appropriate to begin by thinking about the ways in which local religious unity was lacking. One way of doing this is to imagine ourselves in the generic pre-civil war English parish church at service time. And rather than thinking about who is there, let us ponder who is *not* present. First of all, and perhaps most obviously, are the Roman Catholics. While Catholics are inching their way into the mainstream religious history of this period, they are still remarkably absent from many of the major works on the social history of the pre-civil war period. One otherwise excellent and comprehensive recent study of the micro-politics of rural communities in early modern England manages to describe a society in which Catholics appear not to exist at all. Another enormous and formidably researched study of the rites of passage in early modern England restricts Catholics to a tiny handful of sentences over nearly 500 pages of text.[5] Yet there *were* Catholics in pre-civil war England. Identified recusants (that is, those prosecuted for refusing to attend the services of the Church of England) may only have constituted less than two per cent of the entire population, but there were many other Catholics who avoided prosecution for recusancy while still cherishing a Catholic religious identity.[6] Moreover, the symbolic significance of such dissent from religious unity is surely far greater than their precise numbers might suggest.

Catholics need to be placed firmly in our picture, then. But how should we understand their situation vis-à-vis the local community? Were they members of it or were they a separate community altogether? One possible way of thinking about this is by considering how far the position of Catholics could be equated with the phenomenon of 'pillarisation'. This term, a literal translation of the Dutch *verzuiling*, is used by Dutch sociologists to describe the supposedly unique situation in the nineteenth-century Netherlands, where each religious denomination created its own political, social and cultural community, with its own political party, trade union, schools and youth organisation, in a form of social and cultural apartheid.[7] More recently, historians have begun to suggest that this phenomenon might be traced earlier in Dutch history than the nineteenth century, and that versions of it could be said to have existed in the confessional Europe of the seventeenth century.[8] And, certainly, striking echoes of it may be found in Germany and Central Europe – in cities like Augsburg, where each denomination had its own complete social system.[9] These were states where a degree of religious toleration had been formally established, but where toleration essentially fostered segregation, and apartheid.

When attempting to compare this 'pillarisation' model to the behaviour and experience of English Catholics, historians' initial instinct would be to dismiss it as entirely irrelevant. In recent years, a number of scholars have sought to reject the old idea of a hermetically sealed, inward-looking, separated, dissenting Catholic community. Instead, the size, shape and character of the English Catholic community has seemed much more difficult to define, especially once it is recognised that recusancy was a legal offence rather than a confessional calling-card. It has become clear that there was a substantial amount of partial church attendance and conformity among English Catholics. Moreover, it seems less clear that we can impose a rigid distinction between so-called 'church papists' (who attended the protestant church services simply to avoid persecution) and heroic recusants who refused to attend and were fined or imprisoned. Rather, these were categories that constantly shifted, patterns of behaviour that were in a state of flux.[10] Such is the diffuseness of Catholic identity in this period, and the problems in finding a clear definition, that it has even been suggested that we should abandon altogether talk of the existence of a unitary 'English Catholicism' in this period.[11]

Certainly, many Catholics seem well integrated into local society. Catholics have been found acting as local justices, constables and jurors, collecting taxes and even serving as churchwardens. It is hardly a surprise that locals therefore often seem to have assisted in keeping recusancy commissioners at bay. Even in religious matters, too, Catholics can be found going well beyond mere church papistry. Examples can be unearthed of prominent Catholics paying towards the costs of re-edifying their local protestant church, having their wives churched there, their marriages entered in the local register, and being buried in the protestant church (we can even find a Jesuit buried in the local churchyard).[12]

64

It is of course natural that Catholics would have felt a strong desire to maintain links with the local church which their ancestors had attended, and where the graves and monuments of their forebears were located. The social ties of community may also have been very strong. And if we read the casuistical tracts produced by Catholic priests and missionaries, we find that even those lay Catholics with reservations about such involvement with the local church could have their consciences officially assuaged. Catholic casuistical manuals specifically gave their blessing to Catholics to help repair the local church, reflecting that 'the churches are the churches of the true God and Christ . . . it does not matter that the churches are at present held by the heretics'. Besides, 'it is hoped [they] will, God willing, in a short time be restored . . . when the faith is re-established in England'. Catholics were also officially allowed to decorate the parish church 'in the old way with branches, flowers and grasses'.[13] They also allowed the payment of tithes even when a protestant held the benefice 'because they do not pay them to heretics but to the church'.[14] It was also explained that baptism and marriage conducted according to the protestant rite were valid, although Catholic participation in such services was condemned as sinful and scandalous.[15]

Other forms of sociability were not necessarily frowned upon. Roman Catholic casuists were prepared to allow for those occasions when the social demands of the gentry lifestyle and their responsibility to offer hospitality to their neighbours might require Roman Catholic gentlemen to compromise some of their confessional duties. For example, they were permitted to be present at meals in protestant houses when grace was said, and were allowed to bare their heads when the prayers were uttered – partly to conceal their faith but also, it was revealingly conceded, 'out of civility and politeness. For not to bare one's head when everyone else is bareheaded is a sort of incivility and the act of a bumpkin'. While expressing the fear that 'we are easily infected with heresy through familiarity with heretics', the casuists still emphasised that 'we can show them a good deal of familiarity and loyalty without it being too much familiarity'. Moreover, the natural duty of subjection to superiors meant that it was not sinful for wives, children and servants to serve husbands, fathers and masters in some heretical activities (such as preparing meat on fast days).[16] These forms of officially sanctioned sociability conform with the broader phenomenon observed by historians in several European countries which Willem Frijhoff has dubbed 'the ecumenicity of everyday life', where inter-confessional solidarity and sociability was the rule rather than the exception.[17]

But are historians in danger of going too far in emphasising Catholic integration into the local community? Obviously, Catholics' protestant neighbours were not always sympathetic towards them, and patterns of tolerance undoubtedly fluctuated. Moreover, private tolerance often co-existed with forms of official intolerance and anti-Catholicism which could condemn and curb the 'ecumenicity' that can sometimes be observed. Indeed, it was precisely the fact that the theoretical divisions between Catholics and protestants were so often breached in practice that itself prompted more allergic drives against social and cultural links between adherents of the different religions.[18] The behaviour and attitudes of Catholics themselves also displays elements of pillarisation. While they may not have been socially marginalised or excluded from participation in parochial affairs, Catholics did not necessarily see themselves as being integrated, and forms of social apartheid were not alien to Catholic thinking. Catholics were always urged not to attend protestant churches, but these arguments could be placed in a framework that urged far more systematic forms of social apartheid. One paper passed among Catholic gentlewomen around 1628 argued that 'society with those of contrary Religion' was always 'pernicious and unlawfull', and that God's children were enjoined to keep themselves apart from the society of the wicked.[19] These are arguments that we are used to hearing in the mouths of more hardline puritans – it is salutary to remember that Catholics could argue the same. Catholic casuistical manuals insisted that the father 'should labour most diligently' to make his children 'think badly of heretics and avoid their company'.[20] Casuistical manuals warned that it was not lawful to 'associate frequently' with protestants, commenting that this 'does injury to Christ if His enemies are treated with too much familiarity'.[21]

The 1628 paper is also notable in that Catholics are instructed that they should not be buried in the same churchyard as heretics.[22] As has been said, there seems to have been an understandable determination among Catholics still to be buried in the local churchyard where their forebears were (particularly if they were told to regard the churches as still in a sense theirs, and simply on forced loan to the protestants). We may perhaps assume that Catholic ritual was used to supplement protestant ritual in clandestine fashion later on, in very much the same way as happened with baptism and marriage.[23] But problems arose when recusants died who had been excommunicated for their recusancy, and who were therefore not permitted to be buried in the churchyard. Sometimes the solution was to carry out a clandestine burial, such as happened in Allens-Moore in Herefordshire in 1605, when a band of 40–50 Catholics with a 'Saints-bell', cross and burning tapers accompanied the corpse of the excommunicated recusant Alice Wellington to bury it in the churchyard at 6 a.m., when the vicar was still in bed.[24] But a more radical solution was embraced by the remarkable William Blundell of Little Crosby, in Lancashire, who had part of his estate enclosed in 1611 to provide a burial ground for recusants who were prohibited from burial in the parish church. Blundell kept a burial register to record the 80 burials that took place in the first 18 years that the site was used, and it is also notable that bodies were brought to the site from a much wider surrounding area – testimony to the vigour of a Catholic community that transcended the boundaries of parish and immediate neighbourhood.[25]

Is there any clearer way of distancing oneself from the local parish community than being buried elsewhere according to a different funeral rite? Other rites of passage were conducted in ways that defied the local parish community, despite the heavy fines that could be charged. There were clandestine baptisms, christenings and marriages. There is also scattered evidence that wealthier

Catholics might provide relief specifically for poor Catholics, and employment for Catholic servants, as well as providing local 'mass centres' that might also be the venue for clandestine rites of passage.[26]

We can also find putative forms of 'pillarisation' elsewhere, in segregated education, for example.[27] But perhaps most fascinating are forms of pillarised entertainment, such as the troupes of local Catholic actors – notably the Egton Interlude players, whose fame peaked in the Jacobean period. This troupe performed plays and interludes on a circuit of Catholic gentry and yeoman households in the North Riding. Their 'popish playes' often embodied a Catholic political or religious message that would be spelt out in more direct and potent form through the anti-protestant interludes or playlets that the company's members themselves devised.[28]

Nevertheless, my intention here is not to replace an integrationist with a 'pillarised' model. Clearly there is evidence for both models of behaviour, and the degree to which the one form of association was more prominent than the other would have been crucially shaped by local circumstances and the relative intensity of the enforcement of recusancy legislation. On a conceptual level, we might suggest that many Catholics oscillated between these different ways of thinking of themselves as a 'community', that it was a division played out every day in the mind and behaviour of the individual Catholic. The issue of church attendance or non-attendance is not, perhaps, the most useful way into analysing this phenomenon.

Another group of locals who are absent from our generic parish church – at least if it is in London, Norwich, Maidstone, Sandwich or Canterbury – comprises, of course, members of the foreign stranger churches, French and Italian but especially Dutch, where the use of *verzuiling* as a concept seems doubly appropriate. These people *were* members of the local parish community in that they paid the poor rate and other local rates, and yet they also in a sense lived very much apart. Their churches were prominent local statements of religious difference, and they also ran their own poor-relief, plague-relief and education systems.[29] The stranger churches are a reminder that public meetings of congregations acting independently of the state church were visible in several of England's major towns from the reign of Edward VI onwards – they were not a shocking, radical, new departure of the civil war period. Moreover, the existence of those churches helped to confuse still further the notion of clearly defined parochial religious communities. Not only did stranger churches transcend the parish boundaries of the Church of England, but Dutch immigrants and their descendants might oscillate between their local English church and the services of their stranger church. Even one of the leading elders of the Dutch church at Austin Friars made a point of regularly attending his local parish church.[30]

Other groups absent from our notional parish church are also, of course, protestant separatists. By the Caroline period such separatists may well have left the country altogether, to the Netherlands or to New England. Brownism had had its heyday in the 1580s and 1590s, and despite the emergence of Baptist congregations in Jacobean London separatists were not as prominent in the early Stuart period.[31] But for those who remained it is worth remembering that, ironically, their very act of separation from the local religious community left the separatists feeling freer to socialise fully in all secular matters. As the separatist Henry Ainsworth explained, the separatists should have 'no communion with the wicked in their religion', but in 'civill affayres' they were perfectly free to be fully integrated into normal social relationships.[32] There could hardly be a more complete denial of Hooker's assertion of the interdependence of church and commonwealth. Nevertheless, just as remarkable are the sectarian groups which still managed to remain within the established church, incarnating a spiritualising radicalism within a husk of outward conformity.[33] Some of these more exotic and mystical sectarian groups seem to have regularly attended their local churches – a point to which I will return.

There may be other absentees from our generic parish church. Our image of the local church usually includes the prominent, commanding and perhaps elaborately decorated pew of the local great family. Many gentry families did indeed have important pews, and later funeral monuments, in local churches. But were they always there at the Sunday service? Most gentry families would be away from home for part of the year, as business or pleasure took them down to London. But many of the upper gentry and aristocracy also had their own chapels on their estates.[34] John Bowle praised the earl of Kent in a funeral sermon in 1615 for having publicly frequented his local church rather than his private chapel. But clearly this behaviour was regarded as exceptional.[35] Where costly and elaborate chapels had been created, it seems very unlikely that their owners regularly attended the local church instead, except perhaps at the major festivals of Christmas or Easter.[36] These private chapels, attended by the gentry or aristocratic household, in a sense accommodated what was a religious community in its own right – with the servants possibly attending chapel rather than the local church, the services led by the domestic chaplain. The private chapels could also be the venues for more exclusive celebrations of rites of passage, well away from the local parish community. A chapel was not vital for such services: John Evelyn was baptised in the dining room of the family home in 1620.[37] It should be emphasised that this was a form of privatisation, apart from the parish community, that can be observed as a fashion well before the civil war – this was not necessarily a legacy of the assault on parochial norms in the English Revolution.

Others absent from our church service may have 'gadded' to hear sermons elsewhere. This was technically illegal, of course, but in major towns with famous preachers, and most of all in London, it was clearly very common practice. And it was behaviour of which the church might even partly approve – it was not necessary to see such behaviour as expressive of a rejection of the value of public prayer. Notable in this respect is a sermon given by Samuel Gibson at Oundle in 1619. Gibson's sermon was intended mostly to emphasise the importance of public worship, especially the prayers of the minister. But the public worship which he so eloquently praised need not have been attended by the entire local congregation. This is made clear as Gibson goes on positively to exhort his hearers to gad to sermons, chiding them for not daring to 'goe to a Sermon so much as halfe a Sabbath dayes iourney, though they have not at home', and mocking them for pretending that they resisted 'for feare of Apparitors and Churchwardens'. What makes this exhortation all the more remarkable is that it was preached at an episcopal visitation.[38]

In some parishes people might have struggled to find a pew in church even if they had wanted to attend. Church accommodation in towns, and especially in London's suburbs, was often patently inadequate for the increasing population. It is remarkable that even in enormous suburban London parishes such as St Saviour's, Southwark, and St Botolph Aldgate, Jeremy Boulton has calculated that an extraordinarily high proportion of the population (80–90 per cent) attended Easter Communion in the early seventeenth century. Nevertheless, such rates of attendance were achieved only by staggering Easter Communions over many weeks – a practice that Julia Merritt has also documented in the parishes of Westminster.[39] What is proven here is the *lack* of universal attendance at these churches at any one time. Moreover, the enormous efforts made to ensure that all members of the congregation attended Easter Communion were not, could not, be duplicated for the monthly parish communions. In other words, the ideal of each local society united weekly in prayer and communion was simply impossible to achieve in some important parts of the country.

It was not mere shortage of space that prevented some people attending, of course; no picture of church absence would be complete without those who irreligion or the rival attractions of the alehouse kept away, or the sometimes large numbers of excommunicants who were not allowed to attend.[40]

Obviously, not every parish in England would have had separatists, foreigners, Catholics, absent earls and excommunicates among its members. But they might well have played host to at least one of these phenomena. The congregation assembled in the parish church and the local community were not, then, simply co-extensive.

It is also vital to ask how far the people who *are* present at our notional church service constitute a single religious community. We might begin with those whose thoughts were likely to be very much elsewhere – the so-called 'church papists'. Their attendance was reluctant, but they may also have used the opportunity to express their hostility – some read Psalters or chanted Latin psalms.[41] These parishioners can hardly have considered themselves members of the religious community gathered in church on that day.

A more significantly anomalous group consists of those with a good deal more protestant enthusiasm – the puritans. In theory, puritans were wholly committed to the national church. It was puritans who wrote the most persistent and vitriolic works of anti-separatist polemic – indeed, anti-separatism was central to the puritan worldview. Even semi-separatists defended the continuing integrity of the national church, even if some of them chose not to attend it.[42] For all their ideas of themselves as the tiny minority of true believers in an unregenerate world, puritans were also committed to another model, where the whole nation was God's people, an elect nation, modelled on Israel. Two very different notions of the religious community therefore co-existed in the minds of puritans.[43] This is not to say, however, that puritans typically saw themselves as members of the same religious community as the others gathered around them in the local parish church. On the contrary, the community that defined their religious existence was the so-called 'community of the godly', the minority of true believers who could identify each other among the corrupt mass present in the church. It was that community, transcending parochial boundaries, which the godly would seek out, and it was in the company of the fellow-godly, as the puritan preacher Robert Bolton put it, 'their comfortable fellowship in the gospel and mutual intercourse of godly conference, heavenly counsel, spiritual encouragement, consideration one of another, [and] confirmation in grace', that the godly would find a true sense of spiritual fulfilment.[44] And here we might again note some of our 'pillarisation' elements. The 'godly' were involved in distinctive forms of social behaviour and association, might well pursue different education through puritan tutors and puritan foundations, and commonly intermarried, seeking to find godly marriage partners and servants.[45] They also had special charitable duties towards their fellow-godly. As Julia Merritt has noted, the Jacobean puritan preacher Robert Hill instructed his flock that 'especially I must give to the godly' and that when doing good deeds on Sundays 'I must be carefull to provide something, which I may distribute to the necessitie of the saints'.[46]

This was not just a matter of social exclusivity and a recognised shared religious identity. Particularly important is that this exclusive religious identity also took the form of association and meetings of an explicitly religious nature outside the gatherings of the local parish. These meetings for private prayer and sermon repetition might even be participated in by a group that had voluntarily entered into a covenant with each other. As Patrick Collinson has emphasised, these were not 'conventicles', in the sense of direct alternatives to parochial worship. Those taking part in them did not consider themselves to be separating from the national church. Nevertheless, even if there was no liturgical form to these meetings, for those puritans involved one assumes that it was these gatherings of the fellow-godly which more truly approximated to what the 'church' of the New Testament intended. And it is just as notable that, in the 1640s, so many of these covenanted groups made a very smooth transition to acting as full-blown gathered churches.[47] In this sense, the 1640s and 1650s were partly just a rationalisation of what had been happening for a long time.

Just as significant as these gathered assemblies is that notions of godly collectivity were combined with an ethic of social separation from the 'ungodly'. Preachers such as Robert Bolton and Joseph Bentham, successive vicars of Boughton, argued, on the basis of the consideration that there would soon be 'an everlasting separation' between the godly and the profane, that it might be wise to begin this 'disacquaintance' as soon as possible with 'graceless men'.[48] While the puritan must not separate from the congregation in church, yet outside the church, in social relationships and familiar conversation, the godly were actually obliged to cut themselves off from the ungodly as far as possible. As the puritan Thomas Hooker put it: 'I can keep a man out of my house, but I cannot fling him out of the open congregation.'[49] With such ideas of social distancing we are back with the Catholic paper of 1628.

Another important point about the community of the godly was, of course, that it transcended parish boundaries. Thus Peter Lake's study of the 'puritan underground' in early Stuart London has emphasised the degree to which this distinctive religious community operated with scant regard to boundaries of parish and ward.[50]

Our puritan church attenders may therefore have a very different sense of what the service meant than other members of the congregation. Rather than the essence of their religious life being the church service, and voluntary religion in the conventicle a mere supplement or adjunct to it, they may well have seen things the other way round – that the kernel of true religion lay in their covenanted congregations, while public worship in their parish community was the mere husk. But the anti-separatist strain of puritanism should also remind us that there were some very peculiar puritan ideas that might still be compatible with church attendance. We should remember here Patrick Collinson's wonderful example of Randall Bate (who died in prison in 1613). Bate demanded the demolition of parish churches and the abandonment of the practice of burial in churchyards, and yet he condemned separation.[51] The heretical boxmaker John Etherington was, as Peter Lake has pointed out, 'meticulously conformist' in his treatment of ceremonies and church government, and was a regular church attender. Yet he had certainly dabbled in Familist ideas, and his lack of qualms about church ceremonies and readiness to defend the outward ordinances of the Church of England derived from his view of them as almost entirely irrelevant to his religious life, mere external forms compared to 'the inner spiritual realities that alone created and sustained the godly community that remained the true focus of his interest and allegiance'.[52] Of course, the Familists themselves could square their consciences with regular church attendance, and even the holding of the office of churchwarden – but what sort of religious content did they really ascribe to these assemblies?

Even disregarding Randall Bate, John Etherington and their like, we are still faced with the rest of the congregation. Is it here that our true parochial religious community lies? Can we define the rest of the congregation as a religious community defined by their presence at the liturgical service of the Church of England? In the eyes of some historians, we can. Non-puritan English people can be presented as having one voice and one mind. In one working of this position they are even given a new name – 'layfolk'. The 'layfolk' have a single mindset – their 'popular religion' is marked by 'flexibility', 'a syncretic instinct and a reluctance to abandon . . . the middle ground' – most of all this religiosity is marked by tolerance of religious difference and an instinct to create a hybrid religion 'compounded of that which is best in both'.[53] Another rendering of this position presents the liturgy – the Book of Common Prayer – as defining the religious identity of this non-puritan body of people. These are the denizens of 'prayer book protestantism', 'committed conformists', dedicated to an 'habitual, relatively unexacting religion'.[54] The danger is that again we are presented with a mono-lithic core of moderate, instinctively non-doctrinal, English people who inhabit what is presented as a static 'lay religious tradition' which can be found as a sim-ple continuum stretching from the 1550s to the 1650s.[55]

There are many problems with this argument, not least that there is a danger of slippage into discredited notions of an 'Anglican' essence (and while the schol-ars who have coined these terms have used them with care, there is nevertheless a danger that the less sure-footed reader will fall into presupposing this). The main problem here is not the question of whether or not historians specifically use the term 'Anglican', but rather their attempt to impute a single religious identity to everyone who attended church services who was not a puritan. Puritans seems to have a clear, focused identity. The rest of the population, one assumes, are non-puritan. So, the argument runs, what is their identity? But *why* should we assume that there is a single non-puritan identity? And here the attention paid to the liturgy, while salutary, is also part of the problem. We might indeed accept the suggestion that the Book of Common Prayer was central to the experience of English parishioners in this period. But that does not mean that we can read off a universal interpretation of what the Prayer Book meant to people, assuming (as one recent historian has urged) that it conditioned a 'theo-logical response' to doctrine, acting as a prism through which everything else was perceived.[56]

Two particular points seem pertinent for the interpretation of Prayer Book services. First, it is important to remember that, as cultural historians have em-phasised, cultural transmission takes place through complex forms of assim-ilation and appropriation, through which the nature and meaning of the cultural practice may be subtly changed. Those congregated in church were not mere passive recipients of a religious message. Ideas and practices were inevitably refracted through the different ideas, associations and behaviour of the indi-viduals involved.[57] Second, when trying to calculate the meaning that the Prayer Book injected into the service which the parish community attended, we face the fundamental problem that we cannot know how the minister chose to gloss and perform the liturgy – which words were emphasised, which gestures used by the officiating minister, or how far sermons or catechisms primed people to attach specific importance to elements of the liturgy.[58]

Given the impossibility of knowing precisely what was being thought by those attending Church of England services, a more compelling trend in recent scholar-ship has suggested that we should think more of the eclecticism of 'popular' and 'elite' religious beliefs among conforming members of the Church of England.[59] 'Puritan' devotional literature need not be read merely by puritans.[60] The rhythms of the Prayer Book may have had to keep time with the wealth of folk beliefs – of astrology, alchemy, magical healing and divination – that were ever-present in this period. Providentialism, neoplatonism, stoicism and pyrrhonism could all appeal to conforming members of the Church of England, and give their devotions a distinctive inflection. We must be careful not to underestimate the extent to which different potentially heterodox ideas were available to the parishioner prior to the 1640s. Most libraries of the period would have held heterodox religious literature in the form of Roman Catholic writings.[61] But heterodox applications could also be generated by individuals without such assistance. The Bible was a ready source of problematical ideas and examples: a literal reading of the fourth commandment seems to have been enough to give the anti-puritan, impeccably conformist Theophilus Brabourne his conviction that the sabbath must be celebrated on the Saturday.[62] Moreover, private religious duties away from the formal church service might loom large in the lives of non-puritans too. James Howell was no puritan, but he recorded with pride his practice of privately fasting three times a week, as well as praying in seven languages.[63]

It is therefore impossible for us to precisely answer the questions of what the church service meant for those attending it or how far members of the congregation considered themselves to be part of a single religious community. All may have regarded themselves as members of other communities – the puritans as members of the community of the godly, the officiating clergyman as a member of a like-minded clerical association, or profession, the gentry as representatives of a dominant political estate, and so on. We can of course even dispute whether this gathering should be described as 'religious' at all. There are obvious dangers in adopting a socially reductionist view which sees activities within the parish church as fulfilling a purely secular agenda. Nevertheless, precisely because the parish community was notionally present at the service, so the preoccupations and divisions of local society might be performed and displayed in the church service itself – the arrangement of pews and the demeanour of their occupants provided an obvious opportunity for members of the congregation to play out the micro-politics of the parish.

Precise motivations behind church attendance might also vary. Guild members or local office-holders attending a church service might sometimes see themselves primarily as performing a civic duty. Lower down the social scale, regular church attendance was usually required of almsmen, the receipt of poor relief might be conditional on church attendance, and sometimes weekly distributions from endowed charities were made in church.[64] And how should we interpret Easter Communion? For some parishes this would be the only time in the year that the whole parish community was essentially united (and in some, as we have seen, this meeting was still mostly symbolic, as the communion could be staggered over many weeks). Was this more a symbolic annual reassertion of communal harmony encompassing the entire adult population of the parish, rather than a specific feast-day being celebrated by a regularly constituted religious community? Obviously, harmony and charity, too, had religious meaning, and it would be perverse to suggest that a communion service did not have significant religious content, but should the staggered annual Easter Communion also be thought of as serving a social and symbolic purpose very different to that of the weekly church service? Should we also think of them as we think of the perambulations and church ales, May games and revels, midsummer shows and sports – those seasonable occasions when neighbourhood ties were celebrated?[65]

One figure who could crucially influence the way that the church service was perceived and understood was, of course, the minister. For he was the impresario, the master of ceremonies – and the way that the minister chose to pitch the performance could radically change its significance. The nature, style and content of the minister's sermon, even merely the manner and style of his performance of the liturgy, might serve to emphasise certain elements over others. The deployment of liturgical furniture and music, the place where the minister stood at different points in the service, could convey very different meanings. A compelling puritan minister might satisfy the more puritan members of the congregation that their parochial service was starting to approximate to the religious community of the godly (or at least that the disjunction between the godly and the parish community was less stark). Puritan ministers could also (notoriously) seize the opportunity to delineate the boundaries of the religious community by naming local transgressors directly in their sermon.

Those clergy who supported Archbishop Laud could gloss the service in a very different way thanks to some of the rearrangements of church interiors that followed from the Laudian reforms – notably raising the chancel and placing the altar at the east end. But it is also worth noting how Laudian clerics' orchestration of the church service represented a reworking of the local community. It is sometimes suggested that the Laudians emphasised simply hierarchy and order, and that their rearrangement of churches was intended to effect this (thereby, according to one reading, creating division in an otherwise unified community).[66] But Laudian ministers were often providing their own very different reading of the local community. Several Laudian authors pointedly emphasised that the hierarchies of the parish community should be abandoned once the parishioners set foot inside the church. Poorer members of the congregation were specifically told not to stand up and acknowledge deferentially their social superiors when the latter entered the church. It was insisted that all laypeople, whatever their social rank, should be bareheaded in church.[67] Cutting down pews and establishing uniformity in their height and style was intended to create order, but also to prevent the intrusion of civil presumption into the church.[68] The Laudian church was not intended to be a simple reflection of the local commonwealth. Rather, the local religious community was recast, with the laity united in their inferiority, while the cleric was in control, performing in a raised chancel behind altar rails that none but he was allowed to enter.

We should be wary, however, of making Laudianism a strange, inexplicable, new movement that shattered the accepted norms of the local religious community and thereby made inevitable a backlash which would ensure that the parochial religious society would never be reconstructed. It is more apparent that Laudianism emerged from existing tensions and divisions, as a stage in a resurgent clericalism whose spokesmen were arguing as early as 1606 that prayers without a lawful minister never went to God at all.[69] It was one stage in a tense and evolving relationship between the enacting of religious community that took place in the local church and the civil community that existed outside the church door. The opponents of Laudianism attacked it in the early 1640s as an alien force that had disrupted communal norms and local unity, and in the process implied the existence of a unified local religious community. The danger is that we then seek to read that united community back into the earlier period. It may be more useful to think of Laudians working what was only a temporary unity between different groups in the face of their liturgical innovations – rather than artificially radicalising their opponents, they unified radicals who already existed, and intensified ambiguities and inconsistencies in the local religious community that were already well established.

To conclude, given the range of local parishioners who were not attending our notional church service, and the fact that those who were present may have understood the event in very different ways, should we simply conclude that we cannot really talk of a single, parochial, religious community in the pre-civil war period? Of course not. The parish was a vital political and administrative unit, and an important source of local identity, and the church still stood at its ceremonial centre – a place of public witness as well as religious worship.[70] The ideal of the local society unified in prayer was a powerful one that lay at the heart of the whole institution of the parish. And the broader idea that all Englishmen participated in a single, unified, religious community was a fundamental one – sufficiently important that it would not simply retreat in the face of religious diversity and pluralism. It can be found in the eighteenth century as much as the seventeenth, in Cromwell's Protectorate and even in the Netherlands, the 'university of all religions', where the broader community participated in the public rites that were presided over by a public church which did not coerce membership and yet held a monopoly of Christian behaviour in the public sphere.[71]

The point of this chapter has not been simply to juxtapose this ideal with the rather less than perfect reality of our local congregation; rather, it has been to query the assumption that there was one religious community (however imperfect) in England prior to the civil war. Historians of community have warned us against assuming that we can point to a single, essential, local community, and have noted that our tendency to employ the term exclusively in relation to locality and geographical propinquity reflects later usage.[72] Forms of religious community are arguably freer than most from being tied to simple notions of space, whereas civil community in an age when the parish had such administrative importance was inevitably more constricted. It could be suggested, then, that there were a multitude of religious communities in pre-civil war England, located in the household, the conventicle, the community of the godly, the Catholic community, perhaps too in other forms of association and organisation which wielded religious influence, such as livery companies, vestries and so on. A single individual might participate in a number of different religious communities. In fact, different visions of religious community might often co-exist in the mind of an individual. The community gathered in the church is therefore a temporary one – but it reflects a moment when members of these different religious communities come together. It was, in other words, a 'point of contact'. We could, of course, suggest that the congregation gathered in the parish church is made a religious community, not because of shared religious ideas, but rather by the very act of collective participation in the rites of the service.

And in this case, what happened in the 1640s was not so much the creation of new religious communities, but rather the removal of the parochial gathering that could temporarily unite members of these different communities. The most notable new religious community to be born of these events, one might almost suggest, was the new 'Anglican' one.

The result – religious diversity – was hardly something novel in early modern Europe. Part of England's distinctiveness may have been that it had not had to confront religious diversity as directly as had other European countries. Nevertheless, the rise of religious pluralism in the 1640s did have its differences in England compared to other countries. The Netherlands might seem the archetypal home of religious pluralism, but while religious minorities were allowed to exist there, they were expected to remain in theory 'private', and were forbidden from directly attacking the established church.[73] It is the sustained attacks on the public church, the undermining of its dignity and authority, and the very public ways in which the new sectarian groups conducted themselves in the 1640s and 1650s, which make England seem so different from other European countries in this period. And perhaps it is the undermining of the cultural authority of the public church (rather than the simple removal of its power to coerce attendance or the growth of religious diversity) that constitutes part of that elusive legacy of the English Revolution.

Notes

1 *The Folger Library edition of the works of Richard Hooker*, 6 vols (Cambridge, MA, 1977–98), iii. 319.

2 P. J. Norrey, 'The restoration regime in action: the relationship between central and local government in Dorset, Somerset and Wiltshire, 1660–1678', *Historical Journal*, 31 (1988), 789–812.

3 S. Hindle, *The state and social change in early modern England, c. 1550–1640* (Basingstoke, 2000); P. Griffiths, A. Fox and S. Hindle (eds), *The experience of authority in early modern England* (Basingstoke, 1996).

4 J. J. La Rocca, ' "Who can't pray with me, can't love me": toleration and the early Jacobean recusancy policy', *Journal of British Studies*, 23 (1984), 22–36.

5 Hindle, *The state and social change*; D. Cressy. *Birth, marriage and death: ritual, religion, and the life-cycle in Tudor and Stuart England* (Oxford, 1997). For rare examples in the latter work, see 57, 189, 401. While Cressy notes the persistence of Catholic traditions, he is essentially concerned to use these to describe a hybrid protestant culture, rather than the activities of Catholics as such. Catholics (and indeed church papists)

are also absent from Keith Wrightson's famous article 'The politics of the parish in early modern England', in Griffiths et al. (eds), *The experience of authority*.

6 M. B. Rowlands, 'Hidden people: Catholic commoners, 1558–1625', in M. B. Rowlands (ed.), *English Catholics of parish and town 1558–1778*, Catholic Record Society monographs, 5 (Wolverhampton, 1999), 22.

7 A. Lijphart, *The politics of accommodation: pluralism and democracy in the Netherlands* (Berkeley, CA, 1968); J. C. H. Blom, *Verzuiling in Nederland, in het bijzonder op lokaal niveau 1850–1925* (Amsterdam, 1981); S. Stuurman, *Verzuiling, kapitalisme en patriarchaat: aspecten van de ontwikkeling van de moderne staat in Nederland* (Nijmegen, 1983); J. A. Belzen, 'Religion and the social order: psychological factors in Dutch pillarization, especially among the Calvinists', in J. A. Belzen (ed.), *Psychohistory in psychology of religion* (Amsterdam, 2001).

8 S. Groenveld, *Huisgenoten des geloofs: was de samenleving in de Republiek der Verenigde Nederlanden verzuild?* (Hilversum, 1995); W. Frijhoff, *Embodied belief: ten essays on religious culture in Dutch history* (Hilversum, 2002), 277, 280; B. J. Kaplan, '"Dutch" religious tolerance: celebration and revision', in R. P. Hsia and H. van Nierop (eds), *Calvinism and religious toleration in the Dutch golden age* (Cambridge, 2002), 26.

9 A. F. Creasman, '"To instill and preserve the beloved peace": policing public expression across the confessional divide', paper presented at the 'Religion and the early modern public sphere' conference, University of Keele, June 2003.

10 M. Questier, *Conversion, politics and religion in England, 1580–1625* (Cambridge, 1996); and 'Conformity, Catholicism and the law', in P. Lake and M. Questier (eds), *Conformity and orthodoxy in the English Church c. 1560–1660* (Woodbridge, 2000).

11 Questier, *Conversion*, 204.

12 Rowlands, 'Hidden people', and M. Wanklyn, 'Catholics in the village community: Madeley, Shropshire, 1630–1770', in Rowlands, *English Catholics*, 30, 225–6.

13 P. Holmes (ed.), *Elizabethan casuistry* (London, 1981), 25, 110–11.

14 *Ibid.*, 22, 58, 101–2.

15 *Ibid.*, 28–9, 90–1, 99.

16 *Ibid.*, 71, 119, 122–3.

17 Frijhoff, *Embodied belief*, 31; J. Pollmann, 'The bond of Christian piety: the individual practice of tolerance and intolerance in the Dutch republic', in Hsia and van Nierop, *Calvinism and religious toleration*, 55 and *Religious choice in the Dutch republic* (Manchester, 1999).

18 A. Milton, 'A qualified intolerance: the limits and ambiguities of early Stuart anti-Catholicism', in A. Marotti (ed.), *Catholicism and anti-Catholicism in early modern English texts* (Basingstoke, 1999), 107–10.

19 W. Bedell, *An Examination of certaine motives to recusansie* (1628), dedicatory epistle (hereafter, ep. ded.), 1–27.

20 Holmes, *Elizabethan casuistry*, 103.

21 *Ibid.*, 123.

22 Bedell, *Examination*, 8.

23 H. Aveling, *Northern Catholics: the Catholic recusants of the North Riding of Yorkshire 1558–1790* (London, 1966), 148–50, 227.

24 T. Hamond, *The late commotion of certaine papists in Herefordshire* (1605), sigs Dr–Dv.

25 M. Sena, 'William Blundell and the networks of Catholic dissent in post-reformation England', in A. Shepard and P. Withington (eds), *Communities in early modern England* (Manchester, 2000), 64.

26 Rowlands, 'Hidden people'; J. A. Hilton, 'The Catholic poor: paupers and vagabonds, 1580–1780', in Rowlands, *English Catholics*, 28, 30, 125.

27 Aveling, *Northern Catholics*, 291–7.

28 *Ibid.*, 193, 288–90.

29 O. P. Grell, *Dutch Calvinists in early Stuart London* (Leiden, 1989); A. Pettegree, *Foreign protestant communities in sixteenth-century London* (Oxford, 1986); Pettegree, 'The French and Walloon communities in London 1550–1688', in O. P. Grell, J. Israel and N. Tyacke (eds), *From persecution to toleration* (Oxford, 1991).

30 Grell, *Dutch Calvinists*, 3–4.

31 B. R. White, *The English separatist tradition* (Oxford, 1971); S. Brachlow, *The communion of saints* (Oxford, 1988).

32 P. Collinson, 'The cohabitation of the faithful with the unfaithful', in Grell et al. (eds), *From persecution to toleration*, 60–1.

33 P. Lake, *The boxmaker's revenge* (Manchester, 2001), 399–401.

34 On all aspects of gentry and aristocratic chapels I am indebted to Lynn Hulse for her expert advice which has shaped the argument of this paragraph.

35 J. Bowle, *A sermon preached . . . at the funerall of Henrie earle of Kent* (1615), sigs F2v–F3r. Bowle insisted that 'God doth give that blessing to the publike Temple, that he doth not give to a private Chappell; Indeede they are Chappels of ease, more for their ease, then their honor . . . as there is but one common salvation, so there ought to bee a common, and a publique, and a ioynt humble Invocation' (F3r). I am grateful to Dr Hulse for bringing this sermon to my attention.

36 Even if the house had no consecrated chapel, services may have taken place in the great chamber instead, which could even serve as a venue for sermons; I am grateful to Dr Hulse for this point.

37 Cressy, *Birth, marriage and death*, 190.

38 S. Gibson, *A sermon of ecclesiastical benediction* (1620), sigs A2r, 24–5 and generally. It is notable that the sermon carries an endorsement by the three ministers of the Okeham lecture (sig. A2r–v).

39 J. P. Boulton, 'The limits of formal religion: the administration of Holy Communion in late Elizabethan and early Stuart London', *London Journal*, 10 (1984), 135–54; J. F. Merritt, *The social world of early modern Westminster: abbey, court and community, 1525–1640* (Manchester, 2005), 318–20, 327–8.

40 P. Collinson, *The religion of protestants* (Oxford, 1982), 214–17.

41 A. Walsham, *Church papists: Catholicism, conformity and confessional polemic in early modern England* (Woodbridge, 1993), 89–90.

42 P. Collinson, 'Sects and the evolution of puritanism', in F. Bremer (ed.), *Puritanism: trans-Atlantic perspectives on a seventeenth-century Anglo-American faith* (Boston, MA, 1993), 156–60; V. J. Gregory, 'Congregational puritanism and the radical puritan community in England c. 1585–1625', Ph.D thesis, Cambridge University (2003).

43 E.g. P. Collinson, *The birthpangs of protestant England* (Basingstoke, 1988), ch. 1.

44 P. Lake, ' "A charitable Christian hatred": the godly and their enemies in the 1630s', in C. Durston and J. Eales (eds), *The culture of English puritanism 1560–1700* (Basingstoke, 1996), 153.

45 *Ibid.*, 150–6; J. T. Cliffe, *The puritan gentry* (London, 1984), 66, 68, 77.

46 J. F. Merritt, 'The pastoral tight-rope: a puritan pedagogue in Jacobean London', in T. Cogswell, R. Cust and P. Lake (eds), *Politics, religion and popularity in early Stuart Britain* (Cambridge, 2002), 155–6.

47 P. Collinson, 'The English conventicle', in D. Wood and W. Sheils (eds), *Voluntary religion* (Oxford, 1986).

48 Collinson, 'The cohabitation of the faithful with the unfaithful', 66–7.

49 *Ibid.*, 61–2; Lake, 'A charitable Christian hatred', 165–71.

50 Lake, *Boxmaker's revenge*, 170–88, 208–57, 393–6; P. Lake and D. Como, ' "Orthodoxy" and its discontents: dispute settlement and the production of "consensus" in the London (puritan) underground', *Journal of British Studies*, 39 (2000), 34–70.

51 Collinson, 'The cohabitation of the faithful with the unfaithful', 60; and 'Sects and the evolution of puritanism', 157.

52 Lake, *Boxmaker's revenge*, 106, 399.

53 C. Marsh, *Popular religion in sixteenth-century England* (Basingstoke, 1998), 212–13.

54 J. Maltby, *Prayer book and people in Elizabethan and early Stuart England* (Cambridge, 1998), 11, 17; P. Collinson, *Elizabethan essays* (London, 1994), 228.

55 Maltby, *Prayer book and people*, 8.

56 S. L. Arnoult, ' "Spiritual and sacred publique actions": *The Book of Common Prayer* and the understanding of worship in the Elizabethan and Jacobean Church of England', in E. Carlson (ed.), *Religion and the English people, 1500–1640* (Kirksville, MO, 1998), 35.

57 Frijhoff, *Embodied belief*, 53, 286; cf. Cressy, *Birth, marriage and death*, 478–80.

58 This may be compared with Arnold Hunt's recent emphasis on the importance of performance practice in the interpretation of sermons.

59 P. Lake with M. Questier, *The antichrist's lewd hat: protestants, papists and players in post-reformation England* (New Haven, CT, 2002), 315–31.

60 See A. Cambers and M. Wolfe, 'Reading, family religion and evangelical identity in late Stuart England', *Historical Journal*, 47 (2004), 875–96.

61 Milton, 'Qualified intolerance', 91–5.

62 T. Brabourne, *A discourse upon the sabbath day* (1628); and *A defence of . . . the sabbath day* (1632); *ODNB*, entry for: Brabourne, Theophilus.

63 J. Howell, *Epistolae ho-elianae*, 5th edn (1678), 252–5.

64 I. Archer, *The pursuit of stability* (Cambridge, 1991), 91–2.

65 P. Marshall, *Reformation England 1480–1642* (London, 2003), 159–60.

66 S. Hindle, 'A sense of place? Becoming and belonging in the rural parish 1550–1650', in Shepard and Withington, *Communities in early modern England*, 106.

67 J. Swan, *Profanomastix* (1639), 44–5; R. Shelford, *Five pious and learned discourses* (Cambridge, 1635), 14, 16, 19; J. Browning, *Concerning publike-prayer, and the fasts of the church* (1636), 156–7; W. Page, *A treatise or justification of bowing at the name of Jesus* (Oxford, 1631), 6–7; A. Milton, ' "That sacred oratory": religion and the chapel royal during the personal rule of Charles I', in A. Ashbee (ed.), *William Lawes (1602–1645): essays on his life, times and work* (Aldershot, 1998), 84, 95n.

68 A. Foster, 'Church policies of the 1630s', in R. Cust and A. Hughes (eds), *Conflict in early Stuart England* (Harlow, 1989), 208.

69 *Commons journals (CJ)*, i. 312–13.

70 Cressy, *Birth, marriage and death*, 319.

71 Frijhoff, *Embodied belief*, 51; P. van Roden, 'Dissenters en bededagen: civil religion ten tijde van de Republiek', *Bijdragen en Mededelingen betreffende de Geschiedenis der Nederlanden*, 107 (1992), 703–12.

72 P. Withington and A. Shepard, 'Introduction: communities in early modern England', in Shepard and Withington, *Communities in early modern England*, 1–12.

73 P. van Roden, 'Jews and religious toleration in the Dutch republic' in Hsia and van Nierop, *Calvinism and religious toleration*, especially 142–7; B. J. Kaplan, 'Fictions of privacy: house chapels and the spatial accommodation of religious dissent in early modern Europe', *American Historical Review*, 107 (2002), 1031–64.

5

The queen is 'a goggyll eyed hoore': gender and seditious speech in early modern England[1]

Andy Wood

Over a decade ago, Keith Wrightson called for early modern social historians to imitate enclosure rioters and break down boundaries. He meant, of course, not enclosing walls and fences, but conceptual divisions between adjoining sub-fields of the historical enterprise.[2] The second generation of new social historians of early modern England have indeed transgressed many such divisions; but in so doing, we have established some of our own. One of those boundaries separates gender from popular politics.[3] This chapter represents a brief exercise in connecting those two sub-fields; it does so with reference to contemporary popular criticism of early modern monarchs. Along the way, it suggests other areas within which a gendered reading of popular politics might yield results.

In particular, this study of popular political gossip has implications for the theme of this collection of essays: the reconceptualisation of the English Revolution. It is notable that despite its significance to recent cultural and social history, considerations of gender have only rarely influenced studies of the English Revolution.[4] Deploying examples between the early sixteenth century and the early eighteenth century, this essay emphasises the gendered characteristics of popular political language. Since the record of the prosecution of seditious speech has comprised a key source for the history of popular political culture during the 1640s, this study has obvious relevance for research into popular politics during the English Revolution. Other ways in which gendered analysis may bring new perspectives to bear on the English Revolution include, for instance: representations of violence during military encounters; definitions of male and female political duties; sexual stereotypes and the Ranter phenomenon, together with similarly pornographic print representations of other radical organisations; depictions of besieged or looted towns and cities; political language and the deployment of gendered metaphors. This list, of course, is scarcely exhaustive. Rather than laying down any new agenda, I am here seeking to highlight the interpretive possibilities that a gendered analysis can bring to bear on the history of the English Revolution. For gender historians and for historians of the English Revolution alike, there remains, in other words, much to be done.

In recent years, early modern gender historians have written on a diverse range of subjects including crime, the body, constructions of masculinity and femininity, honour, gossip networks, violence and illicit speech.[5] Social historians of popular politics have delved into an equally diverse range of topics, concerning themselves with issues such as rebellion, crowd actions, state formation, parish government, seditious speech, social relations, customary law, popular litigation and political gossip.[6] Only occasionally has there been much cross-fertilisation.[7] Yet the emergence of one distinct sub-literature concerned with gender and another sub-literature concerned with popular politics obscures the many ways in which these areas of everyday life connected. One such avenue by which both areas may be approached is through the history of speech and silence. Just as gender historians have been profoundly interested in gossip networks, the language of sexual labelling and neighbourly arguments, so historians of popular politics have found themselves drawn to plebeian political conversation, rumour, argument and debate. This chapter seeks to connect this mutual interest in the politics of words, and thereby hopes to illustrate one way in which an appreciation of gender may further illuminate the social history of politics. Deploying archival evidence concerning seditious speech, it describes the networks within which men and women spread political gossip and analyses ways in which popular political conversation was gendered. In particular, it looks at the different ways in which assumptions about gender underwrote popular criticism of male and female rulers.[8]

Among other things, this chapter challenges two recent observations concerning gender, speech and popular politics in early modern England. First, it modifies the proposition 'The public sphere . . . was the man's sphere'.[9] Instead, the chapter presents evidence of women voicing political opinions in public, and argues that in both the everyday experience of gender relations and in the articulation of seditious speech ' "public" and "private", "outside" and "inside" the house were, in fact, no more easily separable than "domestic" and "political" '.[10] Secondly, the chapter tempers the claim that 'gossip became politicised . . . on the eve of the civil war'.[11] Rather, the essay is based on two related propositions: first, examples of seditious speech prosecutions from across the early modern period show that concerns over popular political gossip during the 1640s were far from unique;[12] second, since speech was recognised as a sensitive indicator of power relations, it was often 'political' in early modern England.[13]

Speech was not simply a means of communication; it could be an emblem of authority: in standard patriarchal theory, who spoke, with what force, where and when, were supposed to be decided by age, class and gender. That speech was about power is illuminated by the scrutiny of any early modern legal archive. In Archbishop Grindal's visitation records of 1575, detailing his investigations into parochial deviance in the north of England, for instance, we repeatedly find offenders against the local hierarchy singled out for, above all, their *verbal* dissidence. Roger Harrison, of Bridlinton, who gave 'verie obstinate wordes to the churchwarden[s]' offended the rules that governed class relations: it was noted that 'he is verie poore'. Elsewhere, it was hierarchies of gender that were threatened by inappropriately assertive speech: Janet Williamson, of St John's parish in York, was described as 'a notoriowse skolde, a slaunderer of her neighbours'; in the same city, it was noted that Barbara Hunt 'an ungodlie person, offendeth her neighbours by swearinge'.[14]

Within early modern culture, speech was construed as action. The maintenance of order both within and outside the household therefore depended on the policing of speech and the maintenance of silence. But Garthine Walker has recently drawn attention to an important, yet frequently overlooked, aspect of the politics of speech and silence: the criminalisation of certain aspects of plebeian conversation. As she points out, penalties for passing on political gossip or for criticising one's social superiors included a litany of punishments: 'ears were nailed to the pillory and ripped, cropped or chopped off, nostrils were slit, the tongue bored through with a hot iron, cheeks or forehead branded with appropriate letters (such as "F" and "A" for "false accuser", "B" for "blasphemer")'.[15] In particular, such punishments were handed down for seditious speech. Speech deemed treasonable could result even in hanging, drawing and quartering, or, for women, burning.[16] The records of those criminal courts which held jurisdiction over such offences, coupled with reports of seditious speech to the privy council, comprise the documentary foundation of this essay.

Reports and prosecutions of plebeian seditious speech have comprised an important source for social historians, enabling them to illuminate aspects of popular politics and social relations.[17] But, perhaps as another consequence of the unintended separation of gender history from the history of popular politics, the heavy male bias within that material has tended to go unrecognised. Of the 71 cases of treasonable or seditious speech surviving among the depositions for the Northern Circuit assizes between 1640 and 1690, for instance, a total of 69 concerned the errant speech of men. Likewise, the Home Circuit assize indictments for the reigns of Elizabeth I and James I record the seditious and treasonable speech of 154 individuals, of whom 143 were men. Again Tim Harris has found that among the 323 cases of seditious speech from the reign of Charles II, only 37 involved women.[18]

This gender bias within the documentation means that describing plebeian women's political voices is far from easy. The bias most likely springs from a basic disregard for women's voices, which has left its imprint over most of the source material concerning popular politics. Rebellion, for instance, was almost invariably described as a male phenomenon. In Alexander Neville's account of Robert Kett's rebellion of 1549, it is not until an adder bites Mrs Kett's bosom (from which prophetic portent is drawn) that the reader learns there were any women among Kett's camp.[19] In other bodies of source material, such as the depositions concerning customary rights, from which historians of popular politics have gleaned so much, women comprise only a small fraction of those giving evidence: my sample of 3,915 deponents from the Peak Country between 1517 and 1754, for instance, found that 96 per cent were men.[20] Where women's voices surface within such material, they are often muted. When Dorothy Medowe gave evidence concerning the customs of the Norfolk town of Aylsham in 1576, the clerk recorded only: 'To the 1[,] 2 & 3rd [questions] she saith and Affirme as Thomas Medowe hir husbande before hath deposed.'[21] Mostly, this male inattention to women's speech goes undocumented: it can be sensed only through absences. But on occasion that lack of interest accidentally surfaces. When Johan Prowde called Richard Umble 'a stronge theefe and a fals[e] theefe', in October 1549, 'Umble desired her to holde her tonge and sayed he wolde not scolde with her, but wolde rather speake with her husbande'.[22] This male contempt for women's voices also structured the archival record. Again, we catch a brief glimpse of this: one correspondent to Thomas Cromwell cast doubt upon 'a boke conc[er]nyng c[er]tane examynacons for [seditious] wordes spoken' because 'ther is noo witnes but oon woman'.[23]

Yet running alongside this silencing of female speech was a male fear of women's voices. Characteristically, this fear was disguised as contempt. Thus, following the riots of Evil May Day in London in 1517, the authorities sought to control the dangerous spread of rumour by commanding that 'no women should come togither to babble and talke, but all men should keepe their wives in their houses'.[24] Within the dominant norms of early modern society, silence was synonymous with order. Women's speech therefore represented a central battle-ground in the maintenance of established power relations. It was no accident, after all, that Coriolanus calls his wife 'My gracious silence'. It was deemed especially inappropriate for women to discuss politics: Brathwait's 1631 book of conduct *The English Gentlewoman* warned that 'to discourse of state-matters . . . will not become your auditory'. Another widely read conduct book observed in 1612: 'Silence is a gravitie, when she abstaineth and holdeth her peace from speaking when it doth not become her to speake.'[25]

Women, then, were supposed to be 'a model, if not *the* model, of verbal defer-ence in the early modern period'. Moreover, as Catherine Belsey observes, in many circumstances women's speech could be construed as disturbing to the social order as a whole: 'for women to speak [was] to threaten the system of differences which [gave] meaning to patriarchy'.[26] Patriarchy therefore required women's silence on political topics. Yet, as Garthine Walker has recently observed: 'That words were female weapons of choice or necessity was a familiar early modern theme. Vituperation was attributed to virtually every unsympathetic female stereo-type.'[27] The story of the relationship between gender and seditious speech is there-fore a complicated one. On the one hand, the record presents us primarily with male voices, at least partly because of a male disinterest in women's speech. On the other, the evidence seems to suggest profound male anxieties concerning the female voice. If we are to probe the intersection between gender and seditious speech, therefore, we are forced to rely on what can be constructed from fleet-ing archival fragments, combined with a few detailed case studies.

Two especially detailed cases of seditious speech enable us to reconstruct something of how political conversation crossed gender boundaries. The two cases are separated by 132 years, one from the north of England, the other from East

Anglia. Our first story begins on February 19 1685, when the magistrate Sir Richard Neile heard the testimony of Mary Darley, a widow of North Shields. Darley explained that she had recently taken a journey in a wherry from Newcastle to North Shields in the company of a religious nonconformist, Peter Rayning. Darley had overheard a conversation between Rayning and the ship's master concerning the death of King Charles II and their fears that the new king, James II, would bring trouble to the realm. Mary Darley told Neile that, at this, she had risen up and said: 'Here hath bene hard tymes already for a poore widdow to make shift with a charge of children, pray God send us peace and quietnes.' Rayning answered: 'Wee had better have a redd warr then a peace, unles it be to the honor of God.' The following day, back in North Shields, she visited Margaret Atking, who asked her: 'Neighbour, did you not heare the post of last night?' Mary asked Margaret what she meant by this, to which the reply was that the news was very bad, 'for our new King James is dead and they say they have surfeited him, and he hath bene thrice lett blood since his brother died'. Margaret explained that she had responded with the loyal words 'God forbid', before going 'in an amasement' to see the bailiff, James Hebden, and his wife. She told the Hebdens what she had heard, and asked for their advice. James Hebden responded that he had heard no such news, exclaiming, 'God forbid it should be true', and advised her not to repeat the rumour. Finally, Mary Darley told Neile that two local women had condemned her for revealing the rumours going around the town: Abigail Turner had 'abuesed' Darley and her children, saying, 'shee is fitt to be whipped through the towne for informing against her neighbours', and Isabel Trumble had likewise 'abuesed her about the same matter, and badd her goe and forsweare herselfe as she had done'.[28]

Our second story comes from the town of Diss, in 1553, and concerns a scandalous rumour concerning the sexual honour of the recently installed Queen Mary. From the record of examinations taken by the earl of Sussex in early May 1553 a complicated chain of rumours can be reconstructed.[29] The rumour apparently originated with two anonymous men with whom Margery Miles, a widow of Diss, had some conversation at the town's market: 'but what they were she cold not tell nor where they dwelte'. The men told Margery that Queen Mary was pregnant, and that the father of the Queen's illegitimate child was the Lord Chancellor. Margery also heard the same story from the Anne Folfarr the elder. Margery Miles then told this scandalous tale to Robert Bartham and to John Smith, who passed it on to John Wilby, warning him: 'I pray you tell yt no further [but] if you do I will denye yt.'

Despite the warning, Wilby passed the story on to a man called Sheldrake, who in turn told his wife; Sheldrake's wife told the story to the wife of Lawrence Hult, who told her husband; Lawrence Hult then broke the story to the chief constable of Diss, Robert Lowdall. Attempting to trace the origin of the tale, Robert Lowdall spoke to Anne Folfar who explained to him how Anne Clarke, 'somtyme a pore woman in disse', had informed her that the queen was with child. Clarke told Folfar this story while they were sitting in the parish church with Barbara

Gowche; Barbara confirmed the story, declaring 'that the Queanes heighnes was with child by my Lord Chauncellor of Ingland'. Despite Folfar's attempt to shuffle off responsibility, other witnesses confirmed that she had spread the news within the town: Alison Miles, daughter of Margery, described how her mother had gone to Anne Folfar's house; on her mother's return, she told the girl that 'go[o]d wif[e]' Folfar had said that the queen was with child. To complicate the story still further, Barbara Gowche blamed Anne Folfar for the initial conversation in Diss parish church, adding that 'she wold never speak them more and she nev[er] speake them afore to no man therefore she wolde never here more of them'.

Some of the men of Diss also came forward to testify concerning their own conversations. Robert Gowche recalled how Richard Gilbert had entered his house, and after asking him 'if he hard any news', blurted out that 'myn unkle Harry Cowp[er] tolde the Quene was with child'. Like Barbara Gowche, her husband Robert emphasised his distance from the rapidly spreading rumour, insisting that he only 'co[n]fessed' to the magistrates concerning the conversation 'of his mere good will Immedyately after he had hard . . . Richard speak . . . [and] being moved in consiens ded goo unto Robert Lawdale Chief Constable'. Other men of Diss told similar stories of discussing the rumour with local men in fields, on the road, or in their houses.

The conversations going around Diss were dangerous: they could easily be construed as seditious or treasonable, and could therefore result in mutilation or even death for those giving voice to them. The absence of surviving court records makes it impossible to trace the case any further, save only for an angry letter from Queen Mary to the local magistracy, instructing them to punish those who spread 'any vayne p[rop]hesies, sedicous false or untrue rumors'. In particular, Queen Mary observed that she had learnt of many lurid tales being spread concerning 'the estate of o[u]r p[er]son'. Ominously, the queen warned that she was angry that such slander had gone 'unpunysshed', and remained concerned that these rumours were 'wynked at or at lest lytle considered'.[30] Aside from the obvious discomfort that the unrestricted flow of tales concerning Queen Mary's fictitious sexual indiscretions created among the magistracy of East Anglia, what are we to make of this story? It is best understood with reference to our first tale from North Shields in 1685.

Both stories concern male and female involvement in seditious speech; each highlights the importance of both male and female networks in the communication of such seditious speech; and each points towards the interaction of men and women in the dissemination of political gossip. The story from North Shields illuminates how men and women's political conversations overlapped: Mary Darley overhears, and counters, the seditious speech of two men; she then discusses political news with a local woman, before seeking the advice of another woman and her husband. Similarly, the Diss rumour spread from man to woman with ease, albeit sometimes running down channels which were defined by gender. The fact that seditious speech was passed on in company comprising 'diverse and many persons both men and women neighbours' therefore indicates that men and women's political conversations did not occur within separate spheres.[31] Nonetheless this should not be taken to imply that the communication networks along which male and female political gossip passed was not at least *partially* defined by gender: recent work by Bernard Capp has emphasised the significance of gossip networks to the maintenance of female sociability, community and even solidarity. The North Shields tale clearly illuminates forms of local solidarity which could be understood as based on a distinctly gendered sense of women's neighbourly solidarity. When we read that Mary Darley was warned that she was 'fitt to be whipped through the towne for informing against her neighbours', the intimidation mounted against her for informing against her female neighbours seems reminiscent of those forms of mutual protection which Capp has described as an important means of female sociability and solidarity. In this case, Mary Darley appears to have placed herself beyond the bounds of that protective female community.[32]

Unlike the networks through which political information was communicated, a fundamentally important element of plebeian seditious speech was its gendered character. Popular criticism of male rulers was sometimes coloured by sexual politics. George I, notorious for his loss of patriarchal control over his wife, who had cuckolded the king with a German aristocrat, faced constant mockery. Charivaric Jacobite crowds were sometimes led by men wearing horns on their heads, the traditional sign of the cuckold; likewise, he was often burned in effigy, wearing horns. London Restoration Day revellers chanted 'make way for the Cuckoldy King and send him to Hanover'. One ballad taunted the king, declaring his inability to control his wife's sexual behaviour, and exclaiming that the queen had 'play[ed] the Whore'. A London woman, Mary Jones, echoed this view, swearing that 'the Prince of Wales is a bastard, his mother is a Whore, and King George a Rogue'.[33]

Two centuries earlier, Henry VIII's domestic arrangements had incurred similar opprobrium. Following his divorce from Queen Catherine and his courtship of Anne Boleyn, Henry was described by plebeian critics as an 'adulterer'.[34] His later changes of partner also attracted popular criticism. Jane Rattsey, in trouble with the authorities for her conversation with Elizabeth Bassett, diverted the accusation that she had asked 'What if God work of this work to make the lady Anne of Cleves queen again?' by claiming that it was at an 'idle saying'. Clearly under pressure, she insisted that she 'thinks the king's divorce [from Anne of Cleves] good', and insisted, 'upon the sudden tidings declared to her by Bassett', according to which the king was to divorce again, that she had merely exclaimed: 'What a man is the king! How many wives will he have?'[35] Clearly, Jane Rattsey protested too much. The bulk of the evidence points towards considerable popular anxiety concerning, first, the Boleyn match and, later, Henry's subsequent marriage strategies.[36] King Philip's alleged behaviour could also be deployed against Queen Mary's, alluding to her apparent inability to control him. In December 1557, John Capstocke of London stood indicted for claiming that the queen believed that the king will kepe her more companye and love her the better if she gyve hym the crowne, ye[a] will crowne hym to make hym lyve chaste contrary to his nature, for peradventure after he were crowned he wolde be contented with one woman but in the meane space he wolde have choice of three or foure in one night to prove whiche of them he liketh beste, not of ladys and gentlewomen but of bakers daughters and such other poore whores.[37]

In contrast, Edward VI's sullied reputation arose from his mother's alleged adultery and his father's cuckoldery: in 1553, a Dover seaman landed himself in trouble for spreading his opinion that 'the kynge of England was a cuckolds son & a bastard borne'.[38] Likewise, allegations concerning the legitimacy of Charles II spread among the populace: shortly before the coronation of the king, Walter Crompton allegedly said that 'hee hoped the Kinge would never bee crowned, for hee was a bastard'. Around the same time, John Careuth remarked that 'the King was a son of a whore'.[39] Charles II was condemned for his own sexual misconduct as well as that alleged against his mother: one Yorkshire yeoman spoke for many when he remarked in 1677: 'The king mynds nothing but women.' The sexual politics of Restoration royalism also influenced contemporary analyses of popular allegiance: Margaret Dixon stood indicted for claiming: 'There is none that loves [Charles II] but drunk whores and whoremongers.'[40] Nonetheless, the deployment of gendered and sexualised imagery against male rulers represented but one verbal strategy among the many that were available to hostile subjects. Whereas male rulers were condemned according to a variety of reputed characteristics and activities – not only bastardy and adultery, but also tyranny, cruelty, avarice, greed, popery, heresy, murder and (in the case of Oliver Cromwell) regicide – female monarchs were condemned by their gender and sexual reputation alone: as weak rulers; as infertile; as the bearers of secret bastards; and, most frequently, simply as whores.

As we have seen in the case of the gossip going around Diss in 1553, subjects were often keen to discuss the fertility of female monarchs. Two years later, at a time at which the by-then married Queen Mary was making much of her pregnancy, the London woman Alice Perwiche stood indicted for declaring: 'The Quenes grace is not with childe and that another lady shuld be with childe and that ladies childe when she is brought in bedde shold be named the Quenes childe.' Rashly, Perwiche had warmed to her theme:

[T]here be some about the Quenes grace that will make her awaye and that shortly and it shall be done by a certayne lady and she shalbe nameles at this tyme, said she, other ells there be a grete many that be deceaved and then she trust to see the same worlde as it was before her grace beganne to raigne.[41]

In 1687, after the execution of the duke of Monmouth, Stephen Duffield allegedly developed an intriguing theory concerning the queen's fertility, telling his neighbours that

the Queene told the King that she could not conceive unless she dranke Charles Monmouth's blood; upon which the King told her that he would send for him and that he should be lett blood, that she might drinke it: upon which she replyed, that unlesse she might drinke his heart's blood it would doe her noe good.[42]

Separated by a century and a half, in each case, a grotesque tale concerning the queen's fertility was deployed in order to undermine the authority of the regime. Another way of undermining the authority of female rulers was by simply denying that a woman could operate effectively as a monarch. Elizabeth I faced such popular hostility throughout her reign. In 1568, for instance, the Kentish yeoman Bartholomew Taylor was indicted for allegedly expressing the opinion: 'We shall neve have a merye world so longe as we have a woman govener and as the quene lyved.' In 1596, the Beckenham husbandman Edward Ewer likewise stood indicted for his alleged opinion that 'yt would never be a merrye worlde till her majestie was dead or killed; and that her majestie was ruled by her lordes at ther pleasure, but we must not saye soe'.[43] Five years earlier, the Essex labourer John Feltwell was pilloried for initiating a dangerous conversation with the words 'let us praye for a father for we have a mother already'. His neighbour John Thurgood asked, 'What meane you by that?' to which Feltwell replied, 'let us pray for a kinge'. At this, Thurgood retorted, '[we] have a gracious queene already, wherfore wold you praye for a kinge?' Feltwell's response was that

> the Queene was but a woman and ruled by noblemen, and the noblemen and gentelmen were all one, and the gentellmen and fermers wold hold togeyther one with another so that poore men cold gett nothinge amonge them.[44]

Queen Elizabeth's mother had an even harder time of it. It was not only ladies of the court who regarded Anne Boleyn as 'a harlot', and who predicted that she would be burned.[45] The priest Raphe Wyndon was similarly accused of having called Queen Anne 'a hore & harlot', adding that there was a prophecy that a queen would be burned in Smithfield.[46] In 1534, the Suffolk woman Margaret Chaunseler admitted that she had called Queen Anne 'a noughtty hoore' and 'a goggyll eyed hoore & sayd god save queen Kath[r]yn'. Her defence was that she had been 'dronken . . . & that the evill sperite did cause her to speke [the words] & she was very penytent for her offences'.[47]

In the eyes of many of her plebeian subjects, Queen Elizabeth was as disgraceful as her mother. In September 1591, John Massee, a Kentish tailor, was indicted for exclaiming 'by God's wounds, the queene ys a whore'. Likewise, the leatherworker Thomas de Belewe spiced his remark that Queen Elizabeth loved Frenchmen and Walloons more than she did her own subjects with the observation that Elizabeth was a whore who had given birth to two illegitimate children. Similarly, in 1589, the Essex yeoman Thomas Wenden reported that 'the Quenes majestie was an arrant whore'.[48] In 1600, the gardener Richard Maidley had announced that 'what woman soever called him roague, he would call hir whore'. In response, a female neighbour, noticing the presence of John Price, one of the queen's messengers, asked him 'what say you to this mans mystrys[?]' Maidley rashly replied that 'she [the queen] is a whore'.[49]

Throughout her reign, Queen Elizabeth suffered constant popular abuse for the legend that she had given birth to illegitimate children, fathered by the earl of Leicester. In some variations on the tale, Elizabeth had burnt the children in a chimney. Thereby, the queen was presented not only as a whore, but also as an infanticidal mother.[50] Queen Henrietta Maria was similarly dogged by accusations concerning her sexual conduct. In 1646, James Losh, commenting on royalist diplomacy, allegedly remarked that 'the Queene was gone over into Holland to play the whore'. Such allegations were long-lived. Following the Restoration, Jane Blunstone mixed accusations of whoredom with radical protestantism, announcing that Henrietta Maria was 'the great whore of Babylon'. In 1677, John Burnsall stood indicted for his alleged remark that 'the old Queen had severall children in the absence of her husband: one att Pontefract, when her husband had not been with her of a twelve moneth'.[51]

That Elizabeth I, Mary I and Henrietta Maria, despite their very different politics, should all face popular denunciation as whores says much both about gender relations and about popular political language. Most obviously, the denunciation of female monarchs as 'whores' confirms the power of that word within popular culture: it was an ubiquitous insult against women, bordering on the universal.[52] 'Whore', however, was double-edged, both undermining women and enabling them: as Gowing points out, 'it was women, most of all, who hunted out whores and called for their punishment'.[53] The evidence presented here suggests a slight corrective to this view: *both* men *and* women denounced their female rulers as whores. Nonetheless, Gowing's analysis remains perceptive. In labelling female rulers 'whores', subjects did more than simply reach for an easily accessible tag; they also asserted their own authority over the reputation, and hence the power, of their monarch. The evidence of seditious speech prosecutions certainly highlights the ubiquity of the language of whoredom in criticism of women. For female rulers, the label 'whore' identified them not only as unfit rulers, but as dangers to the moral and political security of the realm. Similarly, the accusations of bastardy, adultery and cuckoldry that were levelled against male monarchs labelled them as incompetent, illegitimate or immoral. In both cases, the deployment by subjects of gendered language against their rulers inverted established political hierarchies, establishing the sexual politics of the monarch as a threat to the realm. All of this both helps to establish the usefulness of gender in the analysis of early modern political language and confirms the accuracy of Joan Scott's observation that 'gender is one of the recurrent references by which political power has been conceived, legitimated and criticised'.[54]

Notes

1 I am grateful to John Arnold, Cathie Carmichael, Alex Shepherd, Garthine Walker and Keith Wrightson for their comments on this piece.
2 K. E. Wrightson, 'The enclosure of English social history', in A. Wilson (ed.), *Rethinking social history: English society, 1570–1920 and its interpretation* (Manchester, 1993), 59–77.

3 Although there has been a willingness to recognise gender relations as political, social historians of politics have demonstrated less interest in the converse: the scrutiny of how popular politics might be gendered. Thanks to the influence of feminism, with its insistence that the personal is political, historians of gender have tended to be comfortable with a wide definition of 'politics'. For feminist definitions of politics, see N. J. Hirschmann and C. Di Stefano (eds), *Revisioning the political: feminist reconstructions of traditional concepts in western political theory* (Oxford, 1996).

4 For notable exceptions, see R. Trubowitz, 'Female preachers and male wives: gender and authority in civil war England', and S. Wiseman '"Adam, the father of all flesh": porno-political rhetoric and political theory in and after the English civil war', both in J. Holstun (ed.), *Pamphlet wars: prose in the English revolution* (1992); D. Purkiss, 'Dismembering and remembering: the English civil war and male identity', in C. J. Summers and T. Pebworth (eds), *The English civil wars in the literary imagination* (Columbia, OH, 1999); A. Hughes, 'Gender and politics in Leveller literature', in S. Amussen and M. Kishlansky (eds), *Political culture and cultural politics in early modern England: essays presented to David Underdown* (Manchester, 1995); P. Crawford '"The poorest she": women and citizenship in early modern England', in M. Mendle (ed.), *The Putney debates of 1647: the army, the levellers and the English state* (Cambridge, 2001). In so far as gender has influenced studies of the English Revolution, such work has tended to concentrate on only two themes: radical challenges to patriarchalism and women's participation in the English Revolution: K. Thomas 'Women in the civil war sects', *Past and Present*, 13 (1958), 42–62; P. Higgins, 'The reactions of women, with special reference to women petitioners', in B. Manning (ed.), *Politics, religion and the English civil war* (1973); P. Mack, *Missionary women: ecstatic prophecy in seventeenth-century England* (Berkeley, CA, 1992); P. Crawford, 'The challenges to patriarchalism: how did the revolution affect women?', in J. Morrill (ed.), *Revolution and restoration: England in the 1650s* (London, 1992).

5 See, for instance, G. Walker, *Crime, gender and social order in early modern England* (Cambridge, 2003); L. Gowing, *Domestic dangers: women, words and sex in early modern London* (Oxford, 1996); and *Common bodies: women, touch and power in seventeenth-century England* (New Haven, CT, 2003); B. Capp, *When gossips meet: women, family, and neighbourhood in early modern England* (Oxford, 2003); S. D. Amussen, '"The part of a Christian man": the cultural politics of manhood in early modern England', in Amussen and Kishlansky (eds), *Political culture and cultural politics in early modern England*; E. Foyster, *Manhood in early modern England: honour, sex and marriage* (London and New York, 1999); A. Shepard, *The meanings of manhood in early modern England* (Oxford, 2003); B. Capp, 'The double standard revisited: plebeian women and male sexual reputation in early modern England', *Past and Present*, 162 (1999), 70–100; A. Fletcher, 'Manhood, the male body, courtship and the household in early modern England', *History*, 84 (1999), 419–36.

6 See, for instance, E. H. Shagan, *Popular politics and the English reformation* (Cambridge, 2003); J. Walter, *Understanding popular violence in the English revolution: the Colchester plunderers* (Cambridge, 1999); A. Wood, *The politics of social conflict: the Peak Country, 1520–1770* (Cambridge, 1999); S. Hindle, *The state and social change in early modern England, c. 1550–1640* (Basingstoke, 2000); and 'Persuasion and protest in the Caddington Common enclosure dispute, 1635–1639', *Past and Present*, 158 (1998), 37–78; S. Hipkin, 'Sitting on his penny rent: conflict and right of common in Faversham Blean, 1596–1610', *Rural History*, 11, 1 (2000), 1–35; A. Wood, '"Poore men

woll speke one daye": plebeian languages of deference and defiance in England, c. 1520–1640', in T. Harris (ed.), *The politics of the excluded in early modern England* (Basingtoke, 2001), 67–98; J. Walter, 'Public transcripts, popular agency and the politics of subsistence in early modern England', in M. J. Braddick and J. Walter (eds), *Negotiating power in early modern society: order, hierarchy and subordination in Britain and Ireland* (Cambridge, 2001), 123–48. The field is surveyed in A. Wood, *Riot, rebellion and popular politics in early modern England* (Basingstoke, 2002).

7 See, for instance, S. Hindle, 'The shaming of Margaret Knowsley: gossip, gender and the experience of authority in early modern England', *Continuity and Change*, 9 (1994), 391–419, which addresses the parochial politics of gender; and D. Freist, 'The king's crown is the whore of Babylon: politics, gender and communication in mid-seventeenth-century England', *Gender and History*, 7 (1995), 457–81. For an example of how gender might inform interpretations of politics, see R. Weil, *Political passions: gender, the family and political argument in England, 1680–1714* (Manchester, 1999). For a brilliant discussion of gender and print culture, see P. McDowell, *The women of Grub Street: press, politics and gender in the London literary marketplace 1678–1730* (Oxford, 1998).

8 There are, of course, other ways in which gender structured popular political language. It would be possible to produce studies dealing with, for instance, how male workers claimed political rights by defining skill as a masculine property; how popular rebellion was gendered both in imagery and in organisation; and the different ways in which working men and women claimed a right to political activity on the basis of the need to protect their households.

9 A. Fox, *Oral and literate culture in Britain, 1500–1700* (Oxford, 2001), 173.

10 Gowing, *Domestic dangers*, 26.

11 Freist, 'The king's crown is the whore of Babylon', 466, reiterated at 470 and in D. Freist, *Governed by opinion: politics, religion and the dynamics of communication in Stuart London, 1637–1645* (London, 1997), 212, 238.

12 For the politics of speech and silence in mid-sixteenth century England, see A. Wood, *The 1549 rebellions and the making of early modern England* (Cambridge, forthcoming), ch. 3.

13 This essay therefore represents a contribution to early modern social historians' redefinition of politics, initiated in K. E. Wrightson, 'The politics of the parish in early modern England', in P. Griffiths, A. Fox and S. Hindle (eds), *The experience of authority in early modern England* (Basingstoke, 1996), 10–46.

14 W. J. Sheils, *Archbishop Grindal's visitation, 1575: comperta et detecta book*, Borthwick Texts and Calendars: Records of the Northern Province, 4 (York, 1977), 3, 4, 87.

15 Walker, *Crime, gender and social order*, 100.

16 For a good introduction to the legal basis of such prosecutions, see R. B. Manning, 'The origins of the doctrine of sedition', *Journal of British Studies*, 12 (1980), 99–121.

17 See, for instance, Wood, ' "Poore men woll speke" '; Walter, 'Public transcripts'; E. H. Shagan, 'Rumours and popular politics in the reign of Henry VIII', in Harris (ed.), *The politics of the excluded*, 30–66.

18 *Depositions from the castle of York relating to offences committed in the northern counties in the seventeenth century*, ed. J. Raine, Surtees Society, 40 (Durham, 1861); Fox, *Oral and literate culture*, 339; T. Harris, *London crowds in the reign of Charles II: propaganda and politics from the Restoration until the exclusion crisis* (Cambridge, 1987), 193. In her study of prosecutions for seditious speech in France between 1661

and 1775, Arlette Farge found that women made up a sixth of cases: *Subversive words: public opinion in eighteenth-century France* (Cambridge, 1994), 129.

19 R. Woods, *Norfolke furies and their foyle* (1623), fo. Kr.

20 Wood, *Politics of social conflict*, 132; for the importance of custom in popular polit- ical culture, see A. Wood, 'The place of custom in plebeian political culture: England, 1550–1800', *Social History*, 22 (1997), 46–60.

21 TNA, DL4/18/11. Again, the relationship between gender and custom remains largely unexplored; for an exception, see Shepard, *The meanings of manhood*, 221–30.

22 CLRO, Journal 16, fo. 40r.

23 TNA, SP1/124, fo. 199r.

24 R. Holinshed, *Chronicles of England, Scotland and Ireland*, 6 vols (London, 1807–8), iii. 622.

25 C. Belsey, *The subject of tragedy: identity and difference in Renaissance drama* (London, 1985), 157.

26 J. Kamensky, *Governing the tongue: the politics of speech in early New England* (Oxford, 1997), 134; Belsey, *The subject of tragedy*, 191.

27 G. Walker, *Crime, gender and social order*, 100–1.

28 *Depositions from the castle of York*, 268–9.

29 BL, Cotton MS, Titus, BII, fos 182r–184v.

30 *Ibid.*, fo. 119r.

31 Quoting TNA, SP1/106, fo. 138r; for other examples of men and women discussing politics, see Norfolk Record Office, Norwich City Records 16A/6, p. 40, 12A/1(a), fo. 37r; TNA, E36/120, fo. 176; BL, Cotton MS, Titus, BI, fos 78r–79v; TNA, STAC10/16, fos 133r–200v.

32 Capp, *When gossips meet*, 284–7.

33 N. Rogers, *Crowds, culture and politics in Georgian Britain* (Oxford, 1998), 40, 55, 223.

34 TNA, SP1/125, fos 46r–48v.

35 *Letters and papers of Henry VIII, 1540–41*, no. 1407.

36 S. L. Jansen, *Dangerous talk and strange behaviour: women and popular resistance to the reforms of Henry VIII* (Basingstoke, 1996), 83–9.

37 *CPR, 1557–8*, 150–1.

38 CLRO, Repertory 12 (2), fo. 525v.

39 *Depositions from the castle of York*, 84, 94.

40 *Ibid.*, 6, 83.

41 *CPR (1555–7)*, 184–5; for royal propaganda concerning Mary's pregnancy, see Corpus Christi College, Cambridge, Parker Library, 106, 340/630.

42 *Depositions from the castle of York*, 283.

43 *Calendar of assize records: Kent indictments, Elizabeth I*, ed. J. S. Cockburn (London, 1979), nos 423, 2442.

44 *Calendar of assize records: Essex indictments, Elizabeth I*, ed. J. S. Cockburn (London, 1978), no. 2245.

45 BL, Cotton MS, Cleopatra E. IV, fos 99r–100v.

46 TNA, SP6/7, fos 10r–11r.

47 TNA, SP1/89, fo. 158r.

48 *Calendar of assize records: Essex indictments*, no. 2024; *Calendar of assize records: Kent indictments*, no. 2017; TNA, SP12/190/56.

49 *Calendar of assize records: Surrey indictments*, ed. J. S. Cockburn (London, 1980), no. 3024.

50 Fox, *Oral and literate culture*, 361–2.

51 Capp, *When gossips meet*, 293; *Depositions from the castle of York*, 6.

52 For other insults thrown at women, see G. Walker, 'Expanding the boundaries of female honour in early modern England', *Transactions of the Royal Historical Society*, 6th series, 6 (1996), 235–45.

53 Gowing, *Domestic dangers*, 101.

54 J. W. Scott, 'Gender: a useful category of historical analysis', in her *Gender and the politics of history* (New York, 1988), 48.

6

Politicising the popular? The 'tradition of riot' and popular political culture in the English Revolution

John Walter

In 1639, conversation between an Essex gentleman recently returned from London and a group of women visiting his wife in childbed turned political. The man entertained his audience with talk of negotiations with the Scots which, he said, had led to them demanding the handing over of the archbishop of Canterbury. Asked where he had learnt this 'news', his answer was that it was 'spoken about the Towne'. In another Essex village, Radwinter, a church service was disrupted in March 1642 by a parishioner who tossed to the curate 'a base pamphlet (called *An answer of ye Roundheads to ye Rattleheads*) saying, there is reading work for you, read that'. A few days earlier, a scuffle had broken out during a baptism when the father had asked the curate to omit the sign of the cross, 'according . . . to the Protestation, which we have all taken'. In Ipswich, in November 1642, talk in a shop had turned to discussion of some 'printed passages newlie come to town'. This had led one of those present to say that 'the Kinge was no kinge but a Tyrant'. When challenged and rebuked, his reply had been: 'I can shewe it you in printe.'[1]

Political division and the paralysis this brought to many of the traditional mechanisms by which local society had been policed, and challenges to established order punished, opened up a new political space in the early 1640s. The episodes referred to above are but three of the many that could be advanced to show how mutual interactions between print, rumour, and royal and parliamentary directives politicised local society. Political conflict in the provinces, marked by opposition to the policies of the 1630s, once covert, now open, had damaged that willingness to present and prosecute offenders on which in large part early modern law enforcement depended. The need for both crown and parliament to secure support in a political culture where claims on deference no longer sufficed to mobilise popular support meant that their actions from the elections of 1639–40 on consciously invited popular agency. The paper wars through which these messages were disseminated and the explosion of news-driven print, eased by the collapse of censorship and accelerated by a variety of stimuli (not least commercial gain), effected a transformation in the infrastructure of information and communication.

These developments offered a challenge, both direct and indirect, to many of the norms of a political culture which hitherto had proscribed (at least, independent) popular political agency and which, in theory at least, regarded the *arcana imperii* as the preserve of a political elite. But in so doing, they revealed also the deeper contradictions within the structures of the early modern English state. These contradictions had made maintenance of those norms always problematical, making popular participation in governance a necessary reality well before 1640, necessitating a tradition of political communication with subjects that ran from, *inter alia*, proclamations and judicial charges through to tuning the pulpits.

This chapter examines the impact of this new political space on popular political culture. It concentrates here on developments in popular politics in the early 1640s, a period sometimes neglected in contrast to the attention devoted to the seductive developments later in the decade with the emergence of radical groups, whose status as 'vanguard *political parties*' has undoubtedly been exaggerated and whose problematical relationship to an earlier tradition of protest needs more critical scrutiny. Examining the dominant historiographies within which crowds in the English Revolution have been discussed, the chapter argues for a reading of the *politics* inherent in protest prior to the 1640s. It examines the degree of convergence between 'traditional' crowd actions and the politics of the 1640s, before going on explore the extent to which this new political space offered opportunities for a more formal popular engagement with the politics of the Revolution.

Until recently, there was a tendency in the study of popular politics in the Revolution, as more generally in the historiography of early modern England, to see this as primarily synonymous with the politics of the crowd. This reading sometimes collapses differences between crowds into a hypostatised singular 'early modern crowd': '*the* crowd' acts as surrogate for '*the* people'. The problems this conflation can produce are reflected in discussions of the role of 'the people' in the English Revolution which have seen in the tergiversations of '*the* crowd' evidence either of their fickleness (ironically echoing contemporary early modern prejudices about the irrationality of the 'many-headed monster') or of the linearity of an assumed univocal popular politics, shifting over the course of the Revolution from support for parliament to support for the crown. 'Riot' does of course provide a privileged point of access to popular political culture, providing as it does a moment when the opaque surface of the past is punctured, allowing subordinate groups, rendered otherwise silent by the inequalities in levels of literacy, access to print and to the preserved record, to testify to their attitudes and beliefs. However, the simple stereotype of riot can obscure the often complex and richly symbolic nature of crowd actions, while also ignoring the many forms of popular political action that lay between the polarities of *either* 'riot' *or* political acquiescence.[2]

Echoing tendencies to be found in the historiographies of other periods, political motivation in a popular politics seen through the prism of 'the crowd' could be thought – all too easily – to be explained solely by economic grievance or by the interests of class. This reflected the impact of the convergence of the social history of the 1960s with earlier historiographies, with roots in a liberal or Marxist/radical populism. While this conjuncture helped to promote a serious engagement with crowd actions, a tendency to read those actions in terms of 'knife-and-fork' politics or to read off their motivation from an assumed and reductionist rendering of class interest hampered an understanding of the broader political context and culture within which those grievances were understood as legitimate occasions for collective protest.

The consequences of this development are reflected in Brian Manning's now classic study of the role of the people in the Revolution. Agrarian problems, he argued, led 'many peasants' (a label not without its own problems[3]) to oppose royalist landlords and the king, as landlord, in the civil war and to support parliament. A reversal of expectations in the 1620s and 1630s – the product of higher rents and entry fines, together with the adverse consequences of enclosure, population pressure and industrial depression – saw an alliance of the median and upper strata of 'the peasantry' with smallholders and cottagers in a 'rising tide' of protest in the countryside. In this reading, enclosure was seen as an 'archetypal' act of capitalist appropriation; peasant revolt therefore constituted a 'paradigmatic instance' of class conflict.[4]

Focus on 'the crowd' did reflect the fact that the early 1640s witnessed a concentration of crowd action that had not been seen in number, geographical extent and range of targets since at least the 'commotions' of the mid-sixteenth century and perhaps even the *événements* of 1381. This was certainly the case with agrarian protest. But an emphasis on number and range fails to register some important shifts in the tradition of protest. Whatever the other problems in this reading, Manning's construction of a 'national' crisis depended on the aggregation of examples that in reality reflected the discrete problems of particular regions. Population density and the regional geography of open fields, common rights and enclosure (with open fields largely absent from some areas and others not to experience significant enclosure until after this period) meant that protest had in fact been largely absent from some areas prior to the 1640s. Elsewhere, the changing pattern of enclosure, while increasing popular discontent, had closed down the possibility of open collective protest. The failure of the Oxfordshire rising at the end of the sixteenth century had already signalled the changes largely responsible for this: the recasting of rural social relationships with the middling sort increasingly finding their interests as agrarian capitalists met by promoting, not opposing enclosure, and facilitated by the increasing willingness of the English landed class to seek their returns from land through (co-operative) investment in rising productivity rather than in seigneurial extraction of peasant surplus.

Work since Manning on agrarian crowds in the early 1640s has tended not only to dismiss his classed reading of these episodes but to question whether they can be read as offering evidence of a popular engagement with the politics of the Revolution. This more recent historiography has seen 'riots' as essentially defensive and conservative. Rioters did not give expression to political feelings,

but contented themselves with drawing attention to specific grievances of immediate concern. They manifested positive political indifference. Rural disorders were
'essentially non-ideological and non-revolutionary' in character. In as much, then,
as riot could be said to represent a form of *political* action, it was 'traditional',
'customary' or even 'reactionary', drawing on the legitimising force of custom.[5]
Thus, in this reading, the relationship of agrarian protest to the Revolution was
merely opportunistic.

Despite a tendency to frame studies of the crowd against the then dominant
Marxist historiography in terms of what crowds were *not*, this later work made
an important contribution to our understanding of collective protest in early
modern England. But in arguing against a classed reading of popular political
engagement, the framing of these studies within a particular, but often implicit,
definition of the political obscured the extent to which crowd actions in a culture of obedience which proscribed independent popular action were necessarily political. Labelling protests non-political was accomplished by a questionable
reference to their failure to engage with 'high politics'. Thus 'village revolts' – 'devoid
of political consciousness' – represented 'primitive or pre-political behaviour because
they failed to develop into some modern form of protest or participation in the
political nation'.[6]

If, however, we replace the teleological hierarchies implicit in defining the political with an alternative focus on how power was constituted and contested in early
modern society, then we can begin to understand how crowd actions were
necessarily political, both in the sense of interrogating the everyday exercise of
power *and* in engaging with the politics of the state.[7] More recent work on early
modern crowd actions has offered a richer, if more nuanced, analysis of the
tradition of popular politics prior to the English Revolution. In that tradition,
early modern crowds, operating within a culture of obedience which placed a
premium on securing legitimacy for their actions, sought to defend their rights
and to seek justice by negotiating with, rather than challenging, authority – at
least publicly. Riot was the last, rather than first, resort. Often, resistance took
place in the law courts as well as on the ground, with the precise shaping of actions
within 'riot' deliberately intended to initiate legal action. Crowds consciously fashioned their protest to assert the legitimacy of their actions and demands. In so
doing, their actions often mimicked the role required of the local magistracy by
the English crown, confiscating grain being illegally transported or traded and
returning it to the authorities in pointed criticism of their inactivity, or citing
laws against enclosure while restoring common rights by pulling down hedges.
As this suggests, crowds were necessarily *political*. This was not just because their
actions represented a claim to popular agency and to interrogate the exercise of
power in their lives; nor that in the timing or staging of their actions they sometimes showed a surprisingly developed strategic sense of dislocations in power.
Rather, it was because they often showed a high level of engagement with, and
knowledge of, government policy and priorities, and because their actions
implied a claim to participate in policing the *polis*.

Recognition that protests were inherently political makes it possible to suggest a reading of popular protest in early modern England that offers a more integrated and dynamic understanding of popular politics. English monarchs, all too aware of the limited forces of repression at their command, sought to police social and economic change in order to minimise the threat of popular disorder. They did so within the terms of a public transcript which repeatedly stressed that the rationale for royal policies was to protect their subjects and, in particular, the weak and poor. By so doing, they sought to transmute power into authority and thereby secure popular consent to their rule. A provincial magistracy, drawn from a landed class with attenuated seigneurial powers, also needed to secure their authority by a visible attentiveness to popular grievances, an imperative reinforced by the insistent prodding of central government. Thus, the formal weakness of the state's repressive force, coupled with an acute awareness (even moral panic) about increasing social tensions, made authority ready to respond to popular grievances. In turn, the dependence of power-holders, from monarch to magistrates, on the maintenance of respect for their authority placed a premium on rule by law (and through the law courts). At the same time, lacking a professional bureaucracy, royal government sought to enlist popular support by publicising to the people its policies to police economic change, inviting their co-operation in the detection of wrongdoing. Out of this was created a strong sense of legitimation for those who engaged in protest in defence of what might be termed the 'politics of subsistence'.

Central to popular political culture was a set of expectations about the proper exercise of authority. In turn, central to these was the idea of a just king whose rule, by definition, could not tolerate oppression of his people since monarchy existed to deliver justice to all its subjects. A similar set of expectations was elaborated around the public transcript of the 'good lord', whose right to obedience was contrasted with evil lords whose actions had forfeited the allegiance of tenants and the poor. Protestors, therefore, for the most part invoked, rather than challenged, authority. Petitions which incorporated threats to wreak violence on their manorial lords, or betters, combined these with carefully phrased expressions of loyalty to the monarch, whose person and family they explicitly exempted from such levelling. But this did not mean that there was not an ability to distinguish between monarchy as an institution committed to defending the interests of its subjects and individual monarchs whose policies and practices failed to honour or to achieve that imperative. Public iterations of support for the prince were often, in reality, declarations of support for monarchy as an abstract guarantor of popular rights. Crowds were, then, political not just in terms of seeking to influence power locally, but in expressing political ideas about the proper exercise of that power and of the responsibilities of power and property-holders, up to and including the godly prince, within both the moral economy of the commonwealth and monarchical paternalism.

Seeing crowd actions prior to the Revolution as necessarily political puts the relationship between the tradition of protest and popular politics within the

Revolution in a new and intriguing light. A popular political culture that had at its core a series of expectations about the responsibilities of the good king (or good lord) carried with it the possibility of a rejection of respect for that authority. The growing entanglement with the state that was a consequence of the increasing incorporation of sections of the people as the executors of an increasingly ambitious set of policies offered a political education in loyalty that might also, paradoxically, enlarge the possibilities for a more critical engagement. Magistrates might be understood to be failing in their policies, lords to be flouting royal law and custom (as well as popular expectations), monarchs even to be failing to live up to the role of godly prince and fount of justice.

Another historiographical tradition, with its roots in a liberal-democratic tradition, and strongly represented across the Atlantic, which tried to read out (read back?) the legacies of the English Revolution in terms of religious conflict and its interconnections with the pursuit of liberty has also been influential in studies of popular politics in the Revolution. Although perhaps not directly concerned with popular politics, this historiography sketched the political consequences of religious communities' struggle for toleration. Of course, this alternative rendering of popular politics could fuse with the radical–populist tradition discussed above when, following the contemporary political sociologies of commentators like Richard Baxter and the earl of Clarendon, Marxist historians in particular sought to privilege a social group – the middling sort – as bearers of the (radical) puritan cause. As this parody of a much richer and more nuanced historiography suggests, there was much that was questionable in the approach. At its worst this tradition replaced the teleology of class with the anachronism of democracy. But it could encourage historians of the period to take seriously the larger role that more obviously political conflict, with its roots in confessional strife, played in promoting a popular political culture. More recently, challenges in social theory to an economically reductionist reading of class, and the recognition of a more contingent process of class formation which suggested the need for a greater sensitivity to the role of the political in fashioning collective identities, also underwrote the need to understand popular political culture *in its own terms* and not as a mask for other essentialist interests.[8]

Parallel to the politics of subsistence, then, was another strand of popular politics which saw a more formal engagement with the political and religious policies of the English crown. As work on medieval England has shown, popular politics was not an early modern creation, but the demands of the Tudor state and the confessional consequences of the Reformation increased both its depth and the level of political consciousness it might invoke.[9] These developments too could be located in part in the structural weaknesses of the English monarchy. The communal and associative character of political rule that stemmed in part from the fact that a crown that lacked either a professional bureaucracy or a standing army required, as well as promoted, a high degree of semi-autonomous self-government. The assumption of control over the church by the monarchy *at the same time* as a change in the religion professed within that church inevitably involved a process of conversion and education that afforded the laity a larger role within the advancement and defence of reformation. At best, popular social and economic grievances might produce regional opposition or register some temporal synchronicity under the stimulus of dearth. But action by a state that by contemporary European standards exhibited a high level of political integration could – paradoxically – politicise and unify opposition to it. The potential within the politics of the Reformation to promote popular political awareness had been reflected at a popular level in the rebellions of the sixteenth century, as well as in the litter of libels and seditious talk that religious conflict produced throughout the period. Thus, the popular experience of the 1630s as a period when religious and political liberties were challenged, mediated from 1640 by denunciations in parliament, pulpit and press of popish plots, threatened a more direct challenge to a culture of obedience centred on the monarch as godly prince. There was, therefore, the possibility that the new political space represented by the criticism and collapse of authority at the onset of the English Revolution would see a realisation of the political critique inherent within that strand of popular political culture.

Popular iconoclasm was one of the first expressions of this potential in the 1640s, the attacks on Catholics another. Some political historians of the English Revolution have tended to dismiss the popular iconoclasm of the early 1640s as little more than examples of plebeian disorder. (In so doing, they unwittingly reproduce the attempts of a royalist-inspired campaign to identify such acts as the work of 'the many-headed monster'.[10]) But it is possible to see that iconoclasts, deriving legitimation from the public condemnation of Laudianism in parliament, print and pulpit, were claiming a right to police sacred space and confessional boundaries. As one Essex iconoclast told his examiners, 'the reason of his so pulling downe the railes was, because theye gave offence to his conscience, and that the placeing of them was against Gods lawes, and the King's as appeareth by the twentieth chapter of Exodus, and about the twentyeth verse'.[11] A thickened description of what iconoclasts actually did shows the care with which they spoke through their actions, manipulating their rites of destruction in order to communicate the ideas informing their actions and so distinguish them from mere acts of vandalism.[12] The relationship between crowd, authority and public transcripts to be found in what I have termed the politics of subsistence was also to be found here. The way iconoclasts shaped their destructions often directly reflected the official punishments prescribed for dealing with false beliefs. In purging and purifying churches (and communities) iconoclasts were then extending the role given to them by state and church in policing confessional boundaries within the local community.

There had been earlier episodes of iconoclasm in the sixteenth century, which as yet lack comprehensive histories. But what distinguishes the 1640s is the sheer number of episodes.[13] After attacks on enclosure, this was the second most common occasion of crowd actions (but one with a pronounced regional geography, meaning that in a county like Essex it was the commonest form of crowd action in the 1640s.) We still do not have an accurate sense of the distribution of iconoclasm in the early 1640s. It was clearly more widespread in some areas than others. A variety of factors help to explain its geography. On a regional level the extent and manner of the implementation of Laudian altar policy had some role to play, as did the way regional religious cultures determined the degree of acceptance or resistance, the most obvious contrast here being between the Welsh Marches and eastern England. In the early stages it is perhaps striking testimony to the way in which Laudian bishops and their local clerical allies had been able to cow local opposition, that the presence or absence of troops (*in reality*, locals in uniform) recruited to fight the Scots played an important role, anticipating the role to be played in later iconoclasm by parliamentary forces. But within these broad regional contrasts, there was clearly also a local patterning to iconoclasm where the politics of the parish helped to determine whether popular iconoclasm took place; after 1640, local elites in godly communities could silently reform in anticipation of later parliamentary orders, while in other parishes resistance by aggressive Laudian ministers made popular destruction more likely.

While the extent of conflict reflected the variations in the pace and aggression in implementation across dioceses, the potential for widespread conflict was to be found in the unavoidable physical and visible evidence of change at the level of each and every parish church. It was the changes that Laudianism required in the arrangement of sacred space, the ceremonialism it required in worship within that space, and the doctrinal implications of those changes, that created the possibilities for widespread conflict. The immediate issues of railing and altar worship raised deeper conflicts in which opponents advanced conscience, grounded in scripture and a reading of the Reformation's trajectory as a movement hostile to idolatry and dedicated to enforcement of the second commandment, as a justification for their opposition. Detailed remonstrances, like that from a Colchester churchwarden citing a wide range of authorities and statutes back to Magna Carta, reflected the depth of informed opposition.[14] That ministers might respond by invoking the authority of church and crown and reiterating the obligations of unconditional obedience showed the potential inherent in the Laudian programme for a wider *political* conflict that could reach to every parish, rendering local churches sites for political debate and raising issues of political principle.

As the example of iconoclasm suggests, political events in the early 1640s opened up a new space for popular political agency. Beginning in 1640, the fallout from the Scottish rebellion and growing conflict between crown and parliament saw the further politicisation of the pulpit, with parochial debates about the legality of royal commands and of resistance capable of traversing much the same territory as the more famous and learned discussions among protestant and Catholic theologians from the Reformation on. The failure of parliament and crown to come to a political accommodation saw paper wars in which royalists and parliamentarians were forced to ground appeals for support in ideological statements whose attempt to frame these within a common set of values were undercut by the political context within which they were made. While parliament and crown, and most, *but not all*, of their supporters sought to appeal to a common set of political principles, the cracks quickly showed. At the outset of civil war, competing claims for men and money sharpened recognition of these differences and posed questions of choice against which neutralism and localism proved no defence. The explosion of print and the temporary collapse of censorship saw these messages rehearsed and repeated in a variety of forms, many consciously seeking a popular readership. Printing thus produced a communicative space, one which was public, popular – and critical. Here too, tropes within the battle of print that saw authors giving wider publicity to the ideas against which they wrote helped further to promote a critical reading public.[15]

We can look at two more phenomena of the early 1640s – petitioning and state oaths – to see in detail how these developments impacted on popular political culture. Both may be read as sponsoring a potential reorientation of traditional patterns of political authority since the emergence of cross-petitions and competing oaths reflecting rival sources of authority saw 'subjects' being solicited to give their hands and consent on the basis of reasoned choice, not deferential dependence.

Petitioning, with its unwritten but widely acknowledged linguistic and gestural 'rules', had always provided a privileged political space within which plebeians might enter into a political dialogue with their superiors. But from 1640 the rival political centres of crown and parliament offered competing sites for the rapidly developing practice of 'mass' petitioning.[16] The remarkable level of petitions to parliament, clustered in the early and in the later 1640s, reflects that institution's importance in popular political culture, an importance that stretches back beyond the insistence of sixteenth-century rebels in negotiations with the crown that any resulting political settlement be ratified *by parliament*. But the crowds that accompanied the collective presentation of petitions and the development of parliament as a physical site for political demonstrations represented strikingly new developments in the pattern of popular protest.[17]

Petitions from groups bound together by ties of gender, county, community, confession and craft pulled into the political process those beyond the conventional boundaries of formal political participation. Printing petitions redirected the political messages they contained from their nominal addressees to a larger secondary – 'public' – audience. Printed petitions, with their internal references to counter-petitions and citations of other political texts and authorities, helped to promote what David Zaret has called an 'immanent mode of criticism', imposing 'dialogic order' on political debate, providing readers with the materials to judge between competing claims and promoting the use of reason and informed consent.[18] In the provinces, the importance of securing authoritative backing further politicised institutions like quarter sessions (those provincial parliaments) and assizes, and within them bodies like the grand jury. The role seized by an Essex grand jury in 1641, dominated by godly members, to negate the attempts by proto-royalist magistrates to stage a show trial of a plebeian iconoclast provides a well-documented case of the political conflicts that were happening more generally within these institutional settings.[19] Further such studies are needed to reveal the politics behind the production of petitions emanating from these bodies – and in particular the processes by which they found their way into print.

The widespread popular subscription of competing petitions as their promoters sought the weight of 'noise and numbers',[20] a process about which also we need to know much more, was another important development. Pejorative accounts that seize on contemporary allegations of ignorant and misinformed signings fail to do justice to the role that subscription to petitions could play in promoting and informing local political debate and, as with later Leveller petitioning, creating subscriptional communities which fostered and synchronised political association both within and across traditional political and social boundaries. (The swift dissemination and co-ordination of petitions nationally point to the possibilities afforded for increasingly co-ordinated political action by independent changes in the communication infrastructure linked to a developing 'national' economy.)

State oaths, introduced both by parliament and by royalist authorities to solidify support and identify opponents, also had a role to play in the more formal politicisation of popular protest.[21] Petitioners cited oaths they had taken in justification of their petitioning. Of these, the first, the Protestation of 1641–42, played a major role in promoting political debate at the level of the parish (and in print), a role that has yet to be sufficiently acknowledged. Central to the Protestation was oath-taking at the level of the parish, a practice subsequent oaths were to follow.[22] Originally taken by the members of both Houses in May 1641, subscription came to be required of all adult (male) inhabitants.[23] Taking the Protestation began first in London, then in the boroughs and provinces in the summer of 1641. Legislation to enforce general subscription having failed, the Commons ordered a general taking in response to the king's attempt on the 'Five Members' in January 1642, which met with remarkable success.

The swearing of oaths in early modern society was an act carrying with it onerous obligations. The author of *The nationall covenant* (delivered as sermons in the summer of 1641) emphasised the obligations of keeping an oath – a covenant – sworn before God and warned repeatedly that God himself would punish those who failed to honour their oaths.[24] As a printed declaration appearing at the beginning of August and appealing for support for parliament declared, 'wee are bound by Our Protestation to defend, and woe to us if We do it not, at least to Our utmost endeavours in it, for the discharge of Our Duties, and the saving of our Soules'. That swearing the Protestation by the men of the parish (and sometimes women and youths) took place in the parish church, that it was preceded by a sermon in which the minister was to acquaint the parish with the 'nature of the business' and that it was in places accompanied by the celebration of Holy Communion must have given an added charge to the swearing of an oath before God. In some counties and parishes, the timing of taking the Protestation to coincide with the collection for the relief of distressed protestants in Ireland undoubtedly lent the occasion additional charge and further politicisation, offering as it did a vivid reminder of the nature of the popish threat against which the oath was directed.

Subscribing to (or refusing) the Protestation was of major significance in promoting political debate at the level of local society and in fashioning a pro-parliamentary popular political culture. A lengthy preamble to the oath offered a concise reading of the recent past dominated by a plot to undermine the protestant religion and to introduce tyrannical government. Requiring those who took it to swear actively to defend crown, parliament, protestantism and political liberties against this plot, its focus on the perils of popery allowed parliament to mine the powerful vein of anti-popery, which throughout the period played such a large and protean part in popular political consciousness, serving as a short-hand and explicans for a range of grievances that ran beyond the immediate issue of religious difference.

In the context of the early 1640s the Protestation became an important justification for active popular participation in the work of reformation. Thomas Mockett in his sermons on the Protestation emphasised that taking it imposed an obligation actively to bring to justice those who opposed its terms, while Thomas Robinson drew on it to argue that the removal of altar rails and the casting away of 'all vain ceremonies' must be done 'before our oaths can be fulfilled'. In warming to his theme, Robinson showed the radical potential in popular appropriations of the oath: 'the law of the land therefore is not to be taken principally for the bounds and limits of our Oath, but the law of God; and lawfully may we oppose the law of man so far forth as it opposeth the Law of God'.[25] The oath's capacity to legitimise independent popular action is brought out in the example of popular iconoclasts. At one London church, destruction began with a parishioner on the day of taking the Protestation telling his fellow-parishioners, 'Gentlemen we have heare made a protestation before Almighty god against all popery and popish Inovac[i]ons, and these railes . . . are popish Inovac[i]ons, and therefore it is fitt they be pulled downe'; while at Norwich one of the apprentices who threatened to pull down the rails and the organ in the cathedral claimed that 'the Rayles, and Pipes, and other Innovations, was against the Protestation, and he had sworne against all Innovations and he would pull them downe where-ever he saw them, for so he was bound to doe by the Protestation that he had taken'. Appropriation of the Protestation was widespread enough to be listed by the author of the pamphlet *Certaine affirmations in defence of the pulling down of communion rails, by divers rash and misguided people* as one of the iconoclasts' prime justifications. Perhaps the most potent example of the potential of the Protestation to underwrite popular agency is that of a poor Essex weaver from Ralph Josselin's parish of Earls Colne. Brought to court for stealing and mutilating the Book of Common Prayer, he declared in the face of the leading gentleman of the county 'that it did not repent him that he had so done ffor since he had taken the protestac[i]on he could not sleep quietly till he had done the same'. His act of defiance vividly reflected the danger of a disintegration of the culture of obedience under the questionings of politically informed consciences.[26]

Radical appropriation of the Protestation in this fashion had clearly not been intended by parliament. But parliament's needs to mobilise support could have similar consequences. In the late summer of 1642, parliament had issued a declaration which appeared in print in several forms. In justifying parliament's call to arms, this declaration concluded: 'all which every honest man is bound to defend; especially those who have taken the late Protestation, By which they are more particularly tyed unto it and the more answerable before God, should they neglect it.' As the attacks on Sir John Lucas and Catholic landowners in eastern England and elsewhere showed, an oath which required those who took it to 'oppose, and by all good ways and means endeavour to bring to condign punishment all such as shall by force, practice, counsels, plots, conspiracies or otherwise do anything to the contrary in this present Protestation contained' could legitimise a very active popular agency in the events of the Revolution.[27]

While earlier forms of popular protest reoccurred in the 1640s and, in the case of agrarian protest, on a scale not seen for at least a century, ultimately these failed to mesh with the politics of the Revolution. The potential within protests against enclosure for a more explicit rejection of landlord authority was never realised. The reasons for this are complex. Political division may have legitimised commoners to pursue attacks on their lords as 'enemies of the state', but it did not by definition allow attacks on the landed class as 'enemies of the people'. While the semi-paralysis of authority in the civil war allowed communities to reclaim common rights, after the civil war the balance of power shifted again as the Protectorate acquired armed forces which could be used to suppress protest. A parliament of landowners was to disappoint the expectations of aggrieved tenants in plumping, by and large, for the restoration of the status quo in the countryside, the failure of putative bills for regulating enclosure and the airing of pro-enclosure arguments registering a shift in the public transcript that closed off an important source hitherto of legitimation to would-be rioters. The relative neglect of enclosure as a popular grievance likely to mobilise the largest rural constituency in the 'programmes' of the radical groups effectively denied commoners an alternative leadership. While there are some examples of tenants and commoners locating landlord power in the 'Norman yoke' and seeking its overthrow, and while there is still more to be learned about the Digger communities and their social base, the failure of the group perhaps most likely to have appealed to the constituency of the rural poor – at the hands of local communities (or local elites?) as well as parliament's troops – suggests that a programme of common cultivation of the wastes and commons was at some variance with an earlier tradition of protest in which defence of common rights was intended even for the poorer commoners to sustain diminishing individual holdings. Commoners' support for the moral economy of the commonwealth did not, then, automatically translate into support either for the Commonwealth or its radical critics.

Within the politics of subsistence, harvest failure and dearth had been the other major occasion for crowd actions. The later 1640s saw some of the worst harvests of the century, made worse by successive failures in 1647–49. What is striking is that, with a few exceptions, there was apparently little direct effort made to marry radical political critiques with traditional popular understandings of the causes of dearth. Crowd actions over food in the later 1640s were traditional in form, targeting abuses in the marketing of grain rather than inequalities in command over food stocks, and the evidence would suggest that such incidents were fewer than in earlier periods of dearth. This reflected in large part the ability and willingness of elites at the level of the local community to continue to implement, with little prompting from a now parliamentary regime, measures designed to anticipate and ameliorate popular grievances previously associated with the crown-sponsored policy of the Book of orders. The poor were thus encouraged to identify with their local communities and to choose community over class.

The evidence of sedition both before and during the 1640s and 1650s might suggest the existence of a more radical critique within popular political culture, but it cannot answer the question of how widespread subscription to this otherwise hidden transcript might have been. It was likely however that at the level of local society shifting social alignments underlined the truth of James Scott's observation that subordinate classes while less constrained at the level of thought and ideology were more constrained at the level of political action 'where the daily exercise of power sharply limits the options available to them'.[28] Seen from the centre, the emphasis in the 1640s and 1650s is rightly on the collapse and/or fracturing of traditional institutions and the continuing failure to secure political or religious stability. But how far *at a local level* these operated to open up a new space for radical popular initiatives is uncertain. We still know too little about a radical presence outside the towns and the capital, even less about an *organised* radical presence. Despite the possibilities offered by religious communities, it was probably the case that while print made it possible for radical ideas to circulate more widely, this ran well ahead of the ability of radicals or any radical organisation to make their presence felt at the level of local society. Local ecologies and their interrelationships with patterns of local social and power structures (seigneurial and parochial) clearly had their part to play here in promoting or obstructing such a development. But it is salutary to contemplate how the attempt to proselytise for radical ideas in the Terlings of early modern England would have fared. Change denied the poorer sort, though growing in numbers, the independence necessary to organise open and collective protest in pursuit of their own interests.

In terms of the potential within the politics of subsistence, the Revolution represented a closing down of political space. Clearly, the divergence of popular interests, grounded in the politics of subsistence, from the transcripts of the Revolution also had a part to play in explaining a growing political disillusionment. The impact of the costs of mobilisation, the experience of civil war and of the dislocations in church and society, all both immediately experienced *and* indirectly mediated by discussion (and distortion) in print, helped to promote popular royalism (as well as doubtless apathy and resignation). Class interests were not then to provide a key to popular politics in the Revolution. Recognition of the contingent nature of class formation in early modern England suggests that the provocative inquiry 'what can rich men do against poor men if poor men rise and hold together?'[29] was not a question capable of being answered in the Revolution.

In 1985, David Underdown suggested that there have been three models by which historians have sought to explain the popular role in the English Revolution: deference (which has been largely used to explain royalist success in acquiring an army), localism, and class (which has been used to explain popular parliamentarianism).[30] Since then a whole body of work, Underdown's own later work included, has allowed us to begin to recognise the richness of a popular political culture in early modern England. Educated by the needs of the state through an officially sponsored dialogue of proclamations, policy statements (in the form of judicial charges, etc.), state-sponsored homilies and sermons; entertained by a popular culture in which both the stage and the theatre of authority (royal entries, mayoral shows, 'bonfires and bells', etc.) offered political lessons; informed by texts as diverse as popular ballads, godly sermons, biblical exegesis and cheap print; and incorporated through local office, law enforcement and electioneering – here was a world in which popular political awareness might be displayed in carefully constructed (and sensitively timed) protests which sought to embarrass authority with their knowledge of official discourses.

The English Revolution registered new spaces for forms of protest in which popular agency laid claim to a more formal political role. It is surely possible to see in reactions to a set of cues the (temporary) emergence of citizens from within the earlier chrysalis of subjects. But, as this chapter has suggested, such an outcome had had a much longer gestation. It might be argued that the structures of monarchical rule in early modern England with its participatory 'village republics' and the social depth this gave to politics made this eventuation less surprising than once might have been thought.[31] But the consequences for our understanding of the popular role(s) within the Revolution demand further work. It is perhaps unhelpful in employing a linear chronology and questionable vocabulary to see the Revolution as giving birth *ab initio* to a 'nascent public sphere'. But a sharper sense of the extent and depth of popular political consciousness before the Revolution and of the significant intensification given to this by the events of the early 1640s, enlarges our understandings of the possibilities for popular political action within the Revolution. Popular political agency might be claimed under the powerful notion of a citizenry, mobilised by appeals to conscience, with an active role to play in the preservation of England's liberties and in the rooting out of political and spiritual corruption. Later, in a state in which political control still rested with a landed and mercantile elite, some would seek radically to extend their rights, devising political programmes that both drew creatively on popular experience of the participation in authority before the Revolution as well as on the accelerated politicisation and incorporation that Revolution itself brought. But while developments in the 1640s and 1650s would enlarge the space for an active popular role within the politics of the Revolution, it would also increase the costs of citizenship, both literally in the state's spiralling fiscal demands and in the dislocations to traditional institutions and values. A popular political culture, divided in its political allegiances from the outset of the Revolution, would see increasing numbers decide that the costs outweighed the benefits of citizenship.

Notes

1 TNA, 16/421/21; Bodleian Library, Rawlinson MS D158, fo. 43r; Bankes MS 52/31. For the full history of conflict at Radwinter, see J. Walter, ' "Affronts and insolencies": the voices of Radwinter and popular opposition to Laudianism', *English Historical Review* (forthcoming).

2 For discussion of these other forms, see J. Walter, 'Public transcripts, popular agency and the politics of subsistence in early modern England', in M. J. Braddick and J. Walter (eds), *Negotiating power in early modern society: order, hierarchy and subordination in Britain and Ireland* (Cambridge, 2001), 123–48.

3 J. Walter, 'Changement agraire et disparition de la paysannerie en Angleterre 1500–1800', in H. Frechet (ed.), *La terre et les paysans en France et en Grande-Bretagne de 1600 a 1800* (Paris, 1998), 137–67.

4 B. Manning, *The English people and the English revolution* (1976), ch. 7; and 'The peasantry and the English revolution', *Journal of Peasant Studies*, 2 (1975), 133–58.

5 K. Lindley, *Fenland riots and the English revolution* (London, 1982), 253–8; B. Sharp, *In contempt of all authority: rural artisans and riot in the west of England 1585–1660* (Berkeley, CA, and London, 1980), 7–8; D. Underdown, *A freeborn people: politics and the nation in seventeenth-century England* (Oxford, 1996), vii, ix, 59.

6 R. B. Manning, *Village revolts: social protest and popular disturbances in England, 1509–1640* (Oxford, 1988), 2–3, 309–11, 318–19.

7 For an elaboration of this argument, see J. Walter, 'Crown and crowd: popular culture and popular protest in early modern England', in *Sotsial'naia Istoriia: problemy sintza/Social history: problems of synthesis* (Moscow, 1994), 235–49.

8 J. Walter, *Understanding popular violence in the English revolution: the Colchester plunderers* (Cambridge, 1999), 262–4.

9 I. M. W. Harvey, 'Was there a peasant politics in fifteenth-century England?', in R. H. Britnell and A. J. Pollard (eds), *The MacFarlane legacy: studies in late medieval politics and society* (Stroud, 1995), 155–74; R. B. Goheen, 'Peasant politics? Village community and the crown in the fifteenth-century England', *American Historical Review*, 96 (1999), 42–62.

10 J. Walter, ' "Abolishing superstition with sedition"? The politics of popular iconoclasm in England 1640–1642', *Past and Present*, 183 (2004), 116–21.

11 Essex Record Office, Q/SBa 2/41, Exam. Wm. Skinner, 10 Jan. 1641.

12 Walter, ' "Abolishing superstition with sedition"?', 82–112.

13 For what follows, see J. Walter, 'Confessional politics in pre-civil war Essex: prayer books, profanations and petitions', *Historical Journal*, 44 (2001), 677–701; ' "Abolishing

superstition with sedition"?', 79–123; and 'Popular iconoclasm and the politics of the parish in eastern England, 1640–1642', *Historical Journal*, 47 (2004), 261–90.

14 TNA, SP 16/314/130.

15 J. Raymond, *Pamphlets and pamphleteering in early modern Britain* (Cambridge, 2003), 208–13.

16 A. Fletcher, *The outbreak of the English civil war* (Oxford, 1985), ch. 6.

17 K. Lindley, *Popular politics and religion in civil war London* (Aldershot, 1997), ch. 1; for an interesting discussion of the political significance of the physical site of parliament, see C. R. Kyle and J. Peacey, 'Under cover of much coming and going: public access to parliament and the political process in early modern England', in Kyle and Peacey (eds), *Parliament at work: parliamentary committees, political power and public access in early modern England* (Woodbridge, 2002), 1–28.

18 D. Zaret, *Origins of democratic culture: printing, petitions and the public sphere in early-modern England* (Princeton, NJ, 2000), chs 7–8.

19 Walter, 'Confessional politics in pre-civil war Essex'.

20 Sir Thomas Aston, quoted in J. Maltby, 'Petitions for episcopacy and the Book of Common Prayer on the eve of the civil war 1641–1642', in *From Cranmer to Davidson: a Church of England miscellany*, ed. S. Taylor, Church of England Record Society, 7 (Woodbridge, 1999), 115.

21 D. M. Jones, *Conscience and allegiance in seventeenth-century England: the political significance of oaths and engagements* (Rochester, NY, 1999); E. Vallance, 'Protestation, vow, covenant and engagement: swearing allegiance in the English civil war', *Historical Research*, 75 (2002), 408–24.

22 D. Cressy, 'The protestation protested, 1641 and 1642', *Historical Journal*, 45 (2002), 251–79.

23 For what follows, see Walter, *Understanding popular violence*, 292–6.

24 T. Mocket, *The nationall covenant: or, a discourse on the covenant wherein also the severall parts of the late PROTESTATION are proved to be grounded on religion and reason . . .* (1642), sig A1v, 1, 8, 20–2, 38.

25 BL, E146[24], T. Robinson, *The petitioners vindication from calumnie and aspersion . . .* (1642), 5, 16.

26 House of Lords Record Office, MP HL, 30 June 1641; BL, E140[17], T. L., *True news from Norwich . . .* , 6; I. W., *Certaine affirmations in defence of the pulling down of communion rails, by divers rash and misguided people, judiciously and religiously answered* (1641), 3; Walter, 'Confessional politics in pre-civil war Essex', 688.

27 Walter, *Understanding popular violence*, 296, 330.

28 J. C. Scott, *Domination and the arts of resistance: hidden transcripts* (New Haven, CT, and London, 1990), 91.

29 F. G. Emmison, *Elizabethan life: disorder* (Chelmsford, 1970), 64.

30 D. Underdown, *Revel, riot and rebellion: popular politics and culture in England 1603–1660* (Oxford, 1985), ch. 1.

31 See the comments in P. Collinson, *De republica Anglorum; or, history with the politics put back* (Cambridge, 1989).

7

Religious diversity in revolutionary London

Ann Hughes

On one of the parliamentary fast days of the 1640s, three Londoners – a doctor of medicine, a merchant and a scrivener – sought out an edifying sermon.[1] They went first to hear the Presbyterian James Cranford on the need for conformity and the evils of 'toleration', but finding this tedious they 'went at last to Basing-shaw Church, it being where my Lord Mayor was to be, as expecting to hear some excellent man there'. But again they 'found the matter so lamentable, as we were all three weary of it', and they slipped from the back of the church without causing offence. As Humphrey Brooke, the doctor, later wrote,

> we did all agree, comming afterwards home to Mr Walwyns, that the Ministers did generally spend their time either upon uselesse subjects, such as did little tend to edification, or about advancing their own interests and reputation with the people.[2]

At the home of the merchant, William Walwyn (the future Leveller already notorious for his support for religious liberty), Brooke continued,

> we went on discoursing, from one thing to another, and amongst other things, of the wisdom of the heathen, how wise and able they were in those things, unto which their knowledge did extend; and what pains they took to make men wise, vertuous, and good commonwealths men.[3]

Then Walwyn brought out his books, recommending Lucian's *Dialogues*, especially his account of tyranny, 'for his good ends in discovering the vanity of things in worldly esteem'.[4] By 1649 the third man, Richard Price, scrivener and member of the gathered church led by the maverick Independent John Goodwin, was a committed opponent of Walwyn who, he claimed, had brandished 'that prophane scurrilous Lucians Dialogue', saying 'let us go read that which hath somthing in it, Here is more wit in this ... th[a]n in all the Bible'.[5]

London in the 1640s had become a religious marketplace where sermons according to taste could be found on Sundays and fast days. All parties to this 1649 dispute denied they went from sermon to sermon while accusing their opponents of so doing. It was alleged that Walwyn's 'usual manner was both upon those [fasts] and the Lords days' to go 'from place to place, hearing here a little, and there a little what the Ministers said, making it the subject matter of his prophane scorning and jeering'.[6] Walwyn for his part claimed that members of Goodwin's church went 'to and fro from place to place on the Lords, and Fasts dayes, 4 and 6 of a company spying, watching, and censuring of doctrines'.[7] If such 'gadding' was exceptional, there is much evidence of eclectic sermon attendance. The Presbyterian artisan and parish elder, Nehemiah Wallington, heard Independent preachers like Hugh Peter as well as Presbyterians. In the later 1640s the Worcestershire gentleman Nicholas Lechmere heard a range of city preachers including Richard Vines, Simeon Ashe, Stephen Marshall, Thomas Goodwin, and John Tombes.[8] Sampling sermons, then debating and challenging the views expressed, was central to the urban sociability of engaged citizens, although we should note that, in Walwyn's case, increasingly bitter fragmentation among parliamentarians transformed private, open-minded conversations into partisan recriminations in print. The accounts, both sympathetic and hostile, of William Walwyn's activities in the 1640s echo John Milton's praise in *Areopagitica* of 'the earnest and zealous thirst after knowledge and understanding which God hath stirr'd up in this City'. Milton denounced those who attacked this intellectual speculation under the 'fantastic terrors of sect and schism'.[9]

What Milton celebrated others, indeed, condemned. In 1646 the Presbyterian propagandist Thomas Edwards bemoaned the spread of error in the 'Metr[o]polis . . . and that in the heart of the City'; false doctrines were 'not preached with us in the ear, but on the house-top, we declare our errours, as Sodom, and are not ashamed; yea, abominable errours are Printed, the Books sold up and down in Westminster-Hall, London, and dispersed in all places; yea, given into the hands of Parliament men in Westminster-Hall'.[10] At about the same time, the city's common council evoked the horrors of religious division in similar terms. Private meetings (at least eleven in one parish) were held on the Lord's day; orthodox ministers were 'neglected and contemned' as anti-Christian, as if the 'tirrany of the prelatical government' had never been overthrown, and 'by reason of such meetings and the preaching of women and other ignorant persons, supersticon, heresie, schismes and prophanes are much increased, families divided, and such blasphemies as the peticioners tremble to thinke on uttered to the high dishonour of Almighty God'.[11] Two years later a remonstrance by London Presbyterian ministers similarly complained of 'Grosse ignorance in fundamentalls in Religion . . . dangerous errors and heresies . . . notorious Atheisme and prophanesse'.[12]

Research by modern scholars has confirmed contemporaries' understanding of religious fragmentation in 1640s London.[13] By 1646 there were thirteen 'Independent' congregations meeting in London: among the best known were the church in Stepney, where William Greenhill and Jeremiah Burroughs were pastors, and John Goodwin's gathered church which met first in St Stephens, Coleman Street. The city also contained 7–8 Calvinist, or 'Particular' Baptist, churches that, in October 1644 and January 1646, issued printed confessions of faith, with William Kiffin and Thomas Patient among the most prominent figures. There were some five groups of 'General' Baptists, holding contrasting beliefs in general redemption. The church founded by Thomas Lambe, a cradle of city political radicalism, dominates modern discussions as it dominated Thomas Edwards's fearful accounts: 'There is one Lamb who was a Sope boyler, and a Church that meets in Bell-Alley in Colemanstreet called Lambs Church: This man and his Church are very Erroneous, strange Doctrines being vented there continually.'[14] All these churches had pastors who had been set apart from the rest of the congregation through some process of ordination, but other Londoners argued against any distinction between laymen and preachers. John Spencer, 'Sometime Groome to a Nobleman', insisted that 'the gifts of the Spirit are in every one for the good of the whole body and that there is no private gifts, nor private Christians'. Only those with a 'call' should preach, but such calls were the people's 'great necessity and their great willingnesse to heare them'. By the mid-1640s, at least nine separatist congregations headed by lay pastors were active in London. Spencer had founded a church with a 'felt-maker', John Green, in 1639, while Edward Rosier's and Praisegod Barebone's congregations were among the most notorious.[15]

We must be wary of over-'sectarianising' the situation in 1640s London. The boundaries between different churches were more porous than hostile observers assumed, and the city was an arena for radical preaching and speculation by men (and some women) with no clear congregational affiliations. The charismatic, ordained, Independent preacher Hugh Peter had no pastoral responsibilities in London, but he preached frequently in the city.[16] On the other hand, men with parish livings might preach unorthodox views. Dr Robert Gell somehow managed to combine secure possession of the living of St Mary Aldermary, throughout the 1640s, with open preaching of 'Familist' doctrine. The 'Antinomian' and 'Familist' stress on the immediate inspiration of the spirit that troubled the 'puritan underground' of the 1630s has been brilliantly discussed in recent work by David Como and Peter Lake. From the early 1640s such preaching could emerge more openly than before, not quite free from harassment, but threatened only intermittently and ineffectually as compared to the impact of the bishop of London's courts or the High Commission of the 1630s. One commentator claimed that the Familist 'at this very time . . . doth more hurt in one houre then in ten heretofore', while John Etherington, who was probably an ex-Familist himself, described how the 'blasphemous doctrine' was 'now very boldly taught by one Mr Randall, and sundry others in and about the Citie of London. Whom Multitudes of people follow, and which Doctrine many embrace.'[17]

Religious heterodoxy and sectarian allegiance were not majority or popular positions in the 1640s. The 1648 remonstrance of the city clergy complained of gross ignorance and prophaneness, as well as errors and schism. Keith Lindley has drawn attention to an attack on the house of the Familist Giles Randall in February 1645, perhaps sanctioned in the minds of the boys and women who initiated the assault by official disapproval of Randall's activities. One man was reported to have said: '[W]here are the boys that should pull downe the house according to my Lord Mayors order', with the result that 'a multitude of boys gathered together and broke downe the windowes of Giles Randall'. This attack probably occurred on Shrove Tuesday and mobilised traditional rituals to attack a novel target – another indication of a hankering for a familiar world.[18] Most people very likely remained unconvinced by either mainstream church puritanism or any form of sectarian challenge, but that does not detract from the novel impact of determined minorities.

The intellectual justifications supporting this religious diversity were as complex as the phenomenon itself. Very few argued for broad religious toleration as an inherent good. More commonly a conviction about the corruption of the established national church fuelled the decision to separate and construct a purer way. The veteran anti-Laudian martyr Henry Burton, who decisively rejected a national church in the 1640s, or the increasingly well-organised Calvinist Baptists were examples.[19] Others adopted a broad and flexible notion of religious truth, and argued that there were diverse ways of reaching this truth. It was therefore improper to bridle the individual conscience. John Price, a leading member of John Goodwin's church, wrote, in 1645, 'wee cannot as yet bee all of one minde, which is our affliction as well as our sinne, yet may we be all of one heart', and this stance is associated above all with Oliver Cromwell. It did not involve a commitment to total religious toleration. In the January 1649 manifesto of the army officers (The 'Officers' Agreement of the People') and in the Instrument of Government of December 1653 establishing the Protectorate, a 'public profession' of the Christian religion was to be supported by the state, although no one was to be compelled 'by penalties or otherwise' to adhere to it, but rather to be won over 'by sound doctrine and the example of a good conversation'. Liberty of conscience was offered to many of those who disagreed with the public profession, but supporters of 'popery' and 'prelacy' were expressly excluded and those who denied the Trinity or the validity of the scriptures were by implication not to have liberty of conscience.[20] The ultimate aim indeed was unity on the basis of agreed truths, rather than diversity, although a remarkable range of religious behaviour and opinion was allowed in the meantime.

In contrast to this open-minded drive for unity was a notably relaxed acceptance of the inevitability of division, perhaps less a developed argument than a temperamental disposition. John Spencer's patron, the radical parliamentarian peer Robert, second Lord Brooke, wrote in 1642 that 'it is clear in Reason, that Divisions, Sects, Schisms, and Heresies must come'. There were, Brooke argued, alternative approaches to division and error. There was the forced 'Unity of Darknesse and Ignorance' as found in Spain, or – and much to be preferred – the policy of 'the United Provinces . . . who let every Church please her selfe in her owne way, so long as she leaveth the State to her selfe . . . I wishe heartily, men would remember, that even Nature her selfe as much abhors a forced violent Union, as a Rent or Division.'[21] William Walwyn's *The compassionate Samaritane* (1644) was written out of dissatisfaction with the mainstream

Independents' *Apologeticall narration*. Finding 'that their Apologie therin for themselves and their Toleration was grounded rather upon a Remonstrance of the nearnesse between them and the Presbyterian . . . Finding to my hearts griefe the Separatist thus left in the lurch', Walwyn wrote a broader justification. Like Brooke, Walwyn regarded division as normal: 'All times have produced men of severall wayes, and I believe no man thinkes there will be an agreement of judgement as longe as this World lasts: If ever there be, in all probability it must proceed from the power and efficacie of Truth, not from constraint.'[22] Brooke and Walwyn make an interesting contrast to the fearful paranoia of men like Thomas Edwards, quoted earlier in this chapter. Their attitudes encouraged the view – held by a minority, but a most portentous one – that it was necessary to tolerate erroneous or evil doctrines and, as Brooke implied, to separate religious and civil authority. John Goodwin pointed out in 1644 that punishing error and schism only increased its influence: 'such fetters as these put upon the feet of errors and heresies to secure and keep them under, still have prov'd (and are like to prove no other, but) wings whereby they raise themselves the higher in the thoughts and minds of men'.[23] Slowly arguments were developed for toleration as an end in itself.

The rich variety of congregations and opinions in 1640s London was not novel; many of the ideas, organisations and networks emerged from the intra-puritan ferment described by Como and Lake. Radical impulses often developed from an engagement with mainstream puritan speculation about the nature of individual piety and salvation or the proper form of the visible church. The enthusiastic mysticism of the radical reformation was a rather different influence.[24] Nonetheless the sheer scale and range of action and opinion in London from the early 1640s surely represent a difference in kind whereby religious diversity became unstoppable. The rapid collapse of ecclesiastical authority in the 1640s, the dramatically extended freedom of press and pulpit, and the hopes and fears unleashed by civil war made up a potent environment for sectarian speculation and organisation. Familists (and many others) could thus have as great an impact in one hour as in ten prior to the civil war.

It was in London that such developments reached a spectacular climax, and London is thus the focus for this chapter. Several approaches to religious fragmentation in the 1640s and 1650s are possible. One obvious, but limited, method is to count the adherents of sectarian congregations or opinions. The problems of definition and the elusiveness of source material are but two of the difficulties besetting such an enterprise.[25] We know that most Londoners, like most English people, were not Baptists, Congregationalists or unaligned religious speculators (like Walwyn), but numbers are not the only measure of significance. It is equally clear that a substantial minority of Londoners rejected, in theory and in practice, the notion of a compulsory, inclusive, national church; and that consequently the unity of English protestantism was permanently fractured. Another method is 'archaeological' – the search for the origins of sects and denominations. There is much valuable work within that framework, perhaps especially on the

Baptists, but it can lead to overly neat sectarianised accounts which stress linear or vertical developments at the expense of complex, overlapping, horizontal connections in particular contexts.[26] Finally, intellectual historians have discussed how rationales for full religious toleration emerged in early modern Europe and in seventeenth-century England in particular. William Walwyn, with whom I began, has a place in this very important story, but it is not my concern here.[27]

This chapter offers instead a more prosaic account of how conditions in 1640s London facilitated religious fragmentation and weakened the capacity of any national church to enforce uniformity. The Kent parliamentarian Cheney Culpeper described London to his friend Samuel Hartlib as 'a brave center for all kindes of correspondencey, and a stage' on which men could make names for themselves.[28] Communication both within the city and between London and the rest of the country was transformed in the 1640s, as we can see by exploring the importance of particular spaces and places, the deployment of various media and the role of institutions such as the common council, the Westminster assembly or parliament.

Throughout the city, religious debate flourished in a range of arenas from taverns and bookshops to seats of government. Some London places were in theory private but became public through radical enthusiasm or orthodox attempts at policing: 'Certaine Blasphemies delivered in a private house in a sermon by Mr Webb, in Queen Street, in Covent Garden', in September 1644, were reported to the assembly of divines, and by the latter to the House of Lords.[29] Taverns and other public places became well known for radical speculation: John Lilburne was a 'great stickler' in the rousing meetings at the Windmill Tavern; Hugh Peter preached against the city's Presbyterian authorities at the Three Cranes and the 'Familist' Giles Randall attracted a sort of religious tourist to the Spittle, as on August 30 1646 when '[t]wo persons of quality and worth, a reverend Minister, and another person in publick imployment, went to the Spittle in the afternoone to hear Master Randall . . . having heard many strange things of him'.[30] These examples are from Thomas Edwards's accounts of London in the three parts of his heresiography *Gangraena*. For Edwards the bookshops of Cornhill and St Pauls were crucial sites for the conduct of religious debate. He explained how, in

> December 1644, coming into Mr Smiths shop in Cornhill, neer the Exchange where some persons were, there was some discourse about Liberty of Conscience, and Toleration, whereupon I spake against it, and Mr Cole Bookseller confessed he was against a generall Liberty of Conscience.[31]

Ralph Smith was a Presbyterian book-seller and the publisher of *Gangraena*, whereas his neighbour Peter Coles was a man of more flexible views, sympathetic to a degree to Walwyn. In 1649 Walwyn related: 'Standing in Cornhill, at a Booksellers shop, a man comes and looks at me very earnestly in my face.' After Walwyn had left, the man discussed him with Coles, whose shop it was. He had heard that Walwyn was 'a notorious drunkard, and a whoremaster, and that he painted his face but I see thats false'. Cole, 'troubled on my behalf', reported the conversation to Walwyn.[32] The importance of bookshops is indicated in the here-siographer Ephraim Pagitt's cumbersome observations, where the shop is as prominent as the book: 'For your better information read Mr Gataker's learned booke before named, now set forth, which is to be sold by Fulke Clifton dwelling upon new Fish-street hill'; or 'Of the stirs raised by the Antinomians and Familists in new England' see 'Mr Wells in a booke printed for Ralph Smith at the signe of the Bible in Cornhill, in which you may read a learned confutation of their errors'. Readers are here led to arenas for debate as much as to books to read for information.[33]

Throughout the 1640s religious controversy (and political debate) as much as straightforward instruction were to be found in London's churches. St Stephen Coleman Street, St Mary Aldermanbury and Stepney's church all saw bitter public dispute between Presbyterians and Independents, where clerical rivalries were tangled up with lay mobilisation.[34] Christ Church, in Newgate, where Thomas Edwards preached provocative anti-sectarian lectures, may serve as a detailed example of how the profound religious and political dilemmas of 1640s parliamentarianism were publicly aired in the city. Christ Church was a popular location for the celebration of parliamentarian fast days and special days of thanksgiving or humiliation. On these days an elaborate ceremonial – sermons, speeches, processions, formal dinners – would bring together the city's governors and clergy, with the Westminster Assembly, the two houses of parliament and the representatives of parliament's Scottish allies. The aim often was to reconcile divisions between parliamentarians, but in the process, of course, those divisions were brought before the public gaze. Thomas Juxon, the Independent-leaning London grocer, and the Scots minister Robert Baillie both described the fast day in January 1644, following attempts by the royalists to woo Independent politicians. After a sermon by Stephen Marshall at Christ Church, an elaborate procession moved slowly through the city to a dinner at the Taylors' Hall. With the city's militiamen lining the streets, common councillors headed the procession, on foot in their gowns, followed by the aldermen in scarlet and on horseback. Then came the earls of Essex and Warwick, lord general and lord admiral respectively, followed by the other peers and army officers, also on foot, the House of Commons, the speaker with his mace and the assembly of divines at the rear. At Cheapside, a great bonfire was made of religious pictures, 'relicks, beads, and such trinketts'. Most Londoners, excluded from the good dinner, the psalm and the many toasts enjoyed by Baillie, had been at least spectators of this renewal of the parliamentarian cause as a civic and godly union.[35] The thanksgivings for parliament's crushing victory at Naseby in June 1645, and for the end of royalist resistance in the west in April 1646, were also celebrated at Christ Church. On the latter occasion, the moderate Joseph Caryl, in Thomas Edwards's pulpit, pointedly urged caution in defining and attacking error and insisted: 'I shall never believe all Heresiographers.' On this occasion, too, city governors, peers and MPs, the prince elector and the members of the assembly of divines processed to dinner through 'Cheapside thwackt with people'.[36]

Edwards's weekly lectures were less dignified affairs. In the summer of 1644 the Baptist John Tombes had a bad tempered semi-public exchange with Edwards in the vestry after the sermon. More openly, in November 1644, the Baptist William Kiffin threw a hand-written note into Edwards's pulpit 'to give these leave whom you so brand, as publiquely to object against what you say, when your sermon is ended . . . we hope it will be an encrease of further light to all that feare God'. The note was printed as a cheap handbill for those unable to be present. Argument and heckling made it clear what was at stake in preaching against error, heresy and schism.[37]

Secular public places were also arenas for religious dispute. The Exchange was as important for the spreading of rumour and the mobilisation of support for religious and political positions as it was for economic activity. The Presbyterian clergyman James Cranford was imprisoned by parliament for smearing Lord Saye and other Independent politicians at the Exchange in ostensibly idle talk, while Thomas Edwards described one notable sectary, Clement Writer, as 'an arch-Heretique and fearfull Apostate, an old Wolf and a subtile man, who goes about corrupting and venting his Errors; he is often in Westminster Hall, and on the Exchange', and John Goodwin's associate was simply 'one John Price an Exchange man'.[38] When a Presbyterian petition criticising the August 1645 legislation on church government was voted scandalous by the House of Commons, handbills were pinned up in the Exchange, urging a tax strike because effective measures were not taken against the 'damnable doctrines being broached daily to the scandal of our religion'.[39]

Heated religious lobbying, petitioning and debate took place also at the Guildhall, the seat of city government. The best documented and most bitter encounters took place on 17 March 1646 during a conference between the city authorities and the members of both houses of parliament. Like the high-profile fasts held at Christ Church, this was intended as a reconciliation following the condemnation of the city's petition against Presbyterian legislation as a breach of parliamentary privilege. When the parliamentary delegation came to the city to explain their votes,

> many Sectaries from all parts of the City and Suburbs, came to Guild-hall, where, from about four a clock, till about nine, the Sectaries in severall companies and knots in the Hall, 30, 40 and more in some companies, vented boldly and pleaded for all sorts of opinions, the Antinomian opinions, the Anabaptisticall opinions, etc, pleading for a generall Toleration of all Sects, yea some maintained that no immortall spirit could sinne . . . many other horrid opinions were maintained at the same time, so that 'tis beleeved, that never since Guild-Hall was built, there was so much wickednesse and errour broacht and maintained openly in it.

Thomas Edwards's alarm was shared by another city Presbyterian, John Farthing. This 'so great an appearance of Independants [sic] and separatists' spurred him to denounce one Thomas Hawes, as a blasphemer in 'hot and mallitious expressions', and have him committed to prison.[40]

Westminster Hall, a mile or so from the city, and near the place where parliament met, was the other major location for heated religious argument and the circulation of heterodox books. Thomas Edwards exchanged angry words with Hugh Peter and denounced the sectaries 'walking boldly' there. Books such as *Toleration justifed* were 'openly dispersed . . . given by Sectaries into some Parliament mens hands'. According to the Presbyterian book-seller George Thomason, a second printing of Walwyn's *Word in season* was distributed 'about Westminster Hall by Lilburne the day the cittie remonstrance was presented', and it was there too that Richard Price, a city mercer and the uncle of his scrivener namesake, was warned of Walwyn's pernicious views: 'walking in Westminster hall, he was called from me, and bid beware of me for I was supposed to be a Papist, and a dangerous man'.[41]

The institutions meeting at the Guildhall and Westminster, as well as the spaces they offered for religious lobbying and debate, contributed to the city's religious diversity. There was, in the first place, a significant transformation in the potential power wielded by parliament and by the synod it established, the Westminster assembly. Parliament's defiance of the king and its increasing military success against him ensured that by 1645, at the latest, puritans could realistically look forward to real power to enforce a religious settlement. In the 1630s, when puritans were on the defensive, the emphasis was on maintaining, for the outside world at least, a unity in the face of episcopal harassment. The prospect of power, on the other hand, inevitably exacerbated puritan cleavages over the precise shape of any settlement. The House of Commons, we know, traditionally acted as a 'point of contact', but its relationship with provincial England and with the city authorities in London was necessarily transformed as it became an executive body in permanent session (and one conducting a war), no longer an event rather than an institution.[42]

Religious cleavages were publicised through airings in parliament, and divisions over the future religious settlement became inevitably entangled with differences over the war effort and other 'political' issues. The centrality of London's money and men to parliament's war effort made politically essential the Christ Church or Guildhall ritual niceties of city–parliament feasts, fast days and conferences, which, as we have seen, very easily slipped from occasions for reconciliation into opportunities for gaining support for partisan positions. The Westminster assembly also drew together the centre and the provinces with two clerical members from each county, as well as parliamentary representatives and the Scottish commissioners. As information on dangerous books and heretical preachers would be sent from Yorkshire or Bristol to London, so ministers could relay news of the assembly's own divisions over church government to friends at home.[43]

As a new body charged with the reformation of religion, the Westminster assembly offered an obvious focus for debate over the future of the church. On the other hand, a variety of familiar collectivities, such as companies and wards, formed fertile grounds for building alliances or fomenting division over religion within the new world of the 1640s.[44] Sion College, a library, meeting-place and dining club open to all the city clergy, founded in the 1620s as a relatively uncontroversial focus for clerical collegiality, became a central element in Presbyterian activism.[45] The Stationers' Company has also been seen as a bastion of Presbyterianism but it comprehended Independents such as Henry Overton (a member of John Goodwin's church) as well as Presbyterians such as George Thomason, John Bellamy, Christopher Meredith and Ralph Smith.[46] Everyday trading affairs and civic business could become occasions for religious debate or the building of politico-religious alliances. In describing his subsequent quarrel with the scrivener Richard Price, Walwyn recalled: 'My first acquaintance . . . was by occasion of our parish businesse, in his trade, and that about our Ward; and after that, about a Remonstrance presented to the Common Council'. From the early 1640s, the wards where common councillors were elected annually developed a higher and more politicised profile as the common council overtook the court of alderman as the major institution of city government. Routine business about street-cleaning, local levies and elections brought men of diverse religious opinions together. As leading citizens in Cornhill Ward, for example, the Presbyterian publishers Bellamy and Smith confronted sectaries such as Praisegod Barebone, Benjamin Allen and Nicholas Tew.[47]

As I have indicated, religious controversy was carried on through gesture, speech, writing and print. Oral methods ranged from formal presentations and set-piece sermons to the gossip, speculation and argument found in church vestries, bookshops, the Exchange, the Guildhall or around parliament. After MPs and peers came to the city on 17 March 1646 to explain the condemnation of the Presbyterian petition, the common councillors withdrew and 'there was much debate' before the majority agreed to submit to parliament. Even then the disappointed Presbyterians – 'their friends without and the engaged party within' – complained that 'they had betrayed their friends, had asked pardon when they should have justified the action'.[48] This chapter began with the debates (and alternative readings) that formal sermons could provoke. Manuscript circulation was also important, as much for those who sought to police and limit religious liberty as for those propagating unorthodox ideas. John Tombes tried out his views on baptism through manuscript treatise before being 'provoked' into print by Presbyterian criticism; the 'blasphemies' of Thomas Webbe were noted and reported to the Westminster assembly by the Wiltshire representatives in the assembly. Handbills and petitions were often spread in manuscript form rather than print, as the manuscript material in Thomason's collection demonstrates.[49]

It is difficult, however, to avoid a 'Whiggish' emphasis on the centrality of print to the English Revolution. Walwyn claimed he had 'alwaies said that printing (if any thing in this age) would preserve us from slavery'. In sharp contrast to the 1630s the majority of those contesting among themselves over religion sought the maximum publicity for their views. Why else would Kiffin arrange for his little paper to be printed long after the occasion for its hurling at Edwards in a face-to-face encounter? Why was a petition to the aldermen and common councillors of one city ward printed during the 1645 elections if not to encourage others to petition in the cause of Presbyterianism?[50] A letter delivered to parliament was already a public document, but printing extended its audience, and the form in which a document went into print might itself become a divisive issue. A well-known but instructive instance is Oliver Cromwell's letter of September 1645 to the House of Commons, announcing the fall of Bristol. His postscript rejoiced that

> Presbyterians, Independents, all have here the same spirit of faith and prayer, the same pretence and answer; they agree here, know no names of difference; pity it is it should be otherwise anywhere . . . As for being united in forms, commonly called Uniformity, every Christian will for peace sake study and do, as far as conscience will permit, and from brethren, in things of the mind, we look for no compulsion, but that of light and reason.

According to George Thomason, this 'was printed by the Independent party and scattrd up and downe the streets last night, but expresly omitted by order of the House'.[51] David Zaret's recent work on petitions has drawn attention to the importance of print to political and religious mobilisation in the 1640s, but it is worth stressing that print remained in close interaction with more intimate, face-to-face forms of communication and that there were many other forms of printed material besides petitions.[52] In places all over London, and through talk, writing and the circulation of printed pamphlets, profound religious dilemmas were confronted. As we have seen, conflict might erupt on occasions intended to secure parliamentarian unity, and indeed it was often argued that it was wrong to avoid open debate. Several pamphlets denounced the lord mayor's ban on a public disputation planned for December 1645 between Presbyterians Edmund Calamy and James Cranford, and the prominent Baptists Hanserd Knollys, William Kiffin and Benjamin Cox.[53]

Religious fragmentation hardened in London because religious divisions became emblematic or constitutive of political faction within parliamentarianism; divisions over church government or over theology increasingly merged with politics. In Stepney, where there were inevitably tense relationships between the Presbyterian incumbent Joshua Hoyle and the Congregationalist lecturers Jeremiah Burroughs and William Greenhill, conflict intensified as the city campaign for an effective Presbyterian settlement gathered pace. When Hoyle tried to get the Presbyterian petition of September 1645 read in the church after Burroughs's morning lecture, Burroughs apparently denounced it as an affront to the 'Army that had done so much for us', while his wife 'said it was a second Binions Petition' (after the petition organised by the royalist George Benyon against parliamentarian control of the city militia in February 1642).[54]

The ways in which religious cleavages in London became entangled with different conceptions of the 'parliamentary cause' and contrasting attitudes to parliament's army can be seen in the conflicts over the city's remonstrance to parliament of May 1646. That remonstrance was a response to the repeated failure of city attempts to obtain a stronger Presbyterian settlement through petitioning parliament. It attacked sectarianism and appealed to the Solemn League and Covenant, symbol of parliament's alliance with the Scots, and praised parliament (using the words of its own Grand Remonstrance of November 1641) for its declared determination not 'to lette loose the golden reynes of discipline and Government in the Church'. Yet despite all parliament's ordinances, 'all maner of Herisies, Scismes, and Blasphemies' were boldly maintained by Independents and sectaries. If such men could get into 'places of profitt and Trust in Martiall and Civill affaires' it would 'tend much to the disturbance of the publique peace both of the Church and Commonwealth'. The remonstrance praised 'our Brethren of Scotland' who had come to the aid of the English parliament in its darkest hour and were now scandalously traduced by the enemies of peace and settlement, and so demonstrated a coming together of city concerns with that of the emerging political 'Presbyterian' grouping in parliament, with its stress on the need for a speedy peace and a reduction in taxation.[55]

London campaigns against the city's remonstrance were similarly based on religious affiliations. John Goodwin and members of his congregation were prominent; the 'exchange man' John Price wrote the most extensive attacks on the remonstrance (in response to its defender and probable author John Bellamy) and they were published by another member, the bookseller Henry Overton.[56] William Walwyn's *Word in season*, noted Thomason, was 'Intended against ye Remonstrance now in hand'. In contrast to the praise for the Scots in the remonstrance (reciprocated when the Scots lauded the city and its zeal against error), these supporters of religious liberty urged the delivery of the captured Charles I from his Scottish jailers. They feared that 'a Blew Bonnet' would 'prove as dangerous a fashion as ever was the Episcopall Catter Cap'.[57]

As part of a wide-ranging declaration explaining their plans for government in state and church, the Commons had insisted on 17 April 1646 that it was committed to a Presbyterian church, but not to giving an 'arbitrary and unlimited Power and Jurisdiction to near ten thousand Judicatories' – that is, parochial elderships. Nor, they continued, 'have we yet resolved how a due regard may be had, that tender Consciences which differ not in fundamentals of religion, may be so provided for, as may stand with the word of God and the peace of the kingdom'. Hence the remonstrance's pained expressions of regret that 'the said Sectaries doe encourage themselves, by their misconstruccon of that Expression in the late declaracon concerninge tender consciences to expect a tolleration (contrary to the Nationall Covenant as we humbly conceive)', while petitions and pamphlets against the remonstrance drew attention to the 17 April declaration and urged that parliament be left to manage the affairs of the kingdom in accordance with it. London religious factions thus developed contrasting and complex relationships with parliament itself.[58] Equally, Londoners expressed different attitudes to parliament's New Model Army. In December 1646 a London Presbyterian petition attacked the New Model Army as a hotbed of error and sectarianism while, on the other hand, London sectaries, Independents and those soon to be dubbed 'Levellers' came together in a tense and temporary alliance for their own defence and in support of the much traduced army. The quest for religious liberty or, perhaps more properly, the defence against Presbyterian aggression prompted political mobilisation. A 'large petition' of March 1647, connected with Thomas Lambe's General Baptist congregation, demanded the repeal of all statutes molesting 'religious, peaceable, well affected persons' for their religious views: no 'necessary truths and sincere professors' were to be suppressed as 'errors, sects or schismes'; and certainly religious differences should not be used to justify exclusion from office.[59] After 1649 there were traumatic cleavages between Leveller agitators, General Baptists and the radical Independents of Goodwin's church, which prompted the attacks on Walwyn discussed at the start of this chapter. In 1647 and 1648, however, these groups co-operated sufficiently with members of parliament and the army to defeat a Presbyterian settlement, and by 1649 they had secured a religious freedom unprecedented in England, as Presbyterian legislation remained unenforced while the Elizabethan Act of Uniformity was repealed.

Finally, and paradoxically, it seems that co-operation within compromised the national church even as conflict assaulted it from without. Men and women of widely divergent views co-operated in the organisation of the parish church and even (in the case of the 'Independent' Joseph Caryl) in Presbyterian extra-parochial structures. The Independent pastor Edmund Rosier contributed £8 to the repair of the church (in 1646) and acted as a churchwarden in his parish of Mary Abchurch in 1655; the separatist pastor Praisegod Barebone audited church-wardens' accounts in St Dunstans in the West, as the Independent militia's Colonel Rowland Wilson, a member of George Cockayne's gathered congregation, did in St Martin Outwich. The politically ambitious members of John Goodwin's congregation clearly had to be active in their parish vestry which had a role in common council elections and other civic matters. Furthermore when they were again allowed to meet in St Stephen Coleman Street the gathered church gave half its collection (on fast days or thanksgiving days) to the poor of the parish.[60] William Walwyn, as noted, first met Richard Price the scrivener on the occasion of their parish affairs.

The best-known, or most notorious, example of radical acquiescence in the affairs of the parish is the mystic and future 'Digger' Gerrard Winstanley. His was a frequent presence at vestry meetings in St Olave's Southwark in the early 1640s; although he never attended meetings to choose lecturers or ministers, he participated in discussions about parish property and endorsed the elections of churchwardens and other officials. Later in his life Winstanley served as a 'way-warden' and an overseer of the poor in 1659–60 and as a churchwarden in Cobham in 1667 and 1668. This participation is usually seen as an extraordinary compromise by a Digger turned Quaker: 'It would appear incredible that the outspoken heretical critic of established religion became a churchwarden.' In general the parochial activities of Winstanley, Barebone, Rosier and Wilson are seen as qualifying their radicalism or as evidence of the essential good nature of English people and society.[61] From some perspectives this participation strengthened the unity of the godly, but it is also clear that such men saw the parish as a social community, not as a disciplinary structure enforcing a particular religious vision. Rather than revealing the natural conservative lurking in the breast of every mis- guided heretic, their involvement amounted to a radical departure from conventional understandings of the connections between religion and civil society. Ultimately such developments pointed the way to a separation of religious belief from suitability for civic or public service. His attitude to the parish was indeed one of the constants in Winstanley's remarkably varied life. In an early work demon- strating profoundly heterodox views on God, the Trinity and the scriptures (dis- missed as second-hand testimony) Winstanley denounced those who called a parish a church, or who called on magistrates to enforce church attendance and the payment of tithes. A parish was, on the contrary, 'so called and made for *civil good sake*'.[62]

My account of religious diversity in revolutionary London is a rather optimistic or sanitised one, with little reference made to limits on religious dissent or to the harassment of sectaries. Although church courts and episcopal censorship lapsed in the early 1640s, parliament made regular attempts to suppress unlicensed print- ing, imprisoning radicals such as William Larner, John Lilburne and Richard Overton. Religious dissidents faced intermittent prosecution for blasphemy and separatism throughout the 1640s. In 1643 Nicholas Tew, a General Baptist printer and associate of Lambe and Richard Overton, was presented at the Cornhill Wardmote Inquest 'for admitting assemblies oftentimes into his private house confessing himselfe to be of the Separation'.[63] The Yorkshire preacher Paul Best languished in the Gatehouse for over two years for denying the Trinity, and the Commons voted to bring in an ordinance for the death penalty after being reminded of his anti-trinitarian blasphemies in January 1646. The ordinance for his hanging was read twice in March after 'a very long debate'. Around the same time there began a long Presbyterian agitation for a Blasphemy Act, which finally passed the Commons and the Lords in May 1648. The destruction of presses, the imprisonments and threats should not be ignored, but ultimately these measures were futile. The careers of John Lilburne and Richard Overton demonstrate that imprisonment was no barrier to campaigning through print. Outside Newgate and the Gatehouse, defenders of Best could be found arguing at the Guildhall and rallying support at the Exchange or in Westminster Hall. John Goodwin conducted a strenuous and risky opposition to the Blasphemy Act in pulpit and press. His own *Hagiomastix* had been taken by some to imply that the scriptures were not the word of God, but this did not deter him from raising doubts over the authenticity of the scriptures in his criticism of the proposed ordinance. He also questioned whether opposition to baptism and holding the doctrine of free will were religious errors.[64]

Throughout the 1640s, Londoners like Goodwin challenged fundamental reli- gious ideas; they appealed for support and denounced their opponents through talk, and in print; they founded congregations and sects with attitudes of indif- ference or hostility to a national church, if not to the civic life of their com- munities. Equally vital was the defeat of rival parliamentarian attempts to establish an effective national church. The 1650s provided further breathing space for both ideas and organisations. Despite the intermittent repression that followed the Restoration, the unity of English protestantism was permanently fragmented, and English culture and politics were permanently transformed.

Notes

1 The account of the fast day is taken from the pamphlet controversy surrounding the opinions of the Leveller William Walwyn, in April–May 1649. *Walwins wiles* (1649) attacked him as a crafty atheist; the Preface to this was signed by seven London Independents and Baptists including William Kiffin and Edmund Rosier, but its author was probably another of the seven, John Price, of John Goodwin's gathered congregation. H. Brooke's *The charity of church-men* (1649) and W. Walwyn's *Walwyns just defence* (1649) were produced in defence of Walwyn. All three pamphlets agreed on the events of the fast day, although their interpretations differed. The three works are here quoted from *The Leveller tracts 1647–1653*, ed. W. Haller and G. Davies (Gloucester, MA, 1964 [1944]).

2 *Leveller tracts*, 334, 361.

3 *Ibid.*,362–3.

4 *Ibid.*, 363; cf. Brooke, *Charity of church-men*, 334.

5 *Leveller tracts*, 296.

6 *Ibid.*

7 *Ibid.*, 362.

8 P. Seaver, *Wallington's world: a puritan artisan in seventeenth-century London* (Stanford, CA, 1985), 147–9 and n. 241, 171–2; BL, Add. MSS, 39940–42. I am indebted to Stephen Roberts for giving me a copy of his notes on Lechmere.

9 J. Milton, *Areopagitica*, in *Complete prose works of John Milton*, ed. E. Sirluck (New Haven, CT, 1959), ii. 554.

10 T. Edwards, *Gangraena*, 3 vols (1646), i. 148–9.

11 CLRO, Journal 40, fos 160r–v, 14 January 1646.

12 Dr Williams Library, MS 201.12: C. E. Surman, 'The records of the provincial assembly of London, 1647–1660', as quoted in E. Vernon, 'The Sion College conclave and London Presbyterianism during the English revolution', Ph.D thesis, Cambridge University (1999), 175.

13 This paragraph is based on M. Tolmie, *The triumph of the saints: the separate churches of London 1616–1649* (Cambridge, 1977), 55–65, 94–5, 122; K. Lindley, *Popular politics and religion in civil war London* (Aldershot, 1999), 281–5; and Lindley, 'Whitechapel Independents and the English revolution', *Historical Journal*, 41 (1988), 283–91.

14 Tolmie, *Triumph of the saints*,76; Edwards, *Gangraena*, i. 92–3.

15 J. Spencer, *A short treatise concerning the lawfulnesse of every mans exercising his gift as God shall call him thereunto* (1641), 2, 5–6. He identified himself as groom to a nobleman on the title page of *The spirituall warfare* (1642). The nobleman was Robert Greville, second Lord Brooke; see Tolmie, *Triumph of the saints*, 65–8 for the churches.

16 For the importance of individual preachers see Lindley, *Popular politics*, 287; For Peter see A. Hughes, *Gangraena and the struggle for the English revolution* (Oxford, 2004), 173–4, 247–9.

17 D. Como, *Blown by the spirit: puritanism and the emergence of an Antinomian under-ground in pre-civil-war England* (Stanford, CA, 2004), 444 (for Gell) and generally; P. Lake and D. Como, '"Orthodoxy" and its discontents: dispute settlement and the production of "consensus" in the London (puritan) underground', *Journal of British Studies*, 39 (2000), 34–70; J. Grant, *Truths victory against heresie* (1645), Dedication; J. Etherington, *A brief discovery of the blasphemous doctrine of Familisme, first conceived and brought forth into the world by one Henry Nicolas* (1645); see P. Lake, *The box-maker's revenge: 'orthodoxy', 'heterodoxy' and the politics of the parish in early Stuart London* (Manchester, 2001), for Etherington.

18 London Metropolitan Archives, MJ/SR 962/102, 105; Lindley, *Popular politics*, 302.

19 H. Burton, *The protestation protested* (1641); the Baptists' attempts to shun the cor-ruptions of the world are well illustrated in B. R. White (ed.), *Association records of the Particular Baptists of England, Wales and Ireland to 1660*, 3 vols (London, 1971–74).

20 J. Price, *Unity and duty in twelve considerations* (London, 1645), 5 (recte 3); *The con-stitutional documents of the puritan revolution*, ed. S. R. Gardiner, 3rd edn (Oxford, 1962), 416. The religious clauses of the Instrument (quoted here) were closely modelled on those of the Officers' Agreement; for further discussion see A. Hughes, 'The public profession of these nations', in C. Durston and J. Maltby (eds), *Religion in revolutionary England* (Manchester, forthcoming, 2007).

21 R. Greville, Lord Brooke, *A discourse opening the nature of that episcopacie, which is exercised in England*, 2 edns (London, 1642), here quoted from the facsimile reprint in *Tracts on liberty in the puritan revolution 1638–1647*, ed. W. Haller, 3 vols (New York, 1934), ii. 88, 91.

22 W. Walwyn, *The compassionate Samaritane* (1644),1–3, 53.

23 J. Goodwin, *Theomachia* (1644), 37.

24 Como, *Blown by the spirit*; Lake, *Box-maker's revenge*; see also A. Hughes, 'Religion 1640–1650', in B. Coward (ed.), *A companion to Stuart Britain* (Oxford, 2003), 350–73, for a fuller account of religious radicalism.

25 M. Spufford, 'Can we count the "godly" and the "conformable" in the seventeenth cen-tury?', *Journal of Ecclesiastical History*, 36 (1985), 435–7, offers a critique of a quant-itative approach from a different perspective, while Spufford (ed.), *The world of rural dissenters 1520–1725* (Cambridge, 1995) offers more statistical precision for better documented post-1660 dissent.

26 P. Collinson, 'Towards a broader understanding of the early dissenting tradition', in his *Godly people: essays on English protestantism and puritanism* (London, 1983), 527–62.

27 J. Coffey, *Persecution and toleration in protestant England 1558–1689* (Harlow, 2000) offers an accomplished introduction.

28 'The letters of Sir Cheney Culpeper, 1645–1657', ed. M. J. Braddick and M. Greengrass, *Camden Miscellany*, 33, Camden Society, 5th series, 7 (London, 1996), 266.

29 *Minutes of the sessions of the Westminster assembly of divines*, ed. A. F. Mitchell and J. Struthers (Edinburgh and London, 1874), 10; *LJ*, vii. 71.

30 Edwards, *Gangraena*, i. 96, iii. 121, 25.

31 *Ibid.*, i. 111.

32 Walwyn, *Walwyns just defence*, in *Leveller tracts*, 368–9.

33 E. Pagitt, *Heresiography* (1645), 91.

34 T. Liu, *Puritan London: a study of religion and society in the city parishes* (Newark, NJ, London and Toronto, 1986), 114–16; Hughes, *Gangraena and the struggle for the English revolution*, 51, 167.

35 *The letters and journals of Robert Baillie, A.M.*, ed. D. Laing, 3 vols (Edinburgh, 1841), ii. 134–5; *The journal of Thomas Juxon*, ed. K. Lindley and D. Scott, Camden Society, 5th series, 13 (London, 1999), 39–40; the Scots were due to process between the Commons and the assembly, but not wishing to take precedence over the English ministers they went to the dinner either by coach or on foot.

36 CLRO, Journal 40, fos 134r, 175v; J. Caryl, *Englands plus ultra, both of hoped mercies and of required duties* (1646), 24; *Journal of Thomas Juxon*, 113.

37 J. Tombes, *An apology or plea for the two treatises concerning infant baptism* (1646), 8–9; W. Kiffin, *To Mr Thomas Edwards* (1644).

38 M. Mahony, 'The Savile affair and the politics of the long parliament', *Parliamentary History*, 7 (1988), 212–27; Edwards, *Gangraena*, i. 81, iii. 160.

39 *Journal of Thomas Juxon*, 85; M. Kishlansky, *The rise of the New Model Army* (Cambridge, 1987), 79, followed by Lindley, *Popular politics*, 357.

40 Edwards, *Gangraena*, ii. 8–9; see *Journal of Thomas Juxon*, 109, for a much blander account; CLRO, Journal 40, fo. 175v; Lindley, *Popular politics*, 366–7, 381–2; Kishlansky, *Rise of the New Model Army*, 82–4; *The afflicted Christian justified: in a letter to Mr Thomas Hawes, an honest and godly man* (1646).

41 Edwards, *Gangraena*, iii. 127, i. 119, 149, ii. 155; see Hughes, *Gangraena and the struggle for the English revolution*, 168. The city remonstrance, a Presbyterian manifesto, was presented on 26 May 1646. Thomason's copy of *A word in season* (1646) is BL, E1184 (3); Thomason believed it had been written by John Sadler; *Walwyns just defence*, 369.

42 C. Russell, *The fall of the British monarchies 1637–1642* (Oxford, 1991), 206; and 'The nature of a parliament', in his *Unrevolutionary England* (London, 1990), 1–29, at 29.

43 Hughes, *Gangraena and the struggle for the English revolution*, 137–8.

44 See the authoritative discussion in Lindley, *Popular politics*, ch. 4.

45 Vernon, 'Sion College conclave', 90–1.

46 M. Mahony, 'Presbyterianism in the city of London, 1645–1647', *Historical Journal*, 22 (1979), 93–114; Hughes, *Gangraena and the struggle for the English revolution*, 146–7.

47 Walwyn, *Walwyn's just defence*, 361; Hughes, *Gangraena and the struggle for the English revolution*, 147 (based on Guildhall Library MS 4702/1, Cornhill Ward, Inquest Book).

48 *Journal of Thomas Juxon*, 110.

49 Hughes, *Gangraena and the struggle for the English revolution*, 136–7, 158–9.

50 Walwyn, *Walwyns just defence*, 384; *To the right worshipfull, the aldermen and common counsell-men of the ward of Farrington Within at their ward-moot, 22 December 1645* (1645).

51 The illicit broadside is BL, Thomason 669, fo. 10 (38); the postscript was omitted in the *LJ* and the official publication (Thomason E301).

52 D. Zaret, *Origins of democratic culture: printing, petitions and the public sphere in early-modern England* (Princeton, NJ, 2000); cf. Hughes 'Print, persecution and polemic: Thomas Edwards's *Gangraena* (1646) and civil war sectarianism', in J. Crick and A. Walsham (eds), *Script and print in early modern England* (Cambridge, 2004), 255–74.

53 *A declaration concerning the publike dispute which should have been in the publike meeting-house of Alderman-Bury, the 3d of this instant moneth of December* (1645), 1–2, 4.

54 Edwards, *Gangraena*, i. 109–110; Tolmie, *Triumph of the saints*, 128–9; Lindley, *Popular politics*, 129.

55 The text of this remonstrance is available in pamphlet form (BL, E338 (7), E 339 (1)), in *LJ*, viii. 332–4, and in CLRO, Journal 40, fos 178v–179r; for political divisions among parliamentarians see Hughes, *Gangraena and the struggle for the English revolution*, 346–59.

56 J. Bellamy, *A justification of the city remonstrance and its vindication*; the subheading was *An answer to a book, written by Mr J.P. entituled the city remonstrance remonstrated* (Thomason, dated 21 August); Thomason also noted that J.P. was John Price of John Goodwin's congregation: BL, E350 (23); J. Price, *The city remonstrance remonstrated* (1646).

57 *A word in season* (1646): BL, E337 (25) (18 May 1646); CLRO, Journal 40, fo. 188v (10 July) for the Scots' letter of support for the city. *The afflicted Christian justified*, 18–19; 'catter' or 'cater' meant mitred.

58 *CJ*, iv. 512–13; CLRO, Journal 40, fos 178v–179r; *The humble acknowledgement and petition of divers inhabitants in, and about the citie of London* (1646); *A moderate reply to the citie remonstrance* (1646); and Price, *The city remonstrance*, 14.

59 *To the right honourable the lords assembled in high court of parliament, the humble petition of the lord mayor, aldermen and commons of the city of London, in common council assembled together with an humble representation of the pressing grievances, and important desires of the well- affected freemen, and Covenant-engaged citizens of the city of London* (1646); Tolmie, *Triumph of the saints*, 151–2; Kishlansky, *Rise of the New Model Army*, 190, 329 n. 39; A. Sharp (ed.), *The English Levellers* (Cambridge, 1998), 73–91, at 82.

60 Hughes, *Gangraena and the struggle for the English revolution*, 326; Liu, *Puritan London*, 185–6.

61 For Winstanley specifically, see J. D. Alsop, 'Religion and respectability', *Historical Journal*, 28 (1985), 705–9, at 706; Alsop, 'A high road to radicalism? Gerrard Winstanley's youth', *The Seventeenth Century*, 9:1 (spring 1994), 11–24; Guildhall Library, MS 4415/1, vestry minutes, St Olave, Old Jewry. For a full discussion of the activity of post-1660 dissenters in parochial office (as constables, overseers and witnesses of wills, but not, apparently, as churchwardens) and the general argument about the nature of local communities, see B. Stevenson, 'The social integration of post-restoration dissenters, 1660–1725', in Spufford (ed.), *World of the rural dissenters*, 360–87.

62 G. Winstanley, *Truth lifting up his head above scandals* (1649), 60; my italics.

63 Guildhall Library, MS 4702/1, fo. 228v.

64 See Hughes, *Gangraena and the struggle for the English revolution*, 159–62, 381–4 for Paul Best and the ordinance against blasphemy; J. Goodwin, *Some modest and humble queries* (1646) attacked the proposed Blasphemy Act. John Coffey's forthcoming study of John Goodwin will be of crucial importance for these issues.

8

Behemoth, or civil war and revolution, in English parish communities 1641–82[1]

Dan Beaver

In 1668, Thomas Hobbes reflected on the need for a politics that could communicate the principle that 'the people and the church are one thing and have but one head, the king'.[2] Hobbes believed that the English people would have to be *taught* this principle, perceived as essential to any settled peace in the kingdom, because the common experience of civil war and revolution during the 1640s and 1650s had accustomed a generation to conceive of the church in terms of faction and sect. In this sense, the power of Behemoth, or rebellion, lay in every divided parish as the destructive inheritance of a sacrilegious war. Keith Wrightson, commenting on the implications of religious conflict, has written that 'despite the large literatures which we have on religion, law, and local government, it remains fair to say that the resultant political processes have been little studied in depth or for their own sake'.[3] This chapter discusses this politics of religion in parishes as one of the most important consequences of the English civil war and the Revolution. The ambiguity of this politics has resulted in part from the tendency of social and cultural historians to subsume local experience of politics in general, and local experience of civil war and revolution in particular, in more abstract processes of state and class formation.[4] In this approach, the war and the Revolution become surface events, the discontinuities, paraphrasing Ann Hughes and Richard Cust, that serve at most to reveal long-term continuities in *processes* of social stratification, or in the making of the English polity, a politics often foreign to the language and mentality of the seventeenth century.[5] Analysis of religious divisions in parishes as a consequence of the myriad local experiences of war and revolution begins to restore important contemporary meanings of the mid-century crisis. In many English parishes, a generation of conflict over the meanings of community, the relationship of church and people, constituted the fundamental inheritance of the Restoration from the years of war. An awareness of local and national religious conflict made the very existence of parish communities a political proposition to be defended.[6]

Although this chapter does not presume to identify the causes of the civil war, it does seek to explore the impact of the war on parish communities and to explain some aspects of the violence committed in the course of the war.[7] Even in this narrow sense, however, the English 'wars of religion' began more than a year before the formal outbreak of hostilities.[8] Parishes sustained damage of a cultural order long before shots were fired or pickaxes were raised against religious objects. The politics of religion and the order of parish communities shifted profoundly in 1641. After the many local 'root-and-branch' petition campaigns early in the year, the start on 27 May of the parliamentary debate on a 'root-and-branch' bill against episcopacy, and the withdrawal of penal jurisdiction from the church in the statute against the Court of High Commission, the system of church courts used to enforce conventional standards of ceremony and behaviour in local parishes lost much of its authority and effective power.[9] This suspension of ecclesiastical jurisdiction had a decisive impact on parish communities because, even during the 1630s, diocesan courts served important cultural ends quite apart from the enforcement of the Laudian ceremonial regime. Much of the recent work on church courts has stressed their reinforcement of communal discipline, especially on sexual and matrimonial matters, under the difficult social and economic circumstances of the late sixteenth and early seventeenth centuries. Just as importantly, these courts participated in the cultural process whereby parish communities formed. Among their distinctive qualities as communities was that parishes were dependent on diocesan institutions in matters of authority and symbolism.[10] Parishes by definition participated culturally in the diocesan system, and were neither isolated nor self-contained.

The rituals of penance sanctioned by the church courts had expressed in a powerful visual form the moral boundaries of parish communities. Penitents had stood in their parish church on the sabbath, their status marked by special clothes, props, and forms of demeanor. Most had worn a white sheet, held a white rod, and stood or knelt before the assembled parish to confess their sin, and to implore divine mercy and forgiveness. These rites had aspired to transform the corrupting force of sin into the sanctifying force of love, in the form of absolution or charity. Moreover, the performances had been important religious events, as the spiritual health of parish communities had depended on the identification and correction of sin. Most penitents had been previously identified in the public voice, or everyday talk, of their neighbours as offenders against the public morality of the parish. The confession of sin and the request for pardon in the parish church returned the penitent to the source of accusation, and the rituals of penance served as the means by which the soul and the reputation of suspected neighbours were seen to be healed. The prosecution and visible punishment of the moral offenders previously identified by the collective conscience or 'public voice' of the parish had played an important creative role in social order and community. This punishment, in the form of penance, had made the communal order visible in religious dramas, organised around the detection and destruction of sin.[11]

As this process of symbolising communal boundaries was suspended in 1641 and 1642, a flow of publications increasingly revealed the devilish plots of religion's many enemies. After the news of the Irish rebellion reached parliament on 1 November, pamphlet after lurid pamphlet offered further revelations of a bloody-handed popish conspiracy. This grand popish design may have posed the most obvious dangers to protestant parishes but was not the only enemy in the field. One pamphlet invoked 'Arians, Anabaptists, Brownists, Donatists, Erticheans, Familists, Marcionists, Montanists, Nicolaitans, Pelagians, papists, puritans, nonatians, and all other sorts of heresies and sects' as common enemies of religion. 'Under the colors of a feigned piety,' these 'factions' fought each other 'in a disunion and diversity among themselves' and shared only 'a general, malignant, inveterate hatred' for 'the government, the governors, and the true church'.[12] Richard Baxter later blamed 'separatists, Anabaptists, and the younger and unexperienced sort of religious people' in London for their campaign 'to speak too vehemently and intemperately against the bishops and the church and ceremonies, and to jeer and deride at the common prayer and all that was against their minds'.[13] At least in the short term, the dissolution of diocesan courts could only further the designs of religion's enemies by suspending the primary force for order in local churches. In 1641 and 1642, pamphlets on both sides of the conflict between crown and parliament feared chaos. *Religion's enemies*, published in 1641, lamented the profanation of religion, 'now become the common discourse and table talk in every tavern and alehouse'. Although the Book of Common Prayer had been established by authority of crown and parliament and had served the ceremonial needs of local churches for 80 years, parish communities had lost their boundaries and bulwarks in a 'blind' confusion of the sacred. The pamphlet ended with a 'hearty prayer that, as there is but one shepherd, God in his gracious goodness and mercy would make us all one sheepfold'. Another pamphlet, following its denunciation of the London plot, asked readers to 'pray for the establishment of religion'.[14] A cultural crisis, evident in the dissolution of courts and confusion of symbolic boundaries, joined to fears of powerful religious enemies, may help to explain some of the patterns of violence during the civil war.[15]

Of course, English parishes had never been 'all one sheepfold', and the crisis of the early 1640s occurred in parish communities that, in many cases, had been divided since the Reformations of the sixteenth century.[16] The most recent conflicts had resulted from the efforts of the Laudian bishops during the 1630s to introduce a more uniform ceremonial discipline and strictly to enforce the ceremonial injunctions of the Book of Common Prayer. After his promotion to the archbishopric of Canterbury in 1633, William Laud used his metro-political visitation to enforce the priority of the visible church in its sacraments and festivals; his commissioners moved communion tables to the site of traditional altars, surrounded by protective rails, repaired and 'beautified' the church fabric, and in many places prohibited the customary use of churchyards for pasture.[17] These innovations provoked reactions both as attacks on customary local practices and as assertions of a 'beauty of holiness' that contradicted a strict 'godly' emphasis on scripture and sermons over ceremony and sacred objects in matters of salvation and church order. Laudian visitations divided many parishes and elicited passive and active forms of resistance in both the northern and southern provinces of the church. Despite their seriousness, these conflicts were adjudicated in the familiar arenas of the diocesan courts, as local factions attempted to use networks of influence and the politics of the courts themselves to resist the Laudian innovations in their parish churches.[18] Unlike the crisis of the early 1640s, the conflicts of the 1630s, in most places, produced grievances for parliament rather than violence.

The suspension of ecclesiastical jurisdiction in 1641 dissolved the familiar sites of dispute, and power to adjudicate conflicts over the sacred dropped into the streets of local parishes. In the absence of a settled procedure to identify and prosecute religion's enemies, local factions resorted increasingly to violence. In 1641, parliament itself divided on the issues of iconoclasm and ceremonies in the church, creating an uncertainty in the law. Among many acts of popular iconoclasm in London, Nehemiah Wallington recorded of his own church, St Leonard's Eastcheap, in October 1641, 'the idol in the wall was cut down, and the superstitious pictures in the glass was broken in pieces, and the superstitious things and prayers for the dead in brass picked up and broken, and the pictures of the virgin Mary on the branches of candlesticks was broken'.[19] As recent work by John Walter has revealed, this violence expressed a popular political consciousness and sometimes assumed strikingly conventional forms, such as the use of rough music, or *charivari*, to express a popular desire to restore a traditional protestantism, cleansed of popish influences.[20] A pattern of such disturbances over northern Essex and southern Suffolk, between August and December 1642, included attacks on the estates of prominent Catholics. Shortly before the battle of Edgehill in October, Ralph Josselin, godly vicar of Earls Colne, Essex, observed: 'our poor people in tumults arose and plundered diverse houses, papists and others, and threatened to go farther, which I endeavored to suppress by public and private means'.[21]

After the outbreak of war, this unofficial violence continued. Both sides used stereotypes to promote their campaigns as part of a larger war against religion's enemies: royalists became 'papists' determined to enslave and plunder the people; parliamentarians were 'known to despise the common prayer book and to favour Brownists, Anabaptists, and other disturbers of all order and government'.[22] After 1643, fears of violent disorder informed the grim circularity of parliamentarian iconoclasm. Many on both sides viewed a settlement, a restoration of common boundaries in the sacred, as the only means to forestall the violence of 'profane liberty', yet a settlement required, for a significant proportion of the godly, the destruction of popish remnants in parish churches.[23] As John Morrill has glossed the beliefs of William Dowsing, most notorious of parliamentarian iconoclasts: 'God would build a New Jerusalem, if only the godly would clear the site.'[24] In April, 1643, Sir Robert Harley and his parliamentary committee for 'monuments of superstition and idolatry' put their shoulders to this task in the clearance of Cheapside cross and the windows in Westminster abbey – pulling down there also the altar in Henry VII's chapel – and then entered Whitehall palace in pursuit of 'superstitious pictures'.[25]

This official iconoclasm had its counterpart in judicial violence against 'that grand enemy of the power of godliness.'[26] Laud's trial and execution in January, 1645, occurring at the same time as parliament's suppression of the Book of Common Prayer and the imposition of the Directory of Worship, reiterated the process of violent purification as a prelude to godly settlement in the church. Laud stood accused of high 'traiterous endeavours to subvert God's true religion' and of setting up 'popish idolatry by insensible degrees', as part of a grand scheme 'to reconcile the Church of England to the Church of Rome'.[27] After a lacklustre trial in the Lords between March and October 1644, an unprecedented ordinance of attainder carried the conviction of Laud's guilt from its source in the Commons to the Lords.[28] The sacrificial element in Laud's execution – the parliamentary desire to avoid crowd violence and to make the execution of one 'delinquent' stand for many – lay beneath the surface of William Strode's words of warning to the Lords, in late November 1644, to hasten their action on the ordinance.[29] William Prynne made the point explicit in his prayer for deliverance from 'such an hypocritical, false archiepiscopal generation of vipers, whose heads and hopes of succession we trust your honours have forever cut off in the decapitation of this archbishop of Canterbury, the very worst of his traitorous predecessors, their crimes being all concentred in him'.[30] At the moment of its inception, the new godly order had taken the lifeblood of an antichristian enemy and suppressed the Book of Common Prayer, an instrument of his evil design. After Laud's execution, parliament began a campaign to incorporate parish communities in a presbyterian system of assemblies; a new godly hierarchy would enforce a uniform local conformity to ceremonies prescribed by the Directory of Worship.

The connections among these events were not lost on contemporaries. As Peter Heylyn observed, 'the same day, 4 January, in which [the Lords] passed this bloody ordinance [of Laud's attainder], they passed another for establishing their new Directory [of Worship], which in effect was nothing but a total abolition of the Common Prayer Book, and thereby showed the world how little hopes they had of settling their new form of worship, if the foundation of it were not laid in blood'.[31] Although Heylyn's royalism defined his view of events, Prynne's rhetoric revealed a remarkably similar awareness of the enemy's blood as a prerequisite of godly settlement and the restoration of order.

The crisis and civil war of the 1640s suspended or destroyed many symbols and processes essential to the making of traditional parish communities. Although parliament and civil officers attempted to maintain continuity in the exercise of discipline, and then to impose a new Presbyterian settlement in 1645, many parishes dissolved in factional conflicts and in practice had to find their own informal settlements in the late 1640s and 1650s. These settlements brought an uneasy peace to the multiple protestant communities, the splinters of godliness created by the war and the bitter controversies over the nature of the peace. Among the most important long-term consequences of the civil war and the Revolution was this transformation of religious community from the customary parish, in which shared space suggested a common salvation, to spiritual networks understood in terms of shared beliefs and sympathy of conscience. Yet the destruction of the traditional church as a cultural system paradoxically fostered in many parishes new traditions of loyalty to the Book of Common Prayer and other customary symbols of religious identity. Ann Hughes has suggested, in her work on Warwickshire, how 'the self-confident, demanding and intrusive puritanism' of the revolutionary church 'crystallised and intensified a diffuse body of attitudes and behaviour' which comprised an early form of Anglicanism.[32] In a survey of 150 eastern and western parishes, John Morrill uncovered a pattern of loyalty to the Book of Common Prayer over the new parliamentary Directory after 1645.[33] Yet the newly assertive loyalty to selected 'traditions' of the national church remained a local response to the dissolution of the diocesan system. If some parishes escaped the reality of sectarian conflict, it was impossible to remain unaffected by news of the profound divisions in many other places. In this sense, the informal parish settlements negotiated after the war represent fragile, often combustible, new forms of community made from elements of the traditional system and elements of the radical protestant spiritualism intensified during the 1640s. This patchwork of local settlements became the basis of what was in practice an open church, the revolutionary church of the 1650s.

In the absence of the diocesan system, the disciplinary discourse of print became important in the making and sustaining of communities. Although print had always possessed this power to foster communities among dispersed populations, the circumstances of the late 1640s magnified its significance. Those involved in the great disputes over the nature of the formal settlement after the war 'made the printed book function as a kind of ministerial magistrate', attempting to define and enforce through their texts the terms, symbols and boundaries of new 'reformed' communities.[34] Protestant factionalism became the most serious problem of the peace, its dangers seeming greater to some than the earlier crisis of popery. As Thomas Edwards lamented in 1646, 'our evils are not removed and cured but only changed' from the 'popish innovations, superstitions, and prelatical tyranny' of the early 1640s to the current 'damnable heresies, horrid blasphemies, libertinism, and fearful anarchy'. Edwards viewed 'this last extremity' as 'far more high, violent, and dangerous in many respects' than the former. This way lay madness, 'dressing up a cat like a child to be baptised', 'mechanics and women taking upon them to preach and baptise', 'frogs out of the bottomless pit covering our land, coming into our houses, bedchambers, beds, churches . . . like Africa bringing forth monsters every day'.[35] 'We are gone beyond Amsterdam', a supporter assured Edwards in 1645, 'and are in our highway to Munster.'[36] Edwards and the many local correspondents whose fearful, angry letters were included in his book defended the Presbyterian settlement embodied in the new Directory of Worship as a godly bulwark against the 'devilish' chaos of individual licence and atheism. 'You have made a reformation', Edwards warned parliament, 'but with the reformation, have we not a deformation, and worse things come in upon us than ever we had before?'[37]

Despite its symbolic power, print could acquire magisterial authority only in the aftermath of a settlement. As consensus remained elusive, the printed discourse of the mid-1640s reflected the variety of communities fostered by war. Such polemical writers as Edwards merely intensified the conflict among protestants and offered their opponents opportunities to use print for their own purposes. Edwards himself observed how Independents and sectarians gave 'great and glorious names, swelling titles, to their books', using print and other techniques 'to boast their party to be more and greater than they are, as if parliament, armies, city of London, country, all the godly, wise, judicious men were theirs or would be theirs'.[38] Among the many radical protestant responses to Edwards, a series of pamphlets by William Walwyn in 1646 defined a distinctive form of fellowship in terms of 'liberty of conscience', antithetical to the traditional parish, as 'very many judicious persons' had become, 'through a blessed opportunity, freedom of discourse, and clearer search of scripture than heretofore, fully satisfied in their understandings that to compel or restrain any peaceable person in matters of faith and the worship of God is as real a sin, and as odious in the sight of God, as murder, theft, or adultery'. Simple, powerful images communicated the contrast between such a fellowship of 'liberties' and 'this kind of tyranny, in the bishops and prelatical clergy' and the similar despotism of 'master Edwards his work of bowing all to his rule'.[39] Walwyn, as effectively as Edwards, used imagery which shoved his enemy beyond the bounds of human society. In Walwyn's account, Edwards 'raged like an Irish, ravenous wolf' deprived of its prey, 'the harmless sheep, the Independents and separatists'.[40] The use of print thus served all factions in marshalling support and magnifying importance, shown here in the claim on behalf of gathered churches and sects 'that the numbers of them are daily increased and that their faithfulness to the parliament and commonwealth has caused them to grow in favour with all the people'.[41] The traditional image of the godly 'sheepfold' was recycled in this context to convey a new form of community based on liberty of conscience and protected by parliamentarian soldiers. This brief analysis is not intended to simplify the complex situation after 1645 as a confrontation of sides; it suggests rather an approach to texts that reveals the uses of print in the building and sustaining of communities in the absence of a formal settlement.

Many parishes in the late 1640s contained multiple networks of families defined in terms of community. The more populous urban parishes, especially in London, might conceal a gathered church, and elements of smaller sects, in addition to the faction able to decide the ceremonies used in the parish church. In rural parishes, these networks often comprised small sects sustained by the broader radical discourse in print or sometimes by links to larger groups in nearby towns. If we are to apply the term 'settlement' to English conditions in the late 1640s, it must be explored through a patchwork of informal local settlements. In Kidderminster, Worcestershire, an intensive pastoral discipline enabled Richard

Baxter to build an inclusive godly community. Baxter and his assistant led separate meetings for youths and adults to discuss Baxter's weekly sermons, as well as biweekly catechism sessions for fourteen families. An extraordinary pastoral effort in the cause of Baxter's 'mere catholicism', or aloofness from all parties, resulted in 'freedom from those sects which many other places were infected with'.[42] Yet the distance from traditional parish discipline even in Kidderminster was reflected in Baxter's difficulties with such routine disciplinary problems as 'a common notorious drunkard'.[43]

At the other end of the spectrum, Ralph Josselin, vicar of Earls Colne, Essex, 'began a little to be troubled with some in the matter of separation' as early as summer, 1642, as the godly began to separate from their ungodly neighbours. Josselin could not resolve the resulting problem of 'mixed communion' in the parish and, although troubled by 'our confusions and disorders and want of communion', suspended the ceremony during the 1640s. In 1651, Josselin administered communion to his godly neighbours for the first time in nine years, the group being determined 'to admit none but such as in charity we reckon to be disciples', yet conflict over such ordinances of the church as baptism continued and 'diverse Christians' still refused to help or participate in the ceremony. By the mid-1650s, Quakers had 'set up a paper on the church door' in Earls Colne, and Josselin had to weather a series of confrontations in the parish church, including charges of worldly vanity for his 'cuffs' and verbal abuse sometimes bordering on assault. In 1656, Josselin thankfully recalled being 'in the lane, set upon by one called a Quaker; the lord was with my heart, that I was not dismayed'.[44] During the late 1640s and 1650s, local peace depended all too often on the delicate diplomatic transactions of precisely those kinds of confrontations.

Among the distinctive features of the communites made in the late 1640s and 1650s was the complex sub-cultural interrelationship of parishes and sects. After such missionary campaigns as Samuel Oates's tour of the east Midlands in 1647 and 1648, and the tireless efforts of George Fox and other Quakers in the rural north in 1652, thousands of Baptists and Quakers defined their communities in opposition to the dominant symbolism of parishes.[45] Most protestants feared this dissolution of the parish into multiple communities. Justices of the peace in Rutland accused Oates of 'filling the county with diverse sects and schisms, withdrawing them from their own ministers into mutinous assemblies, and perverting whole families, working divisions even between nearest relatives'.[46] Yet the failure to establish a national settlement fostered a creative interrelationship of parish and sect in fashioning new communities. The dominant factions of Presbyterians and Independents used the war against 'diverse sects and schisms' to build parishes in the new order, just as Baptists evoked 'the hardening of the people in their idolizing of the temple' and Quakers expressed their contempt for the 'priests of Baal' and their 'steeple house,' to create the symbolic repertoire of subcultures and their own new fellowships of interrelated families.[47] These subcultures expressed the efforts of sectarian groups to create a break, an open space, in the conventional order of religion through representations of distinction from this conventional order in symbol, behaviour and ritual.[48] Yet the creation of identity through the rejection of 'idolatry' in the national church formed a subcultural dependence on the symbols of the parish and held the sect in a dialogic relationship to the dominant order. Never did these new sectarian groups demonstrate their dependence on traditional religious culture, nor their part in a new configuration of communities, more powerfully than in their various acts of rejection and separation.

In conclusion, it has become evident that the experience of community in English parishes was fundamentally transformed during the 1640s. Although many elements of traditional parish communities survived the crises of civil war and revolution, their new significance and the loyalty discovered during the 1640s to the customary calendar and ceremonies of the church, even to the church's fabric itself, suggest the impact of war and its disorders on the local experience of familiar symbols and rites. The broad process of change followed an unexpected pattern, as the crisis over popery in the early 1640s helped to precipitate a war among protestants; and a crisis over schism ultimately splintered the movement for further reformation in the aftermath of the parliamentarian victory. Although the despised popish device of episcopacy had ceased its nefarious influence in 1641, the dissolution of the church hierarchy effectively dissolved the cultural boundaries of local parishes. Several important forms of violence during the war, especially the official and unoffical iconoclasm and the judicial murder of 1645, reflect either responses to the absence of boundaries or efforts of reconstruction. After the failure of the Presbyterian settlement in the mid-1640s, new forms of community emerged from myriad negotiations among diverse protestant factions. These factions derived unprecedented disciplinary power and support from the dynamic print culture of the 1640s. A new configuration of communities in many local parishes involved fellowships of sympathetic families defined in terms of church and sect, the symbiotic concerns of uniformity and persecution helping to build communities in the absence of the territorial solidarity of the traditional parish. In 1650, the republic abandoned all pretence of uniformity, as parliament repealed the laws that had compelled attendance of parish churches and left only a blasphemy law to mark the boundaries of protestant community, and the formal toleration of 1653 confirmed this approach to the problem of protestant diversity. Yet the general significance of the changes must be stated in relative rather than absolute terms, as an acute intensification of a process underway since the early Reformation. The result of the crisis during the 1640s was a form of protestant community *more* divided and discursively defined, *more* open to interventions of civil authority in religious matters and *more* sensitive to shifts in the currents of national debates.

Most histories of the Restoration Church in the early 1660s have studied the reestablishment of administrative functions and have not identified the restoration of the parish as a problem distinct from the revival of the institutional structure of the church.[49] When local understandings of events have figured in accounts of the restored regime, attention has usually focused on the corporations because of their rich archives as well as their political importance in the reconstruction of the royal state. Moreover, corporations evoke the crucial problems of culture and identity in the Restoration because, through their charters, they constituted intersections of a kind between local forms of community and governance and the symbolism and authority of the royal state. Historians have approached the local councils as the primary sources of power and identity in their communities, and have tended to understand the Restoration as a royalist invasion of corporate offices, an invasion less successful in some corporations than others but independent of place in its motivations and designs. This approach has defined power and politics in civil terms. If religious issues have been raised, the issues have concerned the ability of specific groups to defy the penal laws and to retain power in their corporations. Despite the impact of civil war and revolution on local experiences of religious community, the restoration of parishes and their distinctive forms of power and identity have received little attention from historians.

The general fear of Quakers as antisocial spiritual levellers has dominated recent discussions of the religious motives for restoration.[50] Although the power of this concern over religious radicalism is not controversial, much remains unclear about the micro-histories of restoration in the parishes. If the fascination of the restoration process lies in its mingling of general and highly specific or local influences, the diversity of local settlements lies very much in shadow. There is remarkably little work on the first wave of episcopal visitations, for example, surely key moments and sites for the making of the first restoration settlements in local parishes. A brief sketch may suggest the benefits of such an approach. A fear of sectarian movements, and Quakerism in particular, formed the context of the first episcopal visitation in Tewkesbury and its neighbourhood, part of Winchcombe deanery in Gloucester diocese. This visitation lasted from December 1661 to September 1662, as convocation revised the Book of Common Prayer, promoted a restrictive Act of Uniformity and created a conservative religious settlement for the national church.[51] At this time, the traditional process of visitation, with its presentment of local offences, reasserted the ceremonial authority and jurisdiction of the territorial church. Just as the local commissioners appointed under the terms of the Corporation Act in 1662 created protective boundaries around restored borough councils, so the presentments made by churchwardens in the course of this visitation formed part of an effort to reconstruct the ceremonial boundaries of parish communities, although the Act of Uniformity was less strictly enforced than the Corporation Act. Between October 1662 and March 1665 the Gloucester consistory court focused almost exclusively on religious offenses and handled seventy presentments from Winchcombe deanery for violations of the ceremonial code in the restored church.[52] Despite the narrowness of the formal settlement in the church, however, churchwardens did not prosecute Presbyterians and Independents in the Vale of Gloucester. On the contrary, the visitation was an unmistakable assault on Baptists and Quakers.[53] Separatism was the principle of exclusion in the restored parish, and Independents in

Tewkesbury were reluctant to separate from a church which had borne their stamp during the 1650s.

This first visitation and its prosecutions thus formed a campaign against Baptists and Quakers, the most visible local separatist communities. Both diocesan and parish officers used the campaign to mark the boundaries of the established church by prosecution of the most conspicuous offenders, but the rank and file separatists were not systematically prosecuted. That method was reflected in the prosecution of villagers known to hold private religious meetings or conventicles in their homes: in 1663, Edwin Millington of Tewkesbury was presented for 'keeping a conventicle of Anabaptists' in his house;[54] the Quakers prosecuted were sufficiently prominent to hold the Stoke Orchard monthly meeting in their Tewkesbury homes.[55] Donald Spaeth has found a similar pattern of exemplary prosecution in the diocese of Salisbury.[56] This assault on separatist leaders and meeting-sites was the primary objective of the visitation. Prosecutions occasionally touched the local rank and file for various offences against the restored parish, including absence from church and more serious transgressions of the ritual cycle, such as keeping infants from baptism. In Winchcombe deanery, at least 17 members of the large Baptist meeting centered on Tewkesbury were prosecuted, 13 per cent of its membership of 135.[57] But the number of prosecutions generally remained small and evenly distributed between movements. Of the 70 presentments made between 1662 and 1665 for violations of the ceremonial code, 35 offenders can be identified positively as either Baptists or Quakers.[58] The small number of known separatists prosecuted suggests that this visitation was an attempt to establish boundaries rather than uniformity. The arrival of the bishop and the preparation of presentments was part of the process of marking the boundaries of the restored church and inducing neighbours beyond the boundaries to cross over.

This pressure on the leadership and margins of separatist communities in the restoration of the parish created and subsequently reinforced the distinction between the church and dissent. The importance of this boundary for local Presbyterians and Independents, as well as the more shadowy community of conformist Anglicans, helps to explain the diverse local support for the Restoration. Protestantism had splintered during the 1640s and 1650s, and a pervasive fear of spiritual levellers induced even Independents to favour the building of formidable boundaries to protect the authority of scripture and the societies of the godly from the destructive power of radical mysticism. This co-operation among Presbyterians, Independents and Cavaliers in the 'royalist restoration' saved the elect from the spiritually and socially subversive force of Quakerism. Yet this fragile alignment of diverse groups produced not the static relationships frequently implied by the concept of the Restoration but a form of belonging characterised as much by unresolved conflicts as by the shared desire to preserve social and religious hierarchy.

The creation of boundaries between church and sect did not imply local consensus on the form of religious ritual to be practised in the restored parish.

Presbyterians, Independents and conformist Anglicans agreed on the necessity of boundaries to protect the formal hierarchy in parishes, but the precise relationship between prescribed forms of prayer and the authority of conscience in this restored hierarchy remained unclear. The parochial restoration thus failed to resolve longstanding conflicts over authority and ceremony in the church. Many nonconformists returned to the parish church in the early 1660s but refused to accept the Restoration settlement as the last word on local religious practice. The first episcopal visitation distinguished Presbyterians, Independents and conformist Anglicans as the restored parish and constructed boundaries to protect this form of belonging from sectarian neighbours. The restoration process thus represented neither a return to homogeneous parish communities nor a decisive break from the experience of the 1640s and 1650s, but rather a redistribution of power among local factions expressed as an assault on sectaries and officers of the protectorate. The fundamental questions of ritual and authority had been rephrased but not resolved.

Parishes in the Restoration church expressed the inheritance of civil war and revolution in patterns of conflict among forms of Anglicanism and in a politics of differentiation between the church and its sectarian neighbors. The most divisive local conflicts concerned the nature of Anglicanism itself. English protestant identity was disputed terrain in the Restoration parish. A sometimes quiescent and sometimes embittered politics of difference culminated in the general crisis of the late 1670s. That crisis divided many parishes into factions marked by passionately held beliefs in, respectively, a church based on law and a church based on conscience, both predicated on cautionary tales drawn from the experiences and memory of civil war, both represented by their advocates as the only legitimate formulae for a national church loyal to the monarchy. The evidence of conflicts to control parishes and to shape their ceremonial discipline, conflicts over the nature of Anglican identity itself, raises important questions about the social depth of doctrinal coherence and 'fundamental principles' in the Church of England.[59] In this context, local ceremonial practice, the exercise of authority by churchwardens and diocesan visitations 'made' parish communities in an overtly political fashion, as local factions negotiated the meanings of English protestantism and thus the boundaries of parish communities.

After the Restoration visitations, the prescriptive code conveyed in such sources as visitation articles represented religious ritual in local parishes as shared and uniform. These sources restored the image of the church as an inclusive institution, an image maintained despite much evidence of local factions marked by opposed views on how parishes ought to be ordered as well as by matters of religious behaviour. Most importantly, *Anglicans* disagreed over the means of restoring order in parishes, and their disagreements reflected conflicts over the meaning of parish communities. In 1670, after the second Conventicle Act, Archbishop Gilbert Sheldon provided a detailed description of church and parish discipline in a letter to William Nicolson, bishop of Gloucester.[60] Sheldon wrote to Nicolson and the other bishops of his province to introduce his plan for 'the peace and settlement of the church and the uniformity of god's service in the same'. He enjoined officers of the church to pursue 'an exemplary conformity in their persons and practice to his majesty's laws and the rules of the church'. He ordered the bishops to direct his letter to 'parsons, vicars and curates', as well as to 'chancellors, archdeacons, commissaries, officials, registers, and other ecclesiastical officers'. This manifesto of hierarchy insisted on the practicability of an inclusive and uniform religious community, if only local officers could be made to 'perform their duty to God, the king, and the church' in their 'several capacities and stations' in parishes and dioceses. An inclusive church would emerge from the local enforcement of law.

According to this hierarchic view of parish discipline, the local minister embodied lawful religion as prescribed by the Book of Common Prayer. His 'reverent performance of so holy a worship' gave 'honour to God' and 'by his own example' instructed the parish in proper doctrine. Divine service consisted of the appointed prayers, read 'without addition or varying in substance or ceremony from the order and method set down by the book'. Ministers further signified their obedience to lawful religion by wearing 'their priestly habit', the surplice and hood. This church of law expressed a fundamental lack of confidence in the lay capacity to govern social and religious behaviour in a responsible manner. On the contrary, the laity needed to emulate a clerical model of proper Christian conduct in order to achieve a virtuous life. The minister furnished such a model both by performing church ceremonies in the lawful manner and by observing a 'strictness and sobriety of life and conversation'. Moreover, an obedient and uniform orderliness in religion and society would inevitably result from a minister's determined efforts to mould parish discipline in his own image by 'checking and punishing such as transgress and encouraging such as live orderly'. A minister became 'a pattern of good living' for his parishioners, inculcating 'virtue and religious deportment' by the force of his own example.

Obedience to the church of law required an assault on religious diversity. Officers of the Anglican Church were missionaries in a wilderness of schism, obliged to 'persuade and win all nonconformists and dissenters to obedience to his majesty's laws and unity with the church'. If persuasion failed, Sheldon ordered his local officers to use 'the censures of the church', but neither persuasion nor the strictures of church courts exhausted the means to enforce uniformity. The second Conventicle Act involved justices of the peace in the defence of religious uniformity. Sheldon directed the officers of the church, from the courts to the churchwardens in their parishes, to identify all 'nonconformists and frequenters of conventicles and unlawful assemblies under pretence of religious worship', particularly the leaders and the locations of the assemblies, and to present the names of offenders to the justices of the peace. A systematic prosecution of religious difference could result, according to Sheldon, only in 'a hearty affection to the worship of God, the honour of the king and his laws, and the peace of the church and kingdom'.

Sheldon himself acknowledged the existence of other Anglican views of parish order. His letter called for obedience to the ritual order prescribed by the Book of Common Prayer, 'wherein I hear and am afraid too many do offend'.[61] Sheldon referred to such clerics as Francis Wells, the curate of Tewkesbury, who adapted the Prayer Book formulae to serve his divided parish and was admonished in the episcopal visitation of 1671 'to read prayers and wear the surplice'.[62] Far from concealing their practices, advocates of this church of conscience used their positions to confront the ecclesiastical hierarchy. In 1676, the ecclesiastical court ordered Wells to read prayers before the bishop and questioned his alteration of the absolution set down in the Book of Common Prayer. Wells replied that 'it never was his custom to read the absolution as the Book of Common Prayer directed'.[63] By modifying ceremonial practice in this way, Wells signified his sensitivity to similar qualms of conscience among his parishioners. Justin Champion and Lee McNulty have attributed similar beliefs and sympathies to Edmund Hickeringill, vicar of Boxted, Essex.[64] The experience of both clerics during the 1640s and 1650s fostered a style of practical divinity suited to the building of communities from factions. This church of conscience required a more indulgent view of religious diversity. In 1669, Bishop Nicolson complained to the lord lieutenant of Gloucestershire and several justices that dissenters assembled 'in greater numbers and more daring than formerly' in the 'hope of impunity from their not being in the least suppressed'.[65] These Anglicans had not, however, abandoned the inclusive understanding of parish community, hoping rather to achieve comprehension by a relaxation of religious boundaries under the law and by an accommodation of the many local expressions of lay piety.

Among Anglicans, the boundaries of the church thus remained a focal point of conflict. As prescriptive codes for the interaction of Anglicans and other groups, however, the church of law and the church of conscience had important implications beyond the boundaries of Anglicanism. The principles at stake in conflicts over Anglican parishes were also confronted in separatist views of religious fellowship. An emphasis on the authority of personal belief among the laity tended to move the church of conscience closer to moderate dissent. The fear and hatred of dissent expressed in the church of law often reflected an awareness of this nonconformist element in the parishes of the national church. Persistent controversies over authority and ceremonies among Anglicans seemed to lend credence to fears of a general nonconformist conspiracy that included dissenters. In the early 1680s, for instance, local anxieties concerning the behaviour of Francis Wells and nonconformist intentions in the parish of Tewkesbury sparked a general prosecution of dissenters. Factional conflicts in Anglican parishes always had the power to incorporate dissenters, the outsiders of the parish.[66]

The notion of a comprehensive parish in both its Anglican forms was challenged by views of community that prescribed separation from the church. After the Restoration, these minority views formed local subcultures, although the process of restoration in the parishes identified these subcultures as dangerous and attempted to isolate their influence. These separatist subcultures comprised a spectrum of positions on the significance of separation that included Presbyterianism, Independence, Anabaptism and Quakerism. In Presbyterian and Independent forms, dissent showed affinities for the restored parish, as each tended to reject the radical sects and to represent its own faction as an alternative vision of the church. Moreover, Presbyterians and Independents had participated actively in the restoration of the monarchy in 1660, in part because of concern over the implications of radical sectarianism. But the distinctive local quality of dissent, common to all its forms, was a process of separation from the restored parish. Despite important evidence of the persistence of neighbourliness among Anglicans and dissenters, this religious separation had a profound impact on the politics of parish communities after the Restoration.[67] The separatism of Quakers expressed the rationale and implications of separation in their clearest forms.

Like their Anglican counterparts, separatist notions of fellowship marked boundaries and attempted to minimise external influences on the behaviour of members. In the justification of their monthly meeting in Stoke Orchard, the main assembly for Tewkesbury and its neighbourhood, for example, Quakers represented the boundary that separated their group from the parish as a wall of blood built during long years of persecution. Ministers of the national church were described as 'the priests of Baal' and 'the fist of wickedness and bloody hands, who have had their hands in the blood of the brethren'. Persecution in the service of the truth was thus a crucial element in Quaker identity. This climate of persecution and the boundaries it produced were maintained and institutionalised through the formal descriptions of the 'sufferings' of their co-religionists collected by Quakers under order as symbols of 'the murdering spirit of this world' from which the group had separated. Those images of persecution and the wall of blood then became the symbolic 'evidence' for the definitive Quaker metaphors of the parish as a modern Egypt and Quakers as the chosen people in captivity. Through the symbolism of captivity and flight, Quaker ritual was distinguished from the ceremonies of the national church as 'the bread of life' from 'the dishes and pleasures' of 'the priest and his company'. These boundaries identified Quakers as the sharers of a hidden truth and as the members of a distinct religious fellowship founded on the unity of the spirit in 'one heart, one mind, and one soul'.[68]

In this prescriptive sense alone, a politics inherited from the civil war made it impossible to restore parish communities after 1660. Common stereotypes tended to complicate and embitter this politics. Anglican notions of the church of law often represented nonconformity and dissent as the deviance of a small number of misdirected Anglicans seduced by malcontents. Although the church of conscience rejected this stereotype, its advocates continued to imagine dissent as the spiritual exile of Anglicans stricken in conscience and driven from the national church by its insistence on submission to the law in ceremonies and discipline. According to both views, if Anglican ministers only performed their proper pastoral duties most of the stray sheep would return to the Anglican fold. These stereotypes may have inspired Anglican fictions of a comprehensive parish but they resulted in a practical politics that consistently underestimated the religious impact of civil war.

Although hardly controversial, it is important to recall the social power of nonconformity in the late seventeenth century. Many illustrations could serve this purpose, but the relations among nonconformists in the parish of Ashchurch, east of Tewkesbury, also reveal the practical fluidity of the boundary between forms of Anglicanism and dissent. Despite a nominal Independency, these nonconformists remained close to their parish church, attending both conventicles and Anglican services. Traces of this faction have survived in church court presentments, parish registers and wills. In 1672, Richard Davison obtained a licence to hold a meeting of Independents in his house in Ashchurch.[69] Davison lived in the hamlet of Natton, close to the centre of the parish,[70] while the other members were dispersed among the hamlets of Pamington, Fiddington and Natton.[71] These families exerted a proprietary influence in Ashchurch, yet their political power transcended their own parish, magnified by links to a similar network of families in Tewkesbury. Richard Davison's brother, William Davison of Tewkesbury, obtained a licence in the early summer of 1672 to hold a meeting of Independents in his house.[72] Henry Lane of Tewkesbury, described as an Independent in the early 1660s, was related by marriage to Richard Haines of Pamington, both having been prosecuted for nonconformity in Ashchurch during the 1630s. Richard's brother William named his 'landlord and very faithful friend' Henry Lane as overseer of his estate in the early 1660s.[73] Although such networks were not invariably the result of civil war, the experience of war and revolution had transformed mere networks into self-conscious factions able to challenge the leadership in restored parishes.

The making of parish communities after the Restoration required officers of the church and lay leaders to manage a dangerous politics of factions and sects, a difficulty compounded by the fluidity of such major factions as Presbyterians and Independents, sometimes seeming to contend for the control of parishes and sometimes resembling sects in their separation from parish affairs. This politics of religion, marked by a simultaneous intimacy and alienation of political enemies, explains a distinctive pattern of relations in many parishes. As Sheldon lamented in his letter to the bishops, many parish officers appeared reluctant to prosecute nonconformity and dissent during the 1670s.[74] This pattern involved more than a disinclination to prosecute neighbours. Many cases came before the courts, but the offenders were prosecuted for such traditional misdemeanours as an absence from church or a failure to receive communion, rather than for attendance at conventicles. Prior to the dramatic increase in overt prosecutions for dissent in 1679, for example, only one case in the Winchcombe deanery of the diocese of Gloucester identified the accused as a participant in a conventicle.[75] Before 1679, churchwardens seldom used the church courts to coerce their nonconformist or separatist neighbours, and this behaviour sheds important light on the significance of the courts in the new politics of the parish.

After the Restoration, few consistory courts regained their jurisdiction over the sexual and matrimonial cases so prominent among their activities during the early seventeenth century.[76] As the rituals of penance assigned by the courts disappeared from parish churches, the courts lost the authority over communal discipline traditionally expressed through the dramas of absolution and charity.[77] Diocesan courts, such powerful instruments of order prior to the civil war, lost much of their customary influence over the forming of parish communities. This important jurisdictional change threw the politics of diocesan intervention on matters of ceremonial conformity and church discipline into sharper relief. The clearly partisan interests of the church courts in the settlement of religious disputes may help to explain the reluctance of local officers to invoke their authority in the delicate factional politics of many parishes. Of 470 cases of absence from church and failure to receive communion prosecuted in Winchcombe deanery between 1671 and 1686, only 63 cases, or 13 per cent, were prosecuted prior to 1678.[78] These cases involved dissenters, but churchwardens would not accuse neighbours of separation in the courts before 1677. During the late 1670s, however, local officers became more systematic, as 407 of the cases from Winchcombe deanery, or 87 per cent, were presented after 1678. In 1680–81 local officers registered Quaker meeting-places and members in the court, and Quakers began to experience in earnest a persecution long anticipated in their records.[79] This evidence suggests the critical influence of the Popish Plot crisis on local decisions to use diocesan courts and coercion to protect the fiction of the comprehensive parish in the Anglican Church.

The Popish Plot and the exclusion crisis of the late 1670s and early 1680s became a crisis of political and religious authority that recalled the experience of the early 1640s. Mark Knights has charted the polarisation of high politics following the dissolution of parliament early in 1679.[80] A similar process of polarisation occurred in parishes, as factions and sects inherited from the 1640s coalesced around the principles of further reform and defence of the king's church in yet another battle over the nature of religious and civil authority. Unfortunately, little microhistorical work has focused on this critical moment in parochial politics. In Tewkesbury and other parishes in northern Gloucestershire, nonconformists and dissenters interpreted the plot as divine retribution for the vile immorality of Charles II's regime. In November 1678 Francis Wells, minister of Tewkesbury, preached a fiery sermon of moral indictment against Charles and his court, reviling the king for 'adultery, whoredom, and fornication', and lamenting those sins as the reason why 'the land mourned' popish atrocities.[81] Despite subsequent suspension from his ministry, Wells became the leader of a local revival of the movement for a further reformation of religious ceremonies in the parish. This reform faction recruited inveterate nonconformists and former parliamentarians, who had returned to the established church in the 1660s, in addition to local dissenters. Wells and his supporters were opposed by a faction loyal to the Restoration settlement, a faction that included the chancellor of the diocese of Gloucester and most of the burgesses of the common council in Tewkesbury. In the early 1680s, this faction of loyalist Anglicans deprived Wells of his benefice, and prolonged controversy finally ended in a reactionary campaign of political and religious exclusion led by former royalists against nonconformists and dissenters.[82] As the parish divided between fear of popery and fear of revolution, churchwardens previously reluctant to prosecute neighbours turned to the partisan power of the church court as the only means by which to defend the parish from subversion.

This chapter has argued for a politics of the parish as the most important impact of civil war and revolution on English local communities. Although religious conflict was hardly a novelty, the war divided families and parishes in an unprecedented fashion, as thousands adjudicated in the courts of personal conscience matters of popery, scriptural authority and the bases of legitimate order in their parishes. The failure of consistory courts in 1641 magnified the crisis, for the courts traditionally participated in the forming of parish communities through the elaborate judicial dramas of penance, contrition, and absolution regularly performed in parish churches. Those courts had never lacked critics, but prior to the civil war parish communities formed in a largely unexamined way, and in most parishes godly networks did not become factions opposed to a church established under the crown. After the Restoration, parishes had to be made in a changed political landscape. Although the visitations of 1661 and 1662 established the boundaries of the restored church, the Restoration in parishes depended on hundreds, perhaps thousands, of fragile negotiated settlements among factions of former enemies. As the church courts came to signify the partisan interest of the Anglican church of law, many churchwardens, especially during the late 1660s and 1670s, became wary of their authority and doubted their power to resolve disputes among neighbours, to make or fabricate parish communities from factions of proprietary families. In this context, parish churches became arenas for local disputes over the meanings of Anglicanism and, ultimately, the religious terms of community. During the Popish Plot crisis, reform and loyalist factions became polarised, and the exclusive local politics of the 1680s starkly reveals the fractured communities inherited from a violent past, perhaps repaired but not rebuilt after the Restoration settlement. Parishes in Restoration England were never effectively taught the Hobbesian notion of one church and one people, under the king, but expressed a politics learned during a generation of civil war and revolution, a politics of religion.

Notes

1 I thank Michael Braddick for his comments on an earlier draft of this essay.
2 T. Hobbes, *Behemoth* (Chicago, 1990), 58.
3 K. Wrightson, 'The politics of the parish in early modern England', in P. Griffiths, A. Fox and S. Hindle (eds), *The experience of authority in early modern England* (New York, 1996), 27.
4 S. Hindle, *The state and social change in early modern England* (London, 2000).
5 R. Cust and A. Hughes, 'Introduction', in Cust and Hughes (eds), *The English civil war* (London, 1997), 1–30.

6 D. Beaver, 'Conscience and context: the popish plot and the politics of ritual, 1678–1682', *Historical Journal*, 34 (1991), 297–327; D. Underdown, *A freeborn people* (Oxford, 1996), 120–2.

7 An excellent introduction that stresses the importance of religious conflict among the causes of civil war is A. Hughes, *The causes of the English civil war* (Oxford, 1998). My analysis of civil war violence includes material from D. Beaver, 'Religion's enemies: parish communities, civil war and religious conflict in England, 1641–1662', in R. P. Hsia (ed.), *Blackwell companion to the reformation world* (Oxford, 2004), 311–31.

8 J. Morrill, 'The religious context of the English civil war', in his *The nature of the English revolution* (London, 1993), 68.

9 There is no general study of this suspension of the jurisdiction of diocesan courts in 1641 and 1642; see, for some local evidence, D. Beaver, *Parish communities and religious conflict in the Vale of Gloucester* (Cambridge, MA, 1998), 191–3, 206–7.

10 *Ibid.*, 81–4, 120–9, 160–5. I understand community as a wide range of common elements, including the sense of belonging, expressed by specific symbols and performances. It was and is common for people to belong to the same community who have never met face to face. This view makes the best sense of the evidence from early modern parishes, often quite dispersed in population and settlement yet revealing powerful evidence of this notion of belonging, for example in mortuary sites and customs. The best introductions to this approach are A. P. Cohen, *The symbolic construction of community* (London, 1985) and C. Bell, *Ritual theory, ritual practice* (Oxford, 1992).

11 Beaver, *Parish communities*, 127–8.

12 *Religion's enemies* (1641), sigs A3–4.

13 *The autobiography of Richard Baxter*, ed. N. H. Keeble (London, 1974), 29.

14 *England's deliverance* (1641), 4.

15 This crisis *within* the culture of English parishes, involving processes and symbols whereby parish communities were made, differs from the notion of a conflict *between* traditional and puritan cultures as a cause of civil war: D. Underdown, *Revel, riot, and rebellion* (Oxford, 1985), 44–72; Hughes, *Causes of the English civil war*, 114–48.

16 Beaver, *Parish communities*, 113–94. An analysis of early Stuart parish churches as points of contact for multiple religious communities is offered in Anthony Milton's contribution to this volume (ch. 4).

17 P. Lake, 'The Laudian style,' in K. Fincham (ed.), *The early Stuart church* (Basingstoke, 1993), 161–85.

18 N. Tyacke, *Anti-Calvinists* (Oxford, 1987), 188–209; Beaver, *Parish communities*, 155–60, 183–9.

19 B. Manning, *The English people and the English revolution* (London, 1976), 46–8.

20 J. Walter, *Understanding popular violence in the English revolution* (Cambridge, 1999), 191–7.

21 *The diary of Ralph Josselin 1616–1683*, ed. A. Macfarlane (London, 1976), 13.

22 Underdown, *Revel, riot and rebellion*, 164–5; Beaver, *Parish communities*, 165–80, 202–3.

23 The words 'profane liberty' are from the frontispiece of *The times displayed in six sestyads* (1646), by royalist poet Samuel Sheppard.

24 J. Morrill, 'William Dowsing and the administration of iconoclasm in the puritan revolution', in *The journal of William Dowsing*, ed. Trevor Cooper (Woodbridge, 2001), 10.

25 M. Aston, *England's iconoclasts* (Oxford, 1988), 76.

26 *Diary of Ralph Josselin*, 31.

27 W. Prynne, *Canterburies doome or the first part of a compleat history of the ... tryall ... of William Laud* (1646), frontispiece.

28 S. R. Gardiner, *History of the great civil war, 1642–1649*, 5 vols (1898), ii. 100; W. Laud, *History of the troubles and trial of William Laud* (1695), 220–431; P. Heylyn, *A brief relation of the death and sufferings of the archbishop of Canterbury* (Oxford, 1645), 7–11.

29 Gardiner, *Great civil war*, ii. 102.

30 Prynne, *Canterburies doome*, 8v.

31 Heylyn, *Brief relation*, 11; Laud, *History of the troubles and trial of William Laud*, 447.

32 A. Hughes, *Politics, society, and civil war in Warwickshire* (Cambridge, 1987), 322.

33 J. Morrill, 'The church in England', in *English revolution*, 163–8.

34 N. Smith, *Literature and revolution in England* (New Haven, 1994), 120–1.

35 T. Edwards, *Gangraena*, 3 vols (1646), i. 58; ii. 29, 58.

36 *Ibid.*, ii. 12–13.

37 *Ibid.*, i, sig. A3v.

38 *Ibid.*, i. 55, 58.

39 W. Walwyn, *An antidote against Master Edwards* (1646), 2.

40 *Ibid.*, 3.

41 *Ibid.*, 3–4.

42 *Autobiography of Richard Baxter*, 80, 84.

43 *Ibid.*, 77–8, 80–2.

44 *Diary of Ralph Josselin*, 12, 77, 96, 234–7, 350, 377, 379, 380, 384, 450; Morrill, 'Church in England', 167; A. Davies, *The Quakers in English society* (Oxford, 2000), 13, 22–3, 181–2.

45 J. F. McGregor, 'The Baptists', and B. Reay, 'Quakerism and society', in J. F. McGregor and B. Reay (eds), *Radical religion in the English revolution* (Oxford, 1984), 32, 141–2.

46 McGregor, 'Baptists', in *ibid.*, 32.

47 Beaver, *Parish communities*, 234–6, 273; Davies, *Quakers in English society*, 77.

48 D. Hebdige, *Subculture: the meaning of style* (London, 1979), 1–19.

49 I. M. Green, *The re-establishment of the church of England* (Oxford, 1978), 1–36, 117–42, 179–201.

50 B. Reay, 'The Quakers, 1659, and the restoration of the monarchy', *History*, 63 (1978), 193–213; B. Reay, 'The authorities and early restoration Quakerism', *Journal of Ecclesiastical History*, 34 (1983), 69–84; J. Spurr, *The restoration church* (New Haven, CT, 1991), 23–4, 27.

51 Gloucestershire Record Office (GRO), Gloucester Diocesan Records (GDR) 209, Episcopal visitation, 1661–1662. The best recent work on the settlement of the national church is Spurr, *Restoration church*, 29–42.

52 GRO, GDR 210, Detection causes, 1662–63; GDR 212, Detection causes, 1663–65.

53 This evidence complicates the interpretation of the Restoration settlement in the church as a general assault by the gentry on puritanism. The practical boundaries of the settlement may have depended on the character of the first visitation: Green, *Re-establishment of the church of England*, 179–80.

54 GRO, GDR 210, Detection causes, 1662–63.

55 *Ibid.*; GRO, D 1340 B2/M1, Stoke Orchard monthly meeting, 19, 24, 41, 47.

56 D. A. Spaeth, *The church in an age of danger* (Cambridge, 2000), 160, 163.

57 The Quakers did not keep a membership list; GRO, GDR 210, Detection causes, 1662–63; GDR 212, Detections, 1663–65; D 4944, Tewkesbury Baptist church book, 38–9.

58 Beaver, *Parish communities*, 257, 423.
59 Spurr, *Restoration church*, 105–65, 379; Beaver, *Parish communities*, 266–81.
60 GRO, GDR 220, Visitation book, 1670–77, fos 2–3; see Spurr, *Restoration church*, 47–8, for Sheldon's view of the church and Restoration Anglicanism.
61 GRO, GDR 220, Visitation book, 1670–77, fos 2–3.
62 GRO, GDR 223, Episcopal visitations, 1671–73.
63 GRO, GDR 227, Detection causes, 1676–77.
64 J. Champion and L. McNulty, 'Making orthodoxy in late restoration England', in M. J. Braddick and J. Walter (eds), *Negotiating power in early modern society: order, hierarchy and subordination in Britain and Ireland* (Cambridge, 2001), 227–48.
65 BL, Add. MS 33,589, fo. 75.
66 Beaver, *Parish communities*, 281–303; see the concise description of the problem of nonconformity in Spaeth, *Church in danger*, 169–71.
67 Bill Stevenson, 'The social integration of post-restoration dissenters', in M. Spufford (ed.), *The world of rural dissenters* (Cambridge, 1995), 360–87.
68 GRO, D 1340 B2/M1, Stoke Orchard monthly meeting, 2–4, 7–8.
69 *CSPD, 1672*, 400, 402.
70 GRO, W 1683/103.
71 GRO, GDR 243, Episcopal visitation, 1682.
72 GRO, W 1683/103; *CSPD, 1672*, 196, 216.
73 GRO, GDR 210, Detection causes, 1662–63; GDR 224, Detection causes, 1671–73; GDR 174, Detection causes, 1631, 1634, 1635, 1636, 1637; W 1663/228.
74 M. Knights, *Politics and opinion in crisis* (Cambridge, 1994), 18; Spaeth, *Church in danger*, 162–3.
75 GRO, GDR 231, Visitation book, 1677–78.
76 The manuscript volumes of presentments for Winchcombe deanery in the diocese of Gloucester for 1671–1708, discussed below, are listed in Beaver, *Parish communities*, 427.
77 Beaver, *Parish communities*, 279–80; see the account of the condition and performance of the courts in Spurr, *Restoration church*, 209–19.
78 See M. Watts, *The dissenters* (Oxford, 1978), 244–9, for the national pattern of prosecutions during the early 1670s.
79 GRO, GDR 241, Detection causes, 1681–82.
80 Knights, *Politics and opinion in crisis*, 107–45.
81 Beaver, 'Conscience and context', 304–5.
82 The terms 'Whig' and 'Tory' were not used in local accounts of faction. Attitudes to the Restoration settlement in the church were the most clearly articulated principles: see the discussion of parties in Knights, *Politics and opinion in crisis*, 355–60.

9

The kings' book: Eikon basilike *and the English Revolution of 1649*

Sean Kelsey

Eikon basilike, the publishing sensation of the seventeenth century, ranks comfortably alongside the King James Bible and the first folio of Shakespeare as the most famous of all early modern publications in English. As a literary artefact it retains much of its undoubted power. The book's transcendence of time and the affairs of men is remarked on by modern literary critics in much the same way it drew contemporary comment.[1] The engagement of this unique and remarkable text with its political context has long been recognised.[2] But modern scholarship has generally placed far greater emphasis on a critical dissection of the literary tropes, artistic devices and rhetorical stratagems which effortlessly transformed one of the most massively public and exhortatory print performances of the age into an ostensibly private, inward-looking manuscript, thus placing the *Eikon* far above the political fray.

This chapter explores further the book's public, political dimension, and my conclusions necessarily remain provisional in the absence of the *Eikon*'s original manuscript. I attempt nevertheless to contextualise what little we do know about the composition, revision and eventual publication of the *Eikon* in order to enhance an appreciation of why it was published when it was, and to what end. It is argued that while preparing for the eventuality of the king's death, Charles I and those of his advisors and supporters who were closest to the writing, compiling, editing and publication of *Eikon basilike* nevertheless did everything they could to prevent it. At the treaty of Newport in the autumn of 1648 and in the final days prior to the king's trial they sought an accommodation with their English opponents in order to save the king's life. Right up until the trial, they deemed publication of the *Eikon* imprudent, fearing lest its forthright rhetoric compromise these last-ditch efforts to save the king and his crown. As I have argued elsewhere, even during the trial attempts were made to reach an accommodation. At this critical juncture, publication of the *Eikon* was finally undertaken, partly as an integral element in the king's negotiating strategy and partly as a form of insurance against the prospect of its failure. The book put in place a set of principles bearing regal imprimatur to which the king's heir might be committed in the event of his father's death and his own succession. *Eikon basilike* was not just the personal testimony of Charles I, but also a skilful gambit in the struggle among partisans of the house of Stuart to help establish and obtain influence over the policy and patronage of his successor. *Eikon basilike* was a book about both the once *and* the future king of England. It was 'the kings' book'.

In essence, it was a book which sought to undermine the case for rebuilding the royalist cause in Scotland, as many of those closest to the prince of Wales, his mother included, would willingly have done, while helping to underpin the case for seeking to revive the interests of the house of Stuart in Ireland instead, a strategy which would place the authority of the English crown and the episcopal Church of England in far less danger than would the conscious resolve to make Charles II a Scottish 'king of presbytery'. This interpretation complicates somewhat the nature of the relationship between *Eikon basilike* and its audience, appreciation of which has been confined hitherto almost entirely to the realm of poetry, aesthetics and prayer. Far from 'timeless', *Eikon basilike* remained relevant only as long as Ireland remained viable as a base for Stuart operations. Thereafter, the emotional authority of the *Eikon* as the personal testimony of a martyr became a particularly heavy burden for a successor who had betrayed so much of his father's extraordinary sacrifice within eighteen months of his own accession. It has been argued that, on publication in 1649, *Eikon basilike* instantly became 'the holy book of royalist politics'.[3] In common with so much holy writ, it was honoured far more in the breach than the observance.

Famously, from the moment of its first publication authorship of the *Eikon* provoked a controversy which epitomises the crisis of truth-telling identified by Michael Braddick as one of the legacies of the English Revolution. It is now universally accepted that the book was a work of collaboration in which the king's own writings, dating from the period of his residence at Holdenby House and Hampton Court in 1647, provided the source material for a finished text compiled and edited very largely by the cleric John Gauden, then finally revised, at least in part, by the king himself.[4] Numerous scholars have asked what purpose the *Eikon* was intended to serve. Many have treated it as a means of maximising sympathy for the late king and his cause in the aftermath of regicide. But, noting its 'active purpose', others have concluded that it was probably intended to influence public opinion in favour of the king during the crisis of 1648–49, a propaganda device which was eventually overtaken by events. The book's original title – *Suspiria regalia*, meaning either 'the royal sigh' or 'plea' – suggests the public presentation of the king's case truly stated. However, the known facts surrounding the book's publication indicate more complex motives.

Gauden had evidently completed his own first draft by the end of May 1648, when he showed it to Arthur Lord Capel, who approved it but advised that Gauden show it to the king before publishing.[5] Gauden's volume was probably not brought to the king's attention before the middle of September, but by early October the publisher Richard Royston had been put on notice to receive the manuscript of the *Eikon*. However, Royston had still not taken delivery of it by the time the treaty of Newport ended, eight weeks later. Another four weeks passed before he received the manuscript, on Christmas Eve 1648. The proofs were ready possibly by mid-January. Accounts are inconsistent but it is possible that an unsuccessful attempt to publish was made shortly thereafter. It is also possible that a first impression of the book was in fact printed but kept under wraps. For whatever reason, *Eikon basilike* would not see the light of day until Charles I himself was dead (the first 'advance' copies going into circulation on the very day of his execution). A comparison between the text and the conduct of its authors, editors and publishers helps to explain why publication was delayed for so long.

Eikon basilike is a book full of ambiguity. This is hardly surprising, given the complexity of its creation, over a period of years, during different stages in its principal author's life, and subject to several phases of editorial intervention. The central theme of *Eikon basilike* – Charles I's conscience and his struggle to act in accordance with its dictates – perforce exposed the ambivalences of the king's spiritual assurance and the concern that pride or vanity might deceive him.[6] However, the text is dominated by certain propositions which lay at the heart of the king's conception of his conscientious duty, about which he entertained very little doubt.

Principal among those propositions were unshakable commitments to the rights and authority of the crown of England and a fundamentalist's devotion to episcopacy and the property rights of the English church. These central tenets of the king's personal credo also manifested themselves in negative form as an equally passionate loathing for strict presbyterianism and its populist, covenant-engaged advocates. In the *Eikon*, Charles acknowledged that true regal strength lay in the rule of law laid down by parliament; repeatedly indicated a willingness to entertain suggestions for the reform of faults which had crept into the Church of England; and even accepted that there was an important role for presbyters therein. But the king remained utterly intransigent in his devotion to the principles of crown sovereignty, the supremacy of episcopal authority and the property rights of the established church, principles for which he professed himself willing to lay down his own life. All throughout he also remained positively contemptuous of the covenanted, populist cliques in England and Scotland on whom he pinned the blame for all his, and his people's, miseries. In his narrative account of the 1640s, the king repeatedly denounced the 'factious combinations' of opportunists who had whipped up 'violent tumults' in the City and at Westminster to their own detestable ends, using religion as a cover for treason – thus employing the stock imagery which had formed the basis of court-backed electioneering in 1640.[7]

At every stage in the process of the book's composition, editing and publication there was good reason why it might have been deemed inadvisable for the king to advertise to the world, by publishing the *Eikon*, the inflexibility with which he held to some or all of those views. At the time Gauden's first draft was being pieced together, Charles himself, the faction of royalists known as the 'Louvre group' – centred on the queen and her chief advisors, Lords Jermyn and Culpeper – and even a significant minority of English parliamentarians were pinning their hopes for the revival of the king's fortunes on the Scots' army of the Covenant commanded by James, duke of Hamilton, with whom Charles had entered into secret agreement in December 1647. The chances of a successful Scottish intervention were undermined by the refusal of Archibald Campbell, marquis of Argyle, and his supporters to back Hamilton's 'engagement' with the English king, on the grounds that Charles had no intention whatever of honouring his undertaking to settle the English Church in accordance with the Covenant. Hamilton's position would not have been helped if Gauden had published the *Eikon* as soon as it was finished. For Gauden's text reverberated with invective which might have been calculated to compromise those attempting to raise Scotland on the king's behalf, and to alienate those Scottified Presbyterians at Westminster and in London who looked to Hamilton for protection from the sectarian New Model Army.[8]

Eikon basilike makes crystalline the king's intense resentment of his treatment at the hands of his Scottish countrymen since 1637, and especially their betrayal of him into the hands of the English parliament in 1647. He did admit that 'my best subjects of Scotland never deserted me', and a majority never went so far from him 'as to make me despair of their return'.[9] But in the *Eikon* the king described the Covenant as an instrument cynically exploited by a faction of Scots to grab and hold on to power 'under the disguises of holy combinations', a faction whose chief design was laid against himself and, above all, the church.[10] Charles particularly detested the Covenanters' zealous compulsion to refashion the Church of England to a wholly inappropriate presbyterian design, especially when that which was hailed as the true object of reformation was a system of church government which had 'too much of man in it to have much of Christ, none of whose institutions were carried on or begun with the temptations of covetousness or ambition, of both which this is vehemently suspected'.[11]

Received wisdom describes the editor of the king's manuscript, John Gauden, as himself a Presbyterian, but there is no adequate evidence for that assertion, and his intimate involvement in the publication of the *Eikon* makes it very hard to believe.[12] In pamphlets published in 1659 and 1661, Gauden himself claimed that he had been a member of the Westminster assembly of divines. In any case, he also claimed that he had been ousted for supporting the reform, rather than the abolition, of episcopacy, while neither his membership nor his ejection is substantiated by the assembly's own records. We know that by the mid-1650s Gauden had begun openly to advocate a primitive model of episcopalian church government. But all that can be said with any confidence about his beliefs prior to that period is that he retained his position as dean of Bocking in Essex by taking the Covenant and conforming to the Directory of Worship.[13] Well might he conform. His living, which he owed to the personal patronage of the earl of Warwick, was one of the most valuable in England, reputedly worth very much more than the £230 per annum at which it was nominally valued.[14]

We do not know whether Gauden himself supported the policy of 'engagement', but it may be revealing that in late May 1648 he chose to show his manuscript to his neighbour Arthur Lord Capel who is known to have shared Sir Edward Hyde's detestation of the Louvre group.[15] In 1648, Capel had been commissioned by the prince of Wales to raise fresh rebellion in England in support of the anticipated Scottish invasion. Presumably Capel recognised the danger of publishing an anti-Covenanter diatribe on the eve of a desperate venture whose slender hopes of success depended almost entirely on Scottish arms and growing Presbyterian disaffection with the parliamentarian regime in England. Certainly he counselled Gauden not to go into print before the king had an opportunity to inspect the manuscript. Once the war of the engagement had fizzled out, and a new round of peace talks between the king and the English parliament got underway, *Eikon basilike* remained in manuscript form for very similar reasons – the king's clear and unequivocal enunciation of his principled convictions would have compromised the efforts he made during the last months of his life to reach an accommodation with his rebellious English subjects. By then Charles was prepared to stake all on the efforts of James Butler, marquis of Ormond, to raise a fresh army in Ireland.[16] He concluded that in the meantime his best hope lay in keeping his English opponents talking, even if that meant the temporary abandonment of the moral high ground which he had spent so much time surveying during the long months of capitivity in 1647.

By the time the treaty of Newport began, the prospects for a peaceful accommodation between king and the English parliament had devolved to the leadership of an uneasy coalition of 'royal Independents' and Erastian Presbyterians at Westminster. Their only hope of conjuring a consensus from the fragments of the parliamentarian cause depended on extracting the king's consent to the abolition of episcopacy, the establishment of presbytery and the sale of the bishops' lands.[17] The parliamentary commissioners sent to Newport had some limited freedom to entertain concessions, but there was little they could do to moderate these key demands, as hard as they might strive to make them seem less unpalatable. Suffering much heartache along the way, Charles slowly edged towards the commissioners, surrendering the entire ecclesiastical hierarchy save for bishops, conceding legislation for the resumption to the crown of legal title to all church lands and, eventually, offering the indefinite suspension of episcopal jurisdiction.[18]

Although it took the threat of a military coup at Westminster to force his hand, before the commissioners left the Isle of Wight on 28 November the king had finally conceded either the letter or the spirit of all their key demands. Unsurprisingly, as they whittled away at the precious stock of principles which had sustained the royalist cause, the king and his advisors were in no rush to publish the manuscript, which had come to their hands as the treaty got started. To commit the book to print at that sensitive moment would have served only to jeopardise the revival of political fortunes which the king's concessions were intended to secure. Several factors rendered *Eikon basilike* inappropriate to the moment, not the least of which was the rather striking contrast between the king's attitude towards the populist Presbyterian clique dominant in England, whom he held in such deep scorn, and the men of the parliamentarian army who had defeated his own forces in battle. He had no illusions about the men who had seized him in June 1647. But he was surprisingly warmly disposed towards his former adversaries in arms, and even went so far as to envisage a settlement which had at its heart the satisfaction of such great patriots as these his old foes and conquerors.[19]

As the king edged himself into a tactical alignment with Presbyterian opinion, he had had little to gain from publishing kind words for the army. Neither was there much wisdom in publishing a book which mounted so determined a defence of the established ecclesiastical order while vehemently denouncing the Covenanters and all their works. In the *Eikon*, the king explained that his coronation oath solemnly bound him to preserve episcopacy, and that to be forced to break that oath would be an 'infinitely greater misery than any hath or can befall me'.[20] By the close of the treaty of Newport, the king had agreed that all episcopal jurisdiction should remain suspended until such time as he and parliament agreed on an alternative, and he told the parliamentarian commissioners that 'the Desire of satisfying his Houses, had made him strayne so far, yea, to slyde by some Things which pertained very much to Conscience'.[21] During the Commons debate on his final answers, Nathaniel Fiennes argued that the king had 'granted all in effect that was desired, and intended not to set up Bishops again, except his Houses at the three years end did agree to it; which amounts to as much as putting them down for ever'.[22] Given that they eventually voted that the king's answers provided grounds for peaceful settlement, a significant majority of his fellow MPs – including arch-Presbyterian William Prynne – clearly wished to believe that Fiennes was right. Yet had the *Eikon* been published while the treaty still held, Fiennes could not possibly have said what he did, nor could Prynne have agreed with him if he had.

If *Eikon basilike* had been published during the treaty the king would not have been able to make a number of other key religious concessions to which he submitted at Newport. In the *Eikon* he had roundly dismissed the Westminster Assembly as illegal, factious, hypocritical, perjured and unrepresentative.[23] He had denounced the Directory of Worship, as well as the assumption that extemporary prayer was any less prone to formality, or any more conducive to piety than the Prayer Book liturgy.[24] Indeed, he had even condemned *de jure* presbyterianism as morally corrupt, intellectually bankrupt and spiritually blank. Yet at Newport he agreed the retrospective approval of the Westminster Assembly's endeavours since 1643, the temporary establishment of the form of worship it had devised and even the proscription of his beloved Prayer Book throughout his dominions, his own court and household included. In the *Eikon*, the king also thanked God for preserving him from the temptation to use his prerogative power to expropriate the churchmen and resume their lands to the use of the crown.[25] By the end of the treaty, the king had accepted that church lands be restored to the crown by act of parliament to hold on trust for the clergy prior to granting ninety-nine-year leases to their purchasers. Of course, Charles had not doubted, even for a moment, the truth of his convictions. His concessions at Newport were intended for no other purpose than to regain the ground from which to vindicate the church and its rights as soon as he was able. But if *Eikon basilike* had been published while he was making his tactical concessions, the effect – which was limited in any case – would have been entirely ruined.[26]

As the king explained to his son, the councillors and divines advising him at Newport had helped him find the resolve to grant away so much, persuading him that in respect of the church, for example, 'the order which we endeavoured to be preserved was more likely to be destroyed by our not complying, than by our suspending it till we and our two Houses agreed on a future Government, which was conceived much differing from abolition'.[27] It is notable that chief among those counselling compromise at Newport were individuals also intimately involved with the final stages of preparing the *Eikon*. Two of them were privy councillors – the marquis of Hertford and the earl of Southampton – one or other of whom had been instrumental in passing Gauden's manuscript of the *Eikon* to the king.[28] Determined to save their royal master if they could, both were subsequently party to the so-called 'Richmond mission' of January 1649 which was intended to avert public proceedings against the king by offering terms for his capitulation.[29] The king eventually received the manuscript of the *Eikon* from the hands of – and indeed first had excerpts from it read to him by – Brian Duppa, bishop of Salisbury. More closely involved in the project of the kings' book than anyone other than John Gauden and Richard Royston, credited with writing two of its chapters himself and responsible for sending the manuscript safely to the publisher, Duppa had once already, in 1646, sanctioned the king's temporary suspension of episcopacy if it helped him to regain the political power with which he might one day fully vindicate and restore episcopal authority.[30] At Newport Duppa was not only one of those who counselled the king once again that he was justified in suspending episcopacy in order to preserve it in the long run, but it was also reported that he and William Juxon, bishop of London, had gone down on their knees to beg that the king yield to the alienation of episcopal lands, 'rather then bring any future hazard upon his Person and People'.[31]

The failure of the treaty of Newport ended any requirement that the king openly court Presbyterian opinion, making it possible to print *Eikon basilike*. However, it is clear that neither the king nor his closest advisors yet believed the game to be up. In the *Eikon*, the king had remarked that his being seized at Holdenby 'tells the world that a king cannot be so low but he is considerable, adding weight to that party where he appears'.[32] Similar thinking is said to have informed his decision not to flee the army in December 1648 when he had the chance.[33] Believing that there was everything still to play for, Charles and his advisors kept the *Eikon* under wraps. Power now lay with the military and those of the Independents who supported it. As we have already seen, in the pages of the *Eikon* itself the king had entertained the prospect of accommodation with the army far more willingly than he could ever have contemplated a compromise with Presbyterians.[34] He also noted that such staunch supporters of freedom of conscience could not in reason restrict his own in the way the Presbyterians would have done.[35] Yet the *Eikon* still offered too many hostages to fortune, and its publication would have closed off too many avenues down which there might yet transpire a route back to the throne of England, and thence to power. In the meantime, there remained little to be gained from making public such an excoriating attack on presbyterianism when pressure from the Scots and their English supporters might actually help to increase the king's chances of striking a deal with the army and the Independents. All that changed with the Commons' appointment of a committee to legislate for the king's trial on 23 December – the before day Royston finally took receipt of the manuscript. But the decision to go into print did not mark the point of no return for the king.

Even after the collapse of the treaty of Newport, several key individuals connected with the composition and publication of *Eikon basilike* continued to search for an accommodation which would preserve Charles I. Even while Duppa was finally sending the corrected version of Gauden's manuscript to the publisher, Richard Royston, the royal chaplain, Jeremy Taylor, would argue passionately, in the face of the overt disgust of his fellow churchmen, that the king was entitled to grant away episcopal estates if that was the price of his life.[36] Back in 1647, Taylor had played a part in efforts to find common ground on which the king might reach an agreement with the army and its sectarian supporters, notably developing a case for religious toleration, said to have been influenced by William Chillingworth.[37] There is no evidence to link Taylor with the king's intimate counsels in the winter of 1648–49, as once again thoughts turned to the possibility of an accommodation with Independent interests. His private musings at this sensitive moment on the king's right, even his duty to expropriate the church for the sake of his own crown, stand in stark contrast with the solemn undertakings given by the king in the manuscript that Royston would shortly print. But this is all the more remarkable as it is Taylor himself who has always been credited with correcting the proofs of the book, and even devising the title under which *Eikon basilike* would attain everlasting fame.[38]

Early in January, John Gauden himself contributed to the concerted effort to create a dialogue between the king and the army, appearing before the council of officers at Whitehall (ostensibly at the invitation of one among them) to plead the case for saving the king's life.[39] The text of his supplication was subsequently printed by Richard Royston, the original publisher of the *Eikon*, who also undertook around that time to print a sermon by another royalist divine favoured by the king, Henry Hammond, in which it was argued that all forms of church government had co-existed in the early days of Christianity, so that none could claim to exist *jure divino*, 'we having no absolute Precept herein, for all men must . . . by the best Reason and revealed light we can, compose things according to our present estates, as we doe in Civill Affaires'.[40] But of all those involved in the publication of *Eikon basilike* who laboured to promote a rapprochement between the king and his captors, the man who did the most was undoubtedly the book's principal author. Charles invited leading Independent divines to discuss points of conscience with him during his final few days at Windsor in mid-January. The day public sessions of his trial commenced, 20 January, the Commons even granted the king's express wish to receive the further ministrations of the bishop of London with a view to settling certain conscientious concerns. By then, such was Juxon's track record as the king's 'conscientious unremembrancer' that the royal request could have been readily interpreted as an invitation to treat.[41]

For the king at least, perhaps the moment had not quite come proudly to hold forth 'I know no resolutions more worthy a Christian king, than to prefer his conscience before his kingdoms.'[42] Once the game was afoot in the great hall at Westminster, the king's finely nuanced performance could only be upstaged by the publication of his claim: 'I would rather choose to wear a crown of thorns with my Saviour, than to exchange that of gold, which is due to me, for one of lead, whose embased flexibleness shall be forced to bend and comply to the various and oft contrary dictates of any factions.'[43] The alchemical transformation of his crown from gold to lead was the final trick up the king's sleeve, and he saw no reason why he should yet forego it.[44] Charles had himself never shown any interest in publishing the *Eikon* under his own name. It is possible that the decision to publish was not his at all, a decision taken by men willing to see the king reach a settlement, but unwilling to see him do so without first 'fixing his negatives' for him.[45]

All the book's main contrivers and abettors, including its principal author, were involved in attempts to prolong the reign of Charles I. But *Eikon basilike* was not devised just as a means of influencing public opinion in the king's favour. It was intended also as the means of inaugurating a martyr cult in the event of his execution. It was more than just 'the king's book': it was also the prince's. If it was a work of spiritual meditation through which the king reconciled himself with the possibility of a martyr's death, then it was also a medium through which some of the king's supporters prepared for the accession of his heir, in the event that their efforts to save the king failed. For all its reflections on the history of the martyr king's own troubles, *Eikon basilike* also incorporated a programme for the future, a programme with all the added authority of a deathbed testimonial.[46] Whatever else the world at large might make of them, these were words which were supposed to weigh particularly heavily on the dead man's eldest son and heir. 'The kings' book' presented to the world a selective image of Charles I in the hope of restricting Charles II to a course of action at the outset of his reign which might honour his father's sainted memory. *Eikon basilike* was not just a work of private meditation, but was also a book of counsel deeply implicated in the factional conflicts which had beset English royalism for years, and which now entered a new and more dramatic phase at this crucial moment of transition.

If the book's contrivers and abettors did more than most to seek to preserve the king, their role in writing, compiling, editing and publishing the manuscript of the *Eikon* nevertheless demonstrates just how little commitment they felt to the search for peaceful accommodation with the English parliament. From their point of view, getting Charles I back on the throne, even as the captive of his English opponents, was evidently preferable to the succession of a king over the water who, although safe, was dangerously exposed to the influence of his mother and her advisors, and their treacherous Scottish friends. Those who fashioned the *Eikon* would have preferred to reach an accommodation with the leaders of the army and the English Independents than with the hated Presbyterians. On the other hand, the book's attitude towards the rebels in Scotland contrasts markedly with the king's opinion of his Catholic Irish subjects. This places *Eikon basilike* firmly on one side of the emergent argument within royalism regarding the relative virtues of two markedly contrasting strategies for restoring the fortunes of the Stuart dynasty.

The policy of engagement had incorporated both Scottish and Irish limbs.[47] The catastrophic failure of that policy dissolved the British coalition into its constituent elements. Royalists were now forced to choose between two irreconcilable strategies.[48] On one side were those who believed that the best hopes for reviving the fortunes of the house of Stuart lay in a military alliance with the confederate Catholics of Ireland (supported by the efforts of the marquis of Montrose to raise forces in the Scottish Highlands and on the Continent), while on the other there stood those who, even after the collapse of the 'engagement', would still have preferred to reach an agreement with elements within the uneasy coalition of Covenanters which held sway at Edinburgh.

Eikon basilike drips with venomous contempt for covenanted presbyterianism and consistently advertises the king's intense resentment of his treatment at the hands of his countrymen. The tone he adopted throughout the book also indicates that he was considerably more warmly disposed towards his Catholic subjects of Ireland as well as those of his Scottish subjects – such as Montrose – who had repented of their initial disloyalty. The king's reflections on the causes of the Irish rebellion appear to have offered sufficient grounds from which to justify the peace talks between the marquis of Ormond and the confederate Catholics on whom the king had pinned his last military hopes. In the *Eikon* it is argued that it was 'the preposterous rigour and unreasonable severity' of some in England which sparked the rebellion in Ireland, 'which wanted not predisposed fuel . . . where despair being added to their former discontents, and the fears of utter extirpation to their wonted oppressions, it was easy to provoke to an open rebellion'. The king effectively blamed the catastrophic spread of the Ulster insurgency on the actions of those 'who think it a great argument of the truth of their religion to endure no other but their own' against those whose religious beliefs and 'natural desires for liberty' made them 'prone enough to break out to all exorbitant violence'. He did not deny that such violence was wrong, but argued that 'next to the sin of those who began that rebellion, theirs must needs be, who either hindered the speedy suppressing of it by domestic dissensions, or diverted the aids, or exasperated the rebels to the most desperate resolutions and actions' by the extremity of their response, 'resolving to destroy' that whole nation.[49]

The king defended the cessation of 1643 as the only way the protestant remnant could save themselves, and also justified his negotiation for Catholic assistance in Ireland.[50]

While tacitly blessing the prospect of a second Ormond peace, *Eikon basilike* made perfectly clear that a deal with Presbyterians was not admissible. In chapter 27 the king addressed the prince of Wales on his duties and responsibilities in the event of his succession, a crucial piece of propaganda for the new reign which was often printed as a separate, or offprint.[51] The king's position was absolutely unequivocal:

> Above all I would have you, as I hope you are already, well grounded and settled in your religion, the best profession of which I have ever esteemed that of the Church of England, in which you have been educated . . . In this I charge you to perservere, as coming nearest to God's word for doctrine and to the primitive examples for government.[52]

The point was rammed home: 'I do require and entreat you, as your father and your King, that you never suffer your heart to receive the least check against or disaffection from the true religion established in the Church of England . . . the best in the world'.[53]

Several editions of *Eikon basilike* were printed in 1649 which incorporated certain 'appendices', most notably the so-called Henderson papers, setting out the king's undying opposition to a Presbyterian church settlement, further suggesting that the book was devised specifically as a piece of propaganda which aimed to influence royalist opinion and to stave off any prospect of an alliance with the Scottish Presbyterians.

All this gives rise to crucial questions about exactly how both the prince and those around him saw his responsibilities in the winter of 1648–49, and the fact is that since the preceding summer Charles had been living up to the standards of the *Eikon* just as badly as had his father. Hyde later recorded that the prince, always prone to listen more attentively to his mother's counsels than anyone else's, had shown himself willing to align with the pro-Scots strategy of Lord Culpeper and Secretary Long, even before the mutiny in the English fleet in the spring of 1648 gifted him the means to put it into action by sailing north. In the middle of August, the earl of Lauderdale came to the royalist fleet riding in the Downs to urge the prince of Wales to come to the head of Hamilton's army. Culpeper persuaded the prince to promise that on doing so he would worship according to the Scottish liturgy and Covenant, and also abandon some of his closest friends, Prince Rupert included, proscribed by a majority of the pro-engagement faction then dominant at Edinburgh.[54]

The prince's counsels were sharply divided at this time over the relative merits of a Scottish or an Irish strategy, with the likes of Lords Cottington, Hopton and Gerrard, and Sir Edward Hyde all vigorously opposing the line adopted by Culpeper and supported by Lords Percy, Willoughby and Wilmot. The failure of the engagement helped shift the balance back towards the strategy of the west.

The 'wholly Scots' Lord Willoughby gave up his command of the royalist navy, which was taken over by Prince Rupert, who began to make preparations to sail for Ireland. But in the winter of 1648–49 there remained a strong Presbyterian influence in royalist counsels, an influence which consistently acted as a check on any active pursuit of an Irish policy. Writing on the last day of October, Sir Ralph Verney was informed from Paris that 'the Scotts say if the King will take the Covenant, they will come into England againe with a stronger Armye then formerly'.[55] To Hyde's irritation, news of the army's *Remonstrance* and the collapse of the Newport treaty served at the Hague 'only to proove that wee must make hast to joyne with the Presbiterians, so that the discourse of Scotland is agayne on foote', and the prince himself became less resolved than he had been to go west.[56] In a letter written from the Hague on 10 January, it was reported that the 'Royal English party here are biding in their hopes, that they shal possible [*sic*] thrive better under a new king, which is, now they say, making way for at Edenburg, by those gon hence'.[57]

Even as Ormond finally concluded his negotiation with the confederate Catholics in Ireland, the northerly drift of royalist strategy gathered momentum. The Whiggamore regime and the kirk had made their first approaches to the prince within weeks of establishing their ascendancy at Edinburgh, and by early December, representatives of the marquis of Argyle were offering to raise an army of 20,000 to vindicate the rights of the king in England.[58] Crucial was the developing rapprochement between Argyle and the former 'engagers' John Maitland, earl of Lauderdale, and William Hamilton, earl of Lanark.[59] Early in January it was reported that Lauderdale had entered the prince's privy council; another leading engager, the earl of Callander, and Sir William Fleming, 'who also ingaged deeply to set Scotland anew in flames', were also at the Hague, as was 'one Mongomery who was sent from Lord Lanerick, also one Carmichell, who brought a Letter from the Committee of Estates to the Prince of Wales'.[60] Callander and Lauderdale appear to have returned to Scotland around mid-January, 'by which it seems more clear they were Agents there'.[61] On 6 January, in the House of Commons, 'letters were read from Holland, advertizing the House, that the Earl of Letherdale, and other Scots were with the English with Prince Charles, And that the Scots have Agents there, and that there are preparations still against England'.

There were also rumours that German and Swedish soldiers would be sent to invade England, 'wherein the Scots are principall Negotiators'.[62] This may be a reference to efforts made by James Graham, marquis of Montrose, to raise levies using the title of 'field marshal' recently granted him by the holy Roman emperor.[63] It is clear that royalists had not yet sunk so low as to contemplate an alliance with hardcore Covenanters, Hyde for instance reporting that the Scots 'are now so weary of my Lord of Argyle, that if the Prince will come to them, he shall have an army ready to conquer the world'.[64] Yet it is also notable that the prince's advisors declined any public concourse with Montrose at this time for fear of the damage it might do him in the eyes of the Covenanters who wished for an alliance with the king but who fought shy of any taint of malignancy.[65] And from Edinburgh it was reported on 30 January that 'if the Prince of Wales declare for Presbytery, we shall cast good looks upon him, which that he may, here are many good wishes'.[66]

In the winter of 1648–49 the Stuarts were obviously in no position to turn their backs decisively on any source of desperately needed help. But there was plenty of evidence to suggest the emergence of a new understanding between the court of Prince Charles and Scottish interests. One consequence of this was disruption to the formulation of a clear policy favouring the Irish along with the projects of Montrose, regardless of where the prince of Wales' own personal preferences may have lain. This was the immediate political context in which *Eikon basilike* was published. Although there exists no clear evidence in support of such an interpretation, it is extremely difficult not to read the book as an extended sermon on the perils of an alliance with Scottish Covenanters and, if only by implication, the relative merits of the alternative Irish strategy. Addressing his son and heir directly in chapter 27 of *Eikon basilike*, the king said that, if needs be, 'I hope God will give me and you that grace which will teach and enable us to want as well as to wear a crown, which is not worth taking up or enjoying upon sordid, dishonourable and irreligious terms'.[67] This seems to bear directly on the prospect that the Scots might crown themselves a new king if the lucky recipient might bend to their 'sordid, dishonourable and irreligious terms'. However, many of those who read this solemn admonition must have been struck forcibly by the gaping chasm between the martyr king's words and the living image which his actions had presented in the last few weeks and months of his life and reign. For instance, as they had watched the progress of the English Presbyterians' talks with the king in the autumn of 1648, many of the king's most prominent and influential supporters – including his lord lieutenant of Ireland, his chancellor of the exchequer and one of his secretaries of state – were shocked to see the king giving away both crown and church in order to cling on to his throne.[68]

After such a performance, it is questionable, perhaps, whether *Eikon basilike* could really have had the moral authority with which it is often credited. Certainly Charles II could be forgiven if his dead father's stern advice had gone in one ear and straight out the other. Barely four months after the execution of Charles I his heir entered abortive talks with the Edinburgh regime. The new king may have found the Scots' overtures repellent, and his own true preferences may well have lain with the policy of the west, whither he eventually departed Holland in June.[69] But it took him five months to take that step not least because his only hope of financial support rested with his host in the United Provinces, his brother-in-law William II, prince of Orange, who continued enthusiastically to promote a presbyterian alliance as part of a dynastic policy involving the marriage of one of his sisters to the new king of Scotland.[70] Equally significantly, Henrietta Maria and her counsellors had made their own support for an Irish policy conditional on a hearing given to the commissioners sent to The Hague by Argyle. This blatant blocking tactic was a source of frustration to those who fervently wished that the young king might join the lord lieutenant at the head of the new Irish army as quickly as possible.[71] Charles lost his opportunity to strike, and set out for Ireland, only to tarry at St Germains all summer. He eventually arrived at Jersey in September. That was as far as he got. Ormond's defeat at Rathmines, and Cromwell's landfall shortly afterwards, had buried the king's prospects in Ireland. Contact was resumed with Argyle's representatives in January 1650, concluding with the treaties of Breda and Heligoland six months later. Charles II had bowed to become a king of presbytery, and on 1 January 1651, he took the Covenant and was crowned in Edinburgh.

The *Eikon*'s vigorous defence of the rights of the Church of England rapidly became an embarrassing reminder of the martyr king's betrayal by his own son and heir. Unable to endure the prospect of a restoration achieved by Scottish arms, many royalists were left with little alternative but to reach an accommodation to new realities in England. Driven as many may have been by the memory of the martyr king's vehement hatred for the Scots Covenanters, ironically it is perfectly possible that *Eikon basilike* made its own powerful contribution to the disaster which befell Charles II at Worcester in 1651. Nine years later, the declaration of Breda skilfully laid the groundwork for a Stuart restoration which had seemed all but impossible even a few short months earlier.

Contrived as the king's return was in collaboration with Presbyterian factions in London, Edinburgh and Dublin, *Eikon basilike* remained an embarrassment. Its publication did not resume until the forcible establishment of an Anglican church got fully under way in 1662. Central to the violent loyalist backlash that now took hold in England, the beatification of Charles I was a development which once again compromised Charles II, undermining his own preference for ecclesiastical 'comprehension', and it is notable just how complicit he was in attempts to call in question the authorship and undermine the credibility of the *Eikon*.[72] Charles II was not the only one who found it difficult to handle his father's ghost and the legacy of the Revolution which had destroyed him. *Eikon basilike*, and its attendant authorship controversy, contributed powerfully to the growing crisis of representation that beset the political discourse of the age.[73] Contemporaries vigorously contested the authenticity of the *Eikon*. The pious authority, or else the fraudulent mendacity of the 'king's book' soon became articles of faith on either side of the political divide.

Eikon basilike was written, compiled, edited and published by a group of statesmen, clerics and politicians – the 'Eikonographers' for short – who were prepared to ignore its central tenets in the course of making strenuous efforts to save the life and prolong the reign of Charles I for fear of something worse. The book was prepared in the meantime with the aim of influencing the policy and patronage of the king's successor if they did not succeed in their primary objective. As at least one contemporary observed, the sanctification of their views by association with royal martyrdom was perhaps their best hope of exercising at least some influence over Charles II, should the crown pass to him.[74] The earl of Southampton had been appointed privy councillor to the prince in 1645, while the king had charged Duppa with the spiritual education of his eldest son around the same time.[75] But in the winter of 1648–49, ensconced across the Channel, the prince seemed far more susceptible to the promptings of his mother and her advisors, and the Scotsmen crowding his court, than was strictly consonant with safeguarding the interests of the crown and the Church of England. If in the interests of an accommodation with the English parliament the Eikonographers might contemplate the king's own temporary betrayal of crown and church with pragmatic resignation, they regarded with alarm the prospect of their alienation into the hands of Scots Presbyterians at the behest of French Catholic interests.

This is certainly not to suggest that the Louvre group was any more sincere in the concessions it was willing to make to Presbyterians than the late king had been, at the time of either the engagement or the treaty of Newport. But their inclination to seek aid in Scotland was a direct challenge to both the beliefs and the authority of one group of royalist counsellors, as well as their influence over the heir to the throne of three kingdoms.[76] It also threatened to undermine the efforts of the marquis of Ormond to re-arm the Stuart cause by forging a military alliance in Ireland. While working hard themselves to resist regicide, the Eikonographers prepared their response to that prospect by simplifying the king's complex and multi-faceted character to a pattern dictated by their own political and ecclesiastical preferences. They depicted him as the implacable defender of an episcopal Church of England who would die to protect it from the presbyterian wolf – a construction which reality was perfectly capable of supporting, but a narrow and selective one nonetheless.[77] They did so partly in order to be able, if and when the need arose, to persuade the successor to the crowns of England, Scotland and Ireland that his best interests, and those of the monarchy itself, the church and their supporters lay not in the north of his dominions, but in the west.

However triumphant its poetic achievement in the long run, however transcendent, sublime or eternal, in the short run *Eikon basilike* was mired in royalist politics and overtaken by events. The book's passionate implication in the partisan struggles which rent post-revolutionary royalism highlights some of the inadequacies in existing discussions of royalist propaganda which neglect the sharp divisions among supporters of the Stuarts and the intense mutual loathing of which they were capable.[78] Were the *Eikon* ever to be judged by its immediate objectives, it would be deemed to have failed. Its power did not last long enough to prevent Charles II from entering a humiliating alliance with the Presbyterian regime in Edinburgh. But with its calculated appeal to English Prayer Book protestantism and its spirited defence of the liturgy and hierarchy of the Church of England, *Eikon basilike* enlisted an audience and conjured a body of opinion so massive that it helped to undermine both this and every subsequent attempt by the new king to derogate, even temporarily (and however insincerely), from the privileges of the Anglican episcopalian establishment.

Notes

1 L. Potter, *Secret rites and secret writing: royalist literature, 1641–1660* (Cambridge, 1989), 160–2; E. Skerpan, *The rhetoric of politics in the English revolution, 1642–1660* (Columbia, 1992), 107–9; T. Corns, *Uncloistered virtue: English political literature, 1640–1660* (Oxford, 1992), 209; S. N. Zwicker, *Lines of authority: politics and English literary culture, 1649–1689* (Ithaca, NY, and London, 1993), 37–59 and generally; K. Sharpe, 'The king's writ', in K. Sharpe and P. Lake (eds), *Politics and culture in early Stuart England* (London, 1993), 117–38; E. S. Wheeler, '*Eikon basilike* and the rhetoric of self-representation', in T. N. Corns (ed.), *The royal image: representations of Charles I* (Cambridge, 1999), 122–40; R. Wilcher, *The writing of royalism, 1628–1660* (Cambridge, 2001); A. Lacey, *The cult of King Charles the martyr* (Woodbridge, 2003).

2 Potter, *Secret rites and secret writing*, 171.

3 Zwicker, *Lines of authority*, 37.

4 F. F. Madan, *A new bibliography of the Eikon basilike of King Charles the First* (Oxford, 1950 [1949]), Appendix 1, 126–63.

5 *Eikon basilike*, ed. P. A. Knachel (Ithaca, NY, 1966), 'Introduction', xxx–ii.

6 See, for example, *Eikon basilike* (1876) (hereafter *EB*), 70, 72.

7 See pp. 47–9 above.

8 D. Scott, *Politics and war in the three Stuart kingdoms, 1637–1649* (Basingstoke, 2003), ch. 6.

9 *EB*, 88.

10 *Ibid.*, 91ff.

11 *Ibid.*, 83–5.

12 *Eikon basilike*, ed. Knachel, xxvii; Wheeler, '*Eikon basilike* and the rhetoric of self-representation', 124 and note.

13 W. A. Shaw, *A history of the English church during the civil wars and under the commonwealth, 1640–1660*, 2 vols (London, 1900), ii. 387; R. S. Bosher, *The making of the restoration settlement: the influence of the Laudians, 1649–1662* (Oxford, 1951), 27–8; *Complete prose works of John Milton*, ed. R. W. Ayers and A. Woolrych, 8 vols (New Haven, CT, 1974), vii. 35; R. Hutton, *The restoration: a political and religious history of England and Wales, 1658–1667* (Oxford, 1993), 143–4; J. Spurr, *The restoration church of England, 1646–1689* (New Haven, CT, and London, 1991), 26, 32; see also H. Smith, *The ecclesiastical history of Essex during the long parliament and commonwealth* (Colchester, nd [1932]).

14 B. Donagan, 'The clerical patronage of Robert Rich, second earl of Warwick, 1619–1642', *Proceedings of the American Philosophical Society*, 120 (1976), 388–419, especially 393, 402.

15 E. Hyde, earl of Clarendon, *The history of the rebellion and civil wars in England*, ed. W. D. A. Macray, 6 vols (Oxford, 1888), iv. 328–9; Scott, *Politics and war*, 166, 176–7.

16 J. Adamson, 'The frighted junto: perceptions of Ireland, and the last attempts at settlement with Charles I', in J. Peacey (ed.), *The regicides and the execution of Charles I* (Basingstoke, 2001), 36–70.

17 D. Underdown, *Pride's purge: politics in the puritan revolution* (Oxford, 1971), 106–42; R. Ashton, *The English civil war: conservatism and revolution, 1603–1649* (London, 1978), 331–42.

18 E. Walker, *Historical discourses* (1705), 42, 64–5, 83–4, 97–8; F. Peck (ed.), *Desiderata curiosa*, 2 vols (1735), ii, lib. x, 7; P. Warwick, *Memoires of the reigne of King Charles I* (1701), 326.

19 *EB*, 185–6, 189.

20 *Ibid.*, 48.

21 Peck (ed.), *Desiderata curiosa*, ii, lib. x, 23.

22 BL, E476(2), *Mercurius pragmaticus*, 5–12 December 1648, sig. Cc2.

23 *EB*, 150–1.

24 *Ibid.*, 115–18.

25 *Ibid.*, 96.

26 The fundamental contradictions between the king's position at the close of the treaty and the opinions published as his in *Eikon basilike* were not lost on contemporary critics: see, for example, *Eikon alethine: the pourtraiture of truths most sacred majesty truly suffering, though not solely* (1649), 52, 80.

27 *State papers collected by Edward, earl of Clarendon*, ed. R. Scrope, 3 vols (1773), ii. 453.

28 *Eikon basilike*, ed. Knachel, xxx–ii; *Burnet's History of my own time*, ed. O. Airy, 3 vols (Oxford, 1897), i. 87.

29 S. Kelsey, 'The death of Charles I', *Historical Journal*, 45 (2002), 727–54, at 740–1.

30 *State papers collected by Edward, earl of Clarendon*, ii. 267–8. For Duppa's supposed authorship of chapters 24 and 28 of the *Eikon*, see Madan, *New bibliography*, 131; and also *Eikon alethine*, 96.

31 BL, E469(10), *Mercurius pragmaticus*, 24–31 October 1648, sig. [Zz]; see also BL, E469(7) and (8*); but cf. E467(4) and E468(17).

32 *EB*, 184.

33 *Memoirs of the two last years of the reign of that unparallell'd prince of ever blessed memory, King Charles I. By Sir Thomas Herbert, Colonel Edward Coke, Major Huntington, Mr Henry Firebrace* (1702), Coke's narrative, 174.

34 See also BL, E469(8), *A terrible thunderclap for the Independent sectaries* (28 October 1648), 2.

35 *EB*, 185.

36 H. Cary (ed.), *Memorials of the great civil war in England from 1646 to 1652*, 2 vols (1842), ii. 75–100.

37 S. R. Gardiner, *History of the great civil war*, 5 vols (London, 1987), iii. 310–12.

38 Madan, *New bibliography*, 131 n., 141–2.

39 BL, E538(11), *The religious and loyal protestation of John Gauden* ([15 January] 1649).

40 BL, E538(14), H. Hammond, *Mysterium religionis recognitum: an expedient for composing differences in religion* ([15 January] 1649), 13–14.

41 Kelsey, 'The death of Charles I', 743.

42 *EB*, 32.

43 *Ibid.*

44 S. Kelsey, 'The trial of Charles I', *English Historical Review*, 118 (2003), 583–616, at 606–8.

45 The tactic had been a familiar characteristic of the king's attempts at accommodation since 1639: R. Cust, *Charles I: a political life* (London, 2005).

46 Potter, *Secret rites and secret writing*, 175; Skerpan, *The rhetoric of politics*, 107–9.

47 Scott, *Politics and war*, 159–60.

48 D. Underdown, *Royalist conspiracy in England, 1649–1660* (New Haven, CT, 1960), 10–12; R. Hutton, *Charles II* (Oxford, 1989), 31; and J. Miller, *Charles II* (London, 1991), ch. 1 and generally.

49 *EB*, 75–9.

50 *Ibid.*, 157–8.

51 *Eikon basilike*, ed. Knachel, 'Introduction', xvi.

52 *EB*, 193–4.

53 *Ibid.*, 202–3.

54 Hyde, *History of the rebellion and civil wars in England*, iv. 341–2; *The Hamilton papers*, ed. S. R. Gardiner, Camden Society, new series, 27 (London, 1880), 241–9; R. C. Anderson, 'The royalists at sea, 1648', *Mariner's Mirror*, 9 (1923), 39; Hutton, *Charles II*, 28.

55 BL, Papers of Sir Ralph Verney, 1648–53, microfilm M636(9).

56 Bodleian Library, MS Firth c. 8, fo. 123v.

57 BL, E538(21), *The moderate intelligencer*, 11–18 January 1649 [1847].

58 Bodleian Library, MS Clarendon 34, fo. 9; BL, Add. MS 18982, fos 144r–v; *State papers collected by Edward, earl of Clarendon*, ii. 460–1; D. Stevenson, *Revolution and counter-revolution in Scotland, 1644–1651* (London, 1977), 126–7.

59 S. R. Gardiner, *History of the commonwealth and protectorate*, 4 vols (London, 1989 [1901]) (hereafter *HCP*), i. 16.

60 BL, E527(6), *Perfect diurnall . . . parliament*, 8–15 January 1649, 2263.

61 BL, E527(8), *Perfect occurrences*, 12–19 January 1649, 803.

62 BL, E527(5), 5–12 January 1649, 791, [796].

63 Gardiner, *HCP*, i. 15; J. N. M. Maclean, 'Montrose's preparations for the invasion of Scotland, 1649–1651', in R. Hatton and M. S. Anderson (eds), *Studies in diplomatic history: essays in memory of David Bayne Horn* (London, 1970), 7–31.

64 Bodleian Library, MS Firth c. 8, fo. 125, Sir Edward Hyde to Prince Rupert, The Hague, Sunday 24 [January] 1648 [n.s.].

65 *State papers collected by Edward, earl of Clarendon*, ii. 466–7, 469–70.

66 BL, E541(27), *The moderate Intelligencer*, 1–8 February 1649 [1883–84].

67 *EB*, 204–5.

68 Bodleian Library, MS Carte 22, fos 645 r–v; *State papers collected by Edward, earl of Clarendon*, ii. 458; T. Carte, *The life of James, duke of Ormond*, 6 vols (Oxford, 1851), vi. 567, 569–71; see also T. Carte (ed.), *A collection of original letters and papers, concerning the affairs of England, from the year 1641 to 1660*, 2 vols (1739), i. 166–7, 168–70, 189–90, 190–1.

69 Gardiner, *HCP*, i. 22, 68–9.

70 P. Geyl, *Orange and Stuart 1641–1672*, trans. A. Pomerans (London, 2001 [1969]), 48–55.

71 Bodleian Library, MS Clarendon 37, fos 30, 49, 64, 65–6, 67.

72 *Burnet's History*, i. 87; Madan, *New bibliography*, 133 note, 151, 156.

73 See pp. 174–81 below.

74 *Eikon alethine*, 40, 96.

74 Clarendon, *History of the rebellion and civil wars in England*, iii. 450. Duppa's pedagogy formed the basis of a long-standing relationship with the prince: K. Fincham, 'Oxford and the early Stuart polity', and M. Feingold, 'The humanities', both in N. Tyacke (ed.), *The history of the university of Oxford*, vol. 4: *Seventeenth-century Oxford* (Oxford, 1997), 209, 241.

76 Scott, *Politics and war*, 176–7. Royalists had been arguing about the legitimacy and propriety of seeking the assistance of the Scots since at least 1645: D. Scott, 'Rethinking royalist politics: faction and ideology, 1642–1649' in J. Adamson (ed.), *The civil wars: rebellion and revolution in the kingdoms of Charles I* (forthcoming). I am grateful to Dr Scott for allowing me to read and to cite his essay in advance of publication.

77 The book's obvious religious and ecclesiastical allegiances were remarked on by contemporaries, and have been mentioned in passing by modern scholars: *Eikon alethine*, 51, 60–3, 70 (correctly 66); J. R. Knott, *Discourses of martyrdom in English literature, 1563–1694* (Cambridge, 1993), 162–3.

78 K. Sharpe, '"An image doting rabble": the failure of republican culture in seventeenth-century England', in K. Sharpe and S. N. Zwicker (eds), *Refiguring revolutions: aesthetics and politics from the English revolution to the romantic revolution* (Berkeley, CA, 1998), 25–56.

10

Public politics in England c. 1675–c. 1715[1]

Mark Knights

In 1584 the government invited subscriptions to a bond of association in the wake of threats to the life of Elizabeth;[2] just over a century later, in 1696, the government similarly invited subscriptions after an assassination attempt against William III, and based the text of the oath closely on the Elizabethan precedent. The invocation of the public made by Burghley and others, through the bond, had some parallel with the actions of the Whigs just over a century later. Each sought to use the pressure of public opinion to advantage. We might see a further similarity in the printed controversies that wracked each era. In 1588–89 when the government was seeking, after the end of the bond movement, to restrict rather than open public debate, seven clandestine tracts, professing to come from one Martin Marprelate, boldly poked fun at the episcopacy in irreverent and satirical polemic.[3] A century later, the revolution of 1688 again prompted the press into action and the inventive invective of Marprelate found plenty of echoes in the theatrical satire of the later Stuarts. And yet, if we compare the late 1580s–early 1590s to the political culture of a century later we find change as well as the apparent continuities. The 1584 bond of association was, for all its novelty, a relatively circumscribed affair. The signatories were mostly men of some substance, able to seal the parchment after their name, and the total number of bonds seems to have been about two dozen. The 1696 oath of association, by contrast, was signed – or marked – by huge numbers right across the nation, not just at county level but in every minor borough in the land. And the presentation of 430 of them to the monarch was carefully recorded for public consumption in the official printed mouthpiece, the *London Gazette*. Similarly, whereas the Marprelate controversy amounted to about 15–16 tracts, the volume of the polemical exchange after 1688 was huge. Mark Goldie counted 128 contributions to the controversy that raged between 1689 and 1690.[4]

One critical difference between the late sixteenth and the late seventeenth century, therefore, has to do with scale. There was a wider public and more print. This quantitative shift is important in its own right, since sheer volume can have structural impact. The enlarged nature of the public and the expansion of the press had qualitative import, as I shall show here. But the question of how far the later seventeenth century's political culture was *qualitatively* different requires us to acknowledge also differences in the nature of the public sphere. Whereas Peter Lake and Michael Questier prefer to talk of a un-Habermasian public for the late sixteenth and early seventeenth centuries, a model of a bourgeois public sphere based on early capitalism, new communicative practices and idealised rational discourse *does* seem to fit the later seventeenth century far more comfortably, an applicability that is symptomatic of change.[5] There was cultural dislocation during the mid-century crisis and that process of transforming the political culture underwent another period of acceleration during the later Stuart period. Whereas the Elizabethan government appears to have imagined the public as a force that could be utilised and then closed down, the later Stuart government was under no such illusion. Indeed, the political parties of the later Stuarts sought to harness the open public sphere for their own partisan purposes – the Whigs, for example, used the association in 1696 to demolish Tory opposition to recognising William III as 'rightful' and 'lawful' king. We might also point to qualitative continuity as well as change in polemical strategy, between Marprelate and his successors, but while admitting this we should also note that the nature of printed debate had changed. While priestcraft was still very much a target in the later seventeenth century, the thrust of polemical attack had also widened. Binary divides and stereotypes persisted, but their characteristics changed. This chapter, therefore, argues that there were both quantitative and qualitative changes over the long seventeenth century, but that there were, as one might expect, also earlier trends that were developed and techniques that evolved.

My argument, covering the neglected period c. 1675–c. 1715, is in two parts. The first considers national politics not just as elite, or high, politics but as a dialogic political process in which the public was fully involved. The public was central to later Stuart politics, not merely an audience but a participant and also a judge. Moreover, the public was, like party, something constructed in rather novel ways. The public as a collective fiction – a definition that appeared in dictionaries only in 1696[6] – could be imagined through truly national political campaigns of unprecedented duration and extent. I suggest that those developments were the result of a number of factors that coincided to impact on political culture. These were the regularity of parliamentary sittings and frequent electioneering; a free press; ideological polarisation; the growth of a fiscal-military state dependent on public credit; and the emergence of political parties. As a result of this powerful combination, I suggest that Whig and Tory were imagined by partisan polemicists to exist in every parish and borough, thereby creating a national political framework within which local factions could exist and through which local tensions could be viewed. This development can be explored by examining the very large number of addresses presented to the monarch by almost every borough – even those that were not enfranchised or that were in Ireland, Scotland and the colonies. Those texts, most of which were published in their thousands, helped embed and foster the appearance of a national public political culture. In other words, into the 'crisis of legitimation' identified by Michael Braddick for the mid-seventeenth century stepped the representational authority of the 'public'.

Having established the enlarged importance of the public, the second part of the chapter considers how the public's role as umpire expanded and how contemporaries viewed the appeal to the people that was inherent in later Stuart politics. I argue that a key problem was that of judgement: the public was now a judge (asked to choose at the polls, when signing addresses, when reading the huge outpouring of the press and so on), but how well could it judge? I suggest that each party viewed the other as intent not on informing or advising the people so that they were better able to judge, but rather on deluding, misleading, misrepresenting and lying to them. I examine perceptions of the degradation of public discourse and conclude that, ironically, the impulse of a participatory representative system was to re-emphasise older notions of the people as an audience that could be all too easily be led astray. Hence limits needed to be placed, either formally or informally, on the public and on public political discourse. This paradox explains in part ambivalences apparent in the political culture of the eighteenth century.

First, then, we need to examine the ways in which the public assumed a new role and was invoked as umpire in partisan politics. The most obvious was at the polls. It is well known that general elections were held, on average, every two-and-a-half years in the period 1679–1716; that electioneering produced bitter feuds affecting nearly every borough and county in the land; and that the electorate was expanding in this period, achieving a higher rate of adult male participation than at any time prior to the 1867 Reform Act. The prolonged frequency of elections and the scale of participation was thus unprecedented. Moreover, parliament sat more regularly and for longer than ever before. It is equally well known that pre-publication licensing lapsed, temporarily in 1679 and then permanently in 1695, so that the press regained and then surpassed earlier levels of output, and a periodical press flourished as never before, in the provinces after 1701 as well as in the capital.

What is less well known is that the period 1660–1720 witnessed a huge outpouring of petitions and addresses presented mostly to the crown but a fewer number also to parliament, on national issues such as war, peace and the succession; most of them were printed, thereby making the public not only their originator but also the secondary audience for which they were intended. Many of the petitions and addresses claimed both to represent the will of the people and to seek to shape the representation of that will by timing their appearance to influence the electorate, thereby making them a form of double representation: representation through text designed, in part, to influence representation at the polls. Compared to earlier campaigns, and even to eighteenth-century ones, the scale of the later Stuart addresses in particular is impressive. Zaret has estimated there were about 500 public petitions that were printed between 1640 and 1660, and individual campaigns were much smaller than their later counterparts.[7] The petitions promoted between December 1641 and August 1642 came from 38 of the 40 counties but only a handful of towns.[8] The highest number achieved before the late Stuart period seems to have been the 94 presented to congratulate Richard Cromwell on his 'accession'.[9] Yet over 4 times as many were presented after Queen Anne's rousing maiden speech to parliament, and those 400 followed hard on the heels of a further 344 addresses that had been presented during the previous 4 months against France's recognition of the pretender. Indeed, between 1679 and 1715 there were well over 5,000 petitions and addresses. The extent of campaigns thus appears to have changed over time.

Electioneering, petitioning and addressing, and pamphleteering on the scale achieved in the later Stuart period had two important consequences. First, it helped to create the sense of a national political culture. If we take the 400 addresses presented in 1702 as an example we find that they came from every quarter of the land, not just from county grand juries and parliamentary constituencies but from tiny non-parliamentary boroughs such as Bradninch in Devon or Maidenhead in Berkshire, or larger ones such as Leeds and Birmingham, from trading companies, from Ireland and from the colonies. And after union with Scotland in 1707, boroughs and counties in northern Britain were also routinely included. Here, then, a very inclusive, national public was being drawn. Indeed, there was now an *expectation* of participation in the national political culture. A delay or failure to draw up an address necessitated public explanation. Moreover, the inclusiveness accentuated individual voices within the collective one, for each of the 400 texts was differently worded, hundreds of variations on a single theme. They thus helped to articulate a national discourse in which certain words and phrases became important codes and badges of ideological conviction. And because they were printed, each locality could both share that language and scrutinise the national discourse. It is also striking how such addresses were a participatory form of representation, suggesting that while the focus of historiographical debate has recently shifted towards studying a negotiated and inclusive state of office-holders we need to add representative practices back into the picture. There may have been 50,000 who held a parish office but there were many times that number who participated through petitioning and addressing, and through local and national elections, or other less formal forms of representation.[10]

Second, electioneering, addressing and pamphleteering could be divisive as well as creating a collective national voice and were thus part of the means by which partisan allegiances were both created and voiced. The campaigns ensured that the fault lines of the national political culture fissured the localities and that local disputes were an intrinsic part of the national divide between Whig and Tory. Thus a controversy over the election of a borough alderman was part of a national struggle between the parties; and national disputes were immediately mirrored in the localities. The clash between the parties, for example, created rival sets of addresses, each claiming a representative voice. In 1710, for example, Whigs and Tories promoted antithetical addresses, one set claiming that the Whig-dominated administration consisted of a bunch of bloodthirsty republicans intent on continuing the war against France merely to line their own pockets, and the other claiming that the high churchmen presented the greatest danger to the country. These disputes had the effect of defining the public still further, since in addition to the majority of a corporation they often claimed to represent the views of the 'principal' or 'chief' inhabitants.[11] And such texts ensured ideological conflict at the local level, helping not only to define the nature of the party conflict but to ensure that a similarity of ideological conflict across the country could produce a sense of a national political struggle between rival parties.

Third, elections, petitions and addresses and the press all offered, or at least claimed to offer, means by which the will of the nation could be judged; but each also required an act of *judgement* on the part of the public. Thus the people had to decide how to cast their votes, whether or not to subscribe to a petition or address, and, as readers, whether or not to believe what they read. In each case the public was also increasingly being asked to choose between rival parties that fielded different slates of candidates, offered rival texts of petitions and addresses and poured out polemical and polarised print. These rival viewpoints created a public dialogue, a dialogue that took place between the various parties but also between the parties and the people, who were invoked both as essential participants but also as an umpire, or judge. A tract of 1689 referred to the 'divine institution of a publick judgment' and John Trenchard argued that 'it is certain that the whole people, who are the publick, are the best judges when things go ill or well with the publick'.[12] The public and public judgement had come of age.

Once the public was routinely invoked as judge, it required counsel about how to exercise its judgement. The first example of printed electoral advice appeared in 1644, but the genre really only blossomed in the later Stuart period, when frequent elections and a free press provided the two essential conditions for its development. There were over 100 titles specifically offering advice to the public in the reign of Anne alone. At the same time we can chart the emergence of the printed division list, again aimed at informing the public and shaping its choice. All such electioneering material was explicitly designed to teach lessons in public judgement. Tract after tract urged voters to rely on their own judgement, and to resist the influence of landlord and pulpit. As one pamphleteer put it, 'he's a free and disinterested elector, that mov'd by no private principle, elects according to the best of his judgment'.[13] Voters, urged another, should choose with 'all the care, caution, deliberation and circumspection imaginable';[14] they should, claimed yet another, take care their votes were 'free, without present, gifts or future promises of reward'.[15] *The best choice of parliament-men* (1701) went on to remind electors: 'you have the balance of power in your hands and may turn the scales to which side you please'.[16] The genre of advice thus both stressed the importance of a rational public capable of making important judgements about the state and fostered the ideal of the rational voter. These were a tremendously creative set of ideas, for the freeholders and burgesses were treated as a national body of men, despite the very significant variations that existed in franchise and local political contexts, and thereby helped to further foster an image of the public and of a national political culture.

There was one further way in which a public worked in a new way and that was public credit. The development of a fiscal–military state began in the 1640s, when innovative methods of raising revenue and improved collection dramatically increased the State's resources.[17] Even so, sustained warfare against France between 1689 and 1713 (with only a short break between 1697 and 1702) fostered a financial as well as a military revolution.[18] Average tax revenue during the war years of the 1690s was £3.64 million, about double the state's tax income prior to 1689. In 1720 the state took 10.8 per cent of income in tax, compared to just 3.4 per cent in 1670.[19] The state's capacity to tax outstripped the growth of the economy, ensuring that a tax-paying public was increasing in importance, not least because taxation was now used to underwrite government borrowing. Public (as opposed to royal) indebtedness, which was unknown before 1689, stood at £16.7 million by 1697, £36 million in 1713 and over £50 million by 1720.[20] Fiscal innovation included the creation of the Bank of England in 1694, paper money and the development of the stock market.[21] Public credit was not only linked to representative politics – credit fluctuated with political power and electoral politics now affected the nation's capacity to wage war – but was itself a representative system, based in part on paper money, exchequer bills and stocks that had representative rather than intrinsic value. The fiscal revolution was a public, representational one.

The public, then, was something different from what it had been in the 1580s or even in the 1640s. By 1700 the sense of the nation not only had a variety of means of articulation, but was a representational interface with the state, a public sphere that could impact on it by altering the composition of parliament, by creating a public discourse that limited or opened political options and by determining public credit. Moreover, it was a public that could not easily be dismissed, not least because the conflict between the parties continually conjured it into being. To be sure, some elements of this public power had been discernible previously and the notion of a *vox populi* was a very old one indeed. We can find similar anxieties about the seditious nature of print, the irrationality of the multitude and the subversion of truth in the sixteenth as well as the seventeenth century.[22] There are continuities at moments of political and religious crisis across time and space. But the collective (albeit, ironically, disputed and divided) voice of the people was, by the later Stuart period, not just a claim made by pamphleteers but a measurable political force intrinsic to the structure of politics. And partisanship intensified earlier concerns and gave them a new context.

My argument is, therefore, not that anxieties about public discourse were necessarily novel. Rather, that the degree of passion aroused by partisanship, the frequency with (and extent to) which the public was being asked to choose, the temptations for corruption offered by an expanded state, the apparent proliferation of plots and the nature of the new public all raised long-standing anxieties to new heights (or at least made their articulation both justifiable and even necessary) and accentuated certain concerns in novel ways. As participants and the umpire of state affairs in an era of publicly adversarial parties, the public's capacity for and exercise of judgement was scrutinised as never before. And by 1715 it had been found wanting, with important implications for the political culture of the eighteenth century.

Why? What was it about party and publicly partisan discourse that was so disconcerting and even dangerous? One answer was the zeal and passion aroused by competitive party politics, which seemed to breed an inveterate hostility to different viewpoints. In 1675 the lord keeper attacked the great heat displayed by those who meddled in public affairs, and in doing so highlighted a shift of culture, from religious to political zeal: 'as there may be a religious zeal, a zeal for God which is not according to knowledge, so there may be a state zeal, a zeal for the public which is not according to prudence, at least not according to the degree of prudence which the same men have when they are not under the transport of such fervent passion'.[23] State zeal was not in itself new but it rose in the later Stuart period to new levels of intensity. *The danger of moderation* (1708) complained that Whig and Tory were so established that there was no possibility of moderation: 'if you come into the Town house, there are but two sides allow'd you to sit down on; and if you pretend to stand in the middle, you'll be continually pelted with some trash or other from both the side-boxes'.[24] Public partisanship was ubiquitous and unavoidable. The very means working to create a national political culture – elections, addresses, the press – simultaneously worked to divide the nation.

Party thus created passions, state zeal, or, in contemporary phrasing, 'rage'.[25] This rage transported men and obscured their ability to discern what was true. Truth became relative to partisan conviction. In what amounted to a vicious circle, having signed up to a party, a partisan's adherence to a party coloured and shaped how he or she viewed the world, leading to interpretations that then reinforced allegiance to that party. As Henry St John, later Viscount Bolingbroke, put it in 1709, 'no man looks on things as they really are, but sees them through that glass which party holds up to him'.[26] Yet, while raising questions about where truth lay, publicly contested partisan politics also undermined the status of monarch and church as arbiters of truth and hence undermined traditional means of validating political truth-claims. Instead (or perhaps more accurately, as well), there was a new, but to many observers, an uncertain or even vacillating umpire, the public. Publicly adversarial politics thus not only institutionalised rival truth claims, but championed as arbiter a public that, it was feared, either lacked the capacity to discern truth or could be manipulated into mistaking truth for error. This was even more dangerous because the public had considerable power to affect public affairs, through the polls, through the public credit necessary to fight war, and through informal pressures, such as petitions and addresses. Truth, then, was a party political issue. As the rage of party increased, all sides began to fear that there was a paradox at the heart of publicly competitive politics: an appeal to the people was an integral part of such politics but it was also the root of the problem. For it was in the very appeal to the public's judgement of what was true that truth could itself become subverted. Truth was both conveyed by public discourse but also undermined by it. This was no abstract problem. For the public was being asked repeatedly, through frequent elections, to judge and make choices, at a time of war against the most powerful military force in Europe. Failure to discern the true choice in these circumstances threatened to be catastrophic.

In what ways, then, was party conflict seen as corrupting public discourse? Or why did party provoke claims that both the public and discourse were threatened? At the heart of contemporary anxieties lay concerns about political language. Party appeared to distort language in a number of ways, which are worth mapping out. Again, it is worth stressing that not all of these were new; but collectively, and over a prolonged period of time (so long that they appeared to become institutionalised in the political system), the claims that they were prevalent helped to shape the prevailing political culture.

First, each party believed the other to be engaged in the deliberate, coordinated manipulation of language, and printed words in particular, for political ends. A Tory tract of 1701 thus identified a number of tracts that could be 'joined together because they were contriv'd, publish'd, and encourag'd by persons in the same interest, and of the same kidney and complexion, that delight in sedition, calumny and detraction'.[27] Similarly the Whigs at the end of Anne's reign believed that, as one tract put it, the weak people had been 'impos'd upon' and 'been made instruments of a great deal of mischief by being hurryed into false cries and misrepresentations of things' by the high-church Tories.[28] Each side feared that the other was engaged in a systematic attempt to mislead the public.

Second, each side accused the other of deploying slogans with charged meanings in order to work on the passions of the public. Thus a 1707 Tory tract suggested that 'liberty and property' was a phrase that 'deluded' the 'weaker sort of people' into 'a misunderstanding of their representatives', as well as fostering 'a disposition to tumults', and that the 'design, by raising of dust, is to throw it in the peoples eyes, that they may not discern right from wrong' and hence allow the Whigs to become, 'by the help of a popular uproar, establish'd in a governing posture'.[29] The Whigs allegedly supposed that the 'the nation, by fine words, may be led about, as the bears are by the fiddle'.[30] The Whigs countered that the 'church in danger' worked in similar ways for the Tories. *The church not in danger* (1707) agreed that the slogan was used by the 'self-designing sophister' who 'prostituted the venerable name of the church to the service of a party' and used an 'equivocating sort of cant . . . to obscure his sordid design of calumniating the Queen and the estates of the realm'.[31] Indeed, pamphleteering was often a case of associating a jumble of pejorative or emotive terms. Thus, as one writer put it:

> Let but any one take a few rattling words for his materials, such as schismatic, atheist, rebels, traitors, miscreants, monsters, enthusiasts, hypocrites; Lord's anointed, sacred

majesty, God's vicegerent; impious, blasphemers, damnation; stir these together in a warm head and after a little shaking, bring them out, scum and all, distribute them into several periods and your work is half done.[32]

Words and phrases were given different meanings by the rival parties purely for partisan ends. Polemicists routinely suggested what John Locke set out philosophically in his *Essay concerning human understanding*, that words were abused and that they often failed to correlate with the idea they represented. That there was a contest over the meaning of words was hardly new. But in the rage of party, it was suggested, the destabilisation of meaning was deliberate partisan misrepresentation perpetrated not against one or two individuals but against the whole nation. The Tories claimed the Whig was a master of sophistry. The Whig thus had a passion for 'confounded jargon . . . and you must always spell him backwards before you can read him'.[33] They were double-dealers 'who paint their faces like Jezabel, and peep into the world with the outside varnish of liberty, moderation, toleration, self-preservation and such like insinuating and deluding Cant'.[34] Party produced a pressure, akin to that of casuistry, by which the meaning of words became subject to private or partisan interpretation. Words and terms acquired specialised and even private meanings. Swift's fears about private, partisan languages are well known.[35] But his anxiety was widely shared. The world seemed upside down, claimed one tract sympathetic to dissent, because people misapplied meanings: 'behold on the one hand vertue termed vice, sobriety debauchery, religion faction, pious and peaceable assemblies riots and routs and punished as such'.[36] As one critic of a clerical address put it, talking to the people in 'a language in which the sense of words is perverted' and words understood in one sense nevertheless 'made to speak another sense and to signifie the direct contrary . . . serv'd not only to *distinguish* but even to *form* and *make* parties'.[37]

Third, parties perfected the art of political lying. One pamphleteer observed: 'Almost every age hath been remarkably infamous for some prevailing iniquity more than other; and how justly this we live in may be call'd by way of eminence, the Lying age, you all I presume very well know.'[38] This was an exaggeration, of course. As Nigel Smith has shown, the association of lying and print was made in the 1640s when the freedom of the press 'radically destabilised conceptions of truth, trustworthiness and authority'.[39] Even so, political lying did seem to be even more worrying in the later Stuart period, perhaps because of the danger it posed to the electoral system. Thomas Rawlins, a Norfolk parson, lamented in 1713 (as an election loomed) that 'never in any place or time did the spirit of lying become so daring and impudent, as it has of late among us; it appears openly, without veil or masque, and flies in the face of our superiors at noon-day, without fear or shame, at least without fear of punishment'.[40] Political lying, complained another cleric, John Edwards, led to a perjured form of modern politics. 'The chiefest art of state', he lamented,

hath been generally to dissemble. The great mystery of it is to keep the ignorant and vulgar (who are always the most) in false apprehensions of what is to be done and

177

never to let them know the true measure of things. This in plain English is politic lying, [for] the study hath been to appease the people, not to make them happy. I appeal to impartial minds, whether in such politicks there be any thing solid and certain, any thing to be depended upon.[41]

Thus Tory critics of the infamous 'Legion memorial' of 1701, sometimes said to be written by Defoe, saw it as a 'meer piece of forgery', the natural outcome of a party dedicated not to 'honesty and truth', as Legion claimed, but to lying (Legion, after all, was the biblical devil who aimed to 'misrepresent actions and be a false accuser').[42] Whig and Tory saw each other as liars. And this was the inevitable consequence of partisan politics, for 'when there are two different parties in a nation, they will see things in different lights'.[43] The divided political culture thus dealt in what everyone agreed to be delusions and fictions even if they could not agree on what was real.

Fourth, these fictions and uncertainties became part of the political contest. Parties were representational creations with identities that were constructed by adherents but also by their rivals. The parties and their critics were locked into a struggle to define and redefine themselves. This might not matter too much were it not for the fact that when voters chose candidates they often did so assuming that there was a correlation between a party's name and the identity of the party. Yet contemporaries increasingly doubted whether this was the case. The party label was either used as a cover to advance private interest or the nature of the party identity had shifted. This was dangerous because the public used party names to aid their judgement of candidates. As one tract put it, 'the general method of enquiry about members for parliament is whether they are Whigs or Tories'.[44] Whig and Tory were thus set up 'as the Tower-mark to warrant the value and weight of all the current men in the kingdom; so that every man now passes or is cry'd down in the country, is receiv'd or rejected above; according as he is tender'd under one of these names'.[45] The problems inherent in the names of Whig and Tory struck de Rapin-Thoyras, who sought to explain the terms to both a foreign and an English audience at the end of our period. Rapin feared that the 'the names Whig and Tory inspire certain confused ideas, which few people are able rightly to disentangle'.[46] Distinguishing what the parties really stood for from the fictional depictions of them was nevertheless made difficult by the claims to impartiality that could be invoked in order to disguise Whig or Tory positions. In January 1713, for example, a new periodical, The Britain, claimed to want to reconcile Whig and Tory.[47] Yet this pose of impartiality was in fact a veneer to woo the reader. As early as the fourth issue Narcissus Luttrell detected its partisan bent, dismissing it as 'a silly Whig paper'.[48] The guise of impartiality could thus itself be a partisan fiction. Correctly defining the parties was almost impossible because the process of definition was part of the political game; and such definitions varied according to the perspective of writer and reader.

The meanings of Whig and Tory are evidently crucial to understanding the politics of the period. Sir John Plumb claimed that the contours of the two parties were always apparent to contemporaries. Unlike historians, he suggested, who are often bewildered by the complexities of party politics, 'contemporaries were less distracted and they rarely had difficulty, at least after the middle 1690s, in distinguishing Whig from Tory'.[49] This is true, in the sense that for most of the period contemporaries did discern a bipartisan struggle. But it obscures a contest that permeated the printed polemic of the period about what precisely Whig and Tory meant. In other words, the identity of Whig and Tory can be confusing to students of the period precisely *because* the labels Whig and Tory were themselves contested terms with fluid meanings.

Fifth, partisan polemic also fostered fictional worlds. This was particularly apparent in the use made of imagined dialogues between ideologues. One pamphlet purported to be *A certain information of a certain discourse. That happen'd at a certain gentleman's house in a certain county. Written by a certain person then present, to a certain friend now at London. From whence you may collect the great certainty of the account* (1713). This tract played with the truth-claims it made, for as its dialogue is about to begin the author interjects:

> [H]old, he shant begin, till I have answered an objection which may be made by the reader how I came to be present and not say a word all the time. Why perhaps I am the spectator, who never talks in any company; no, that, says my reader, I'm sure you are not. Well then perhaps ... I am one that listened at the door, or perhaps, I spoke and wont tell you what I said, or perhaps I held my tongue.[50]

Here the 'certain discourse' was filtered by the reporter – or 'spectator' – who intrudes himself into the print only to offer no explanation of his part and remain unidentifiable – even though it is on his credibility that the 'certain' account rests.[51]

These partisan dialogues often used the genre to play on the disparity between public and private motives, and it was here that the greatest fictional potential existed, because the exposé of an individual's inner (and real) self necessarily meant some attempt at prose character sketches. Dialogue could thus be used as public exposure of confessions made in the 'privacy' of intimate conversations. Speech that emulated private dialogue could thus give additional validity to admissions that one of the participants – and hence one of the parties – had base and sinister motives. Private speech thus conferred authenticity on a fabricated confession of evil motives. The dialogue thus leant itself to the suggestion that parties operated conspiratorially; the reader was temporarily placed as an eavesdropper on the seditious confessions of plotters. The most important example of this type of confessional dialogue was a series written by Charles Davenant, who dramatised politics in prose just as his father Sir William Davenant had dramatised for the Caroline stage.[52] The brilliance of the dialogues lay in their creation of a fictional Whig character, Tom Double, whose name epitomised his ability to pursue private designs under the cover of party and the public interest. The reader is allowed to hear Tom's 'private' spoken explanation of his double-dealing. Tom's designs are thus exposed in public, to the reader, though the conversation remains 'private' between the two characters who meet away from public gaze.

Finally, the partisan political culture, as this suggests, created the space to explore fictionalised selves. Perhaps the best example is William Fuller, who first wormed himself into the court of James II and subsequently became a double-agent for the Williamite regime.[53] Fuller maximised his revelations through a very skilful use of the press, issuing a number of sensationalist tracts that sought to prove that the 'pretender' (the future 'James III') was, as the Whigs claimed, a 'sham'. Yet Fuller was himself a sham, spending a lifetime extorting money by pretending to be all sorts of people who he was not: Fuller gent, Sir William Fuller and even the Right Honourable Lord Fuller. Many of his pamphlets were autobiographical – his 'evidence' could not be told without some account of his personal activity (not least to explain how he could both be loyal to William and be able to reveal conspiracy), but the versions of his life were fluid, dramatic and sometimes contradictory.[54] Parliament condemned him as 'a notorious impostor, a cheat and a false accuser', King's Bench found him guilty in 1703 of being a 'common liar' and a series of pamphlets, written both by Jacobites and Williamites, sought to expose him as such, delighting in uncovering the cheats he had performed on the public.[55] Yet the possibility that he might just be telling the truth meant that it was always impossible to dismiss what he said as a pack of lies. Fuller knew this and exploited that anxiety and uncertainty to the full. Indeed, he seems to have relished the fictions he wove and his repeated stabs at autobiography became exercises in rogue romance. When hostile biographers sought to expose him, Fuller in turn called them 'snarling, impudent liars'.[56] Fuller was a convicted fraud who nevertheless offered his testimony of Jacobite plotting and the warming-pan baby as though his word was truth and claimed all his detractors were liars. He then disowned his claims, reclaimed them and then claimed their falsity again, as the political wind dictated. When we re-read the pamphlet storm about either him or his claims, we appear to have entered a world in which truth and even self-identity have become mere playthings.

The epistemological uncertainties, rival truth-claims and fictionality of the later Stuart period were not unprecedented in early modern England. Nor was uncertainty merely the creation of party politics. But partisan conflict led to an important *intensification* of longer term phenomena, to quite unprecedented proportions, so that preoccupation with the abuse of language for political ends and with the fictional impulse of partisan politics became commonplaces, *embedded* in the political culture and part of the representational politics that was gaining hold. Partisan and public politics constituted a threat to fixed and secure notions of truth, knowledge, certainty, meaning and understanding. And this threat *was part of* everyday political struggle and hence exported throughout the land by means of the national political culture already identified. Party intruded into almost every minor borough in the kingdom, rendering the problems of truth and judgement real and routine. The public was a rational umpire the decisions and opinions of which were fundamental to the structure of politics; but the public was also an irrational tool in the hands of manipulative politicians and frauds. The public was judge, but, many felt, its judgement was liable to be warped either by its own passions or by the manipulative language that surrounded it. In an entry for February 1708 Sarah Cowper, the wife of Hertford's Whig MP Sir William Cowper and keen observer of both partisan and print culture, noted in her diary: 'The Publick is made to be Cheated in many Things, and Some take Advantage of its Disposition.'[57] But it was the Tory landslide electoral victories in 1710 and 1713 that were most profoundly disturbing to a Whig sympathy for the judgement of the people, for the apparent public support for the high church between 1710 and 1716 imperilled all revolution principles. In 1688 the public had judged correctly; but during the elections of 1710 and 1713, and then the riots of 1715–16, it seemed to many Whigs that the people had succumbed to the lies and manipulations of their opponents.

John Edwards, the cleric we met earlier worrying over the prevalence of political lying, claimed that 'there are no certain rules in policy now'.[58] This was not quite true. For the debased nature of public discourse gave rise to both formal and informal rules that, in reaction against the rage of party, strove after an idealised form of political dialogue. In 1716 the Whigs, now convinced that the public had been temporarily seduced by high-church and Jacobite lies and misrepresentations, repealed the Triennial Act and introduced an act requiring general elections only once every seven years. Public judgement at the polls was thus neutered. But there were also informal strategies to contain an abusive and irrational public discourse. One was the ever-stronger stress on reasoned and polite argument as a counter to the emotive passion aroused by party allegiance. Another was critical advice to the public about how to judge men and how to deconstruct texts. Yet another was to develop ways of using an ostensibly free press to regulate itself, with print censoring print for the benefit of the public. In other words, the reaction against party rage and its consequences provoked ideals and strategies aspired to and even implemented during the eighteenth century.

Notes

1 This chapter summarises some themes explored in more detail in my *Representation and misrepresentation in later Stuart Britain: partisanship and political culture* (Oxford, 2005). Many people who influenced my thinking are acknowledged there, but I am grateful also to the AHRB for providing the period of study leave during which this was written.

2 P. Collinson, 'The monarchical republic of Queen Elizabeth I', *Bulletin of the John Rylands University Library of Manchester*, 69 (1987), 394–424; D. Cressy, 'Binding the nation: the bonds of association, 1584 and 1696', in D. J. Guth and J. W. McKenna (eds), *Tudor rule and revolution* (Cambridge, 1982); E. Vallance, 'Loyal or rebellious? Protestant associations in England, 1584–1696', *The Seventeenth Century*, 17 (2002), 1–23; D. M. Jones, *Conscience and allegiance in seventeenth-century England: the political significance of oaths and engagements* (Rochester, NY, 1999).

3 P. Collinson, 'Ecclesiastical vitriol: religious satire in the 1590s and the invention of puritanism', in J. Guy (ed.), *The reign of Elizabeth I: court and culture in the last decade*

(Cambridge, 1995); J. Raymond, *Pamphlets and pamphleteering in early modern Britain* (Cambridge, 2002).

4 M. Goldie, 'The revolution of 1689 and the structure of political argument: an essay and an annotated bibliography of pamphlets on the allegiance controversy', *Bulletin of Research in the Humanities*, 83 (1980), 477.

5 P. Lake with M. Questier, 'Puritans, papists, and the "public sphere" in early modern England: the Edmund Campion affair in context', *Journal of Modern History*, 72 (2000), 587–627; and *The antichrist's lewd hat: protestants, papists and players in post-reformation England* (New Haven, CT, 2002).

6 G. Baldwin, 'The "public" as a rhetorical community in early modern England', in A. Shepard and P. Withington (eds), *Communities in early modern England* (Manchester, 2000), 209.

7 D. Zaret, 'Petitions and the "invention" of public opinion in the English revolution', *American Journal of Sociology*, 101 (1996), 1507. The number of petitions produced in this period is the subject of ongoing research and Zaret's figures may well represent an underestimate of the real figure. Even so, the national coverage achieved by later campaigns seems generally to have been unmatched.

8 A. Fletcher, *The outbreak of the English civil war* (New York, 1981), 192.

9 *A true catalogue, or an account of the several places . . . where . . . Richard Cromwell was proclaimed lord protector* (1659).

10 It may also be that we need different models for rural and urban communities.

11 H. French, 'Social status, localism and the "middle sort of people" in England 1620–1750', *Past and Present*, 166 (2000), 66–99.

12 *A discourse concerning the nature, power and proper effects of the present conventions in both kingdoms call'd by the Prince of Orange 1688/9*, in *State tracts*, 3 vols (1705), i. 219; *London Journal*, 21 January 1721.

13 *Enquiry into the inconvenience of public and the advantages of private elections with a method of a ballot* (1701), 9.

14 *The subjects case: or serious advice to all Englishmen who have the right of electing members to serve their country in the next parliament* (1701), 1.

15 *The best choice of parliament-men* (1701), 1.

16 *Ibid.*, 6.

17 M. J. Braddick, *The nerves of state: taxation and the financing of the English state 1558–1714* (Manchester, 1996).

18 J. Brewer, *The sinews of power: war, money, and the English State, 1688–1783* (New York, 1989); P. G. M. Dickson, *The financial revolution in England: a study in the development of public credit, 1688–1756* (London, 1967); M. Duffy, *The military revolution and the state 1500–1800* (Exeter, 1980); D. W. Jones, *War and economy in the age of William III and Marlborough* (Oxford, 1988); P. K. O'Brien and P. Hunt, 'The rise of a fiscal state in England 1485–1815', *Historical Research*, 66 (1993), 129–76; B. Carruthers, *City of capital: politics and markets in the English financial revolution* (Princeton, NJ, 1996); C. Brooks, 'Public finance and political stability: the administration of the land tax 1688–1720', *Historical Journal*, 17 (1974), 281–300.

19 P. K. O'Brien, 'The political economy of British taxation, 1660–1815', *Economic History Review*, 2nd series, 41 (1988), 1–32.

20 A distinction should be made between a royal and a national debt.

21 Besides the works cited above see also M. Li, *The great recoinage of 1696–9* (London, 1963); P. Laslett, 'John Locke, the great recoinage and the origins of the Board of Trade,

1695–1698', *William and Mary Quarterly*, 3rd series, 14 (1957), 370–402; J. E. T. Rogers, *The first nine years of the Bank of England* (Oxford, 1887); W. Scott, *The constitution and finance of English, Scottish and Irish joint-stock companies to 1720* (Cambridge, 1951); J. K. Horsfield, *British monetary experiments, 1650–1710* (1960).

22 D. Zaret, *Origins of democratic culture: printing, petitions, and the public sphere in early-modern England* (Princeton, NJ, 2000); A. Wood, *Riot, rebellion and popular politics in early modern England* (Basingstoke, 2002); P. Collinson, *The puritan character: polemics and polarities in early seventeenth-century English culture* (Los Angeles, CA, 1987); P. Zagorin, *Ways of lying: dissimulation, persecution, and conformity in early modern Europe* (Cambridge, MA, 1990); C. Condren, *Satire, lies and politics: the case of Dr Arbuthnot* (Basingstoke, 1997); E. Skerpan, *The rhetoric of politics in the English revolution, 1642–1660* (Columbia, MO, and London, 1992); S. Achinstein, 'The politics of Babel in the English revolution', in J. Holstun (ed.), *Pamphlet wars: prose in the English revolution* (London, 1992), 14–44; and 'The uses of deception: from Cromwell to Milton', in K. Z. Keller and G. J. Schiffhorst (eds), *The witness of time: manifestations of ideology in seventeenth-century England* (Pittsburgh, PA, 1993); B. Vickers, 'The Royal Society and English prose style: a reassessment', in B. Vickers and N. Streuver (eds), *Rhetoric and the pursuit of truth: language change in the seventeenth and eighteenth centuries.* (Los Angeles, CA, 1985); Q. Skinner, *Reason and rhetoric in the philosophy of Hobbes* (Cambridge, 1996); R. Ashcraft, 'The language of political conflict in Restoration literature', in R. Ashcraft and A. Roper (eds), *Politics as reflected in literature: papers presented at a Clark Library Seminar 1987* (Los Angeles, CA, 1989).

23 *LJ*, xii. 654.

24 *The danger of moderation* (1708), 4–5.

25 Dryden in 1681 referred to the 'civil rage' – in the epilogue to *Tamerlane the great*, spoken to Charles II at the opening of the Playhouse in Oxford, on 19 March 1681: *Dryden: a selection*, ed. J. Conaghan (London, 1978), 224.

26 'The letters of Henry St John to the earl of Orrery, 1709–1711', ed. H. T. Dickinson, *Camden Miscellany*, 26, Camden. Soc., 4th series, 14 (London, 1975), 147 (1 September 1709).

27 *England's enemies exposed* (1701), Preface.

28 *Reflections on the management of some late party-disputes* (1715), 1–2.

29 *The true picture of a modern Whig reviv'd* (1707), 38–9, 43.

30 *Ibid.*, 36.

31 *The church not in danger* (1707), 4–5.

32 T. Bradbury, *The lawfulness of resisting tyrants*, 2nd edn (1714), Preface.

33 *The character of a Whig, under several denominations* (1709 [1700]), 3–4, 22, 30.

34 H. Pugh, *The true nature of religious zeal* (1710); the tract is quoted in W. Kennett, *The wisdom of looking backward* (1715), 70–1.

35 D. Eilon, *Faction's fictions* (Newark, NJ, 1991); *Examiner*, 16 November 1710.

36 *The second part of the peoples antient and just liberties asserted* (1670), 4. The difference over the word 'riot' was particularly important, since it was the basis for legal prosecution of religious conventicles in the 1680s – for a discussion see T. Ellwood, *A discourse concerning riots* (1683).

37 *The objection of the non-susbscribing London clergy* (1710), 3–4, 10.

38 Kennett, *Wisdom of looking backward*, 180–1, citing R. L. Lloyd, *A sermon preach'd at St Paul's Covent-Garden, on the 30th of January, 1711* (1712), 6. For other remarks by Lloyd about lying see Kennett, *Wisdom of looking backward*, 258–9.

39 N. Smith, *Literature and revolution* (New Haven, CT, 1994), 28, 358.

40 T. Rawlins, *Truth and sincerity recommended in a sermon against lying* (1713), 18–19.

41 J. Edwards, *Some new discoveries of the uncertainty, deficiency and corruptions of human knowledge and learning* (1714), 64.

42 *England's enemies exposed*, 26, 28–30.

43 *Freeholder*, no. 17, 17 February 1716.

44 *A letter to the gentlemen and freeholders of the county of Dorset* (1713), 28.

45 *Danger of moderation*, 4, 6.

46 P. de Rapin-Thoyras, *The history of Whig and Tory from the conquest to the present time* (1723) (written February 1716), 57–8.

47 *The Britain*, no. 19, 7–11 March 1713.

48 BL, Burney Collection, endorsement on no. 4, 10–13 January 1713; the paper may have been written by John Oldmixon, who had assisted Arthur Mainwaring in refuting and out-arguing the Tory *Examiner* in their periodical *The Medley*. Manwaring was defended in no. 12, 11–14 Feburary 1713.

49 J. Plumb, *The growth of political stability in England, 1675–1725* (London, 1967), 130.

50 T. Burnet, *A certain information of a certain discourse* (1713), 5–6.

51 Cf. the *Spectator* periodical.

52 Davenant senior urged the utility of poetry in producing virtue. Charles Davenant's dialogues are: *The true picture of a modern Whig, set forth in a dialogue between Mr Whiglove & Mr Double* (1701), which ran to seven editions by 1705; *Tom Double return'd out of the country* (1702), 2 editions; and *Sir Thomas Double at court* (1710). Another tract which appropriated Tom Double – *The true picture of a modern Whig reviv'd* (1707) – was probably not Davenant's work.

53 For a biography see G. Campbell, *Impostor at the bar: William Fuller 1670–1733* (London, 1961). Fuller used 'cant' in his letters to ministers: Nottingham University Library, Portland papers, PwA447–50.

54 *The life of William Fuller, gent. (1701); Mr William Fuller's trip to Bridewell* (1703); *The whole life of Mr William Fuller* (1703); *The sincere and hearty confession of Mr William Fuller* (1704); *The truth at last or Mr William Fuller's free account of his books (or narratives) and public transactions* (1702).

55 *The life of William Fuller* (1692); *The truest account of Mr Fuller's discovery of the true mother of the pretended prince of Wales* (1696); R. Kingston: *The life of William Fuller, alias Fullee, alias Fowler, alias Ellison etc* (1701); *The cheaters speculum, or, the new English rogue* (1700); *The English rogue reviv'd: or the life of William Fuller, cheat-master-general of Great Britain* (1718).

56 Campbell, *Impostor at the bar*, 154.

57 Hertfordshire Record Office, Panshanger MSS, D/EP F32, p. 165.

58 Edwards, *Some new discoveries*, 63.

11

'My Kingdom is not of this world': the politics of religion after the Revolution

Justin Champion

Much has been written about the ecclesiological consequences of the English Revolution.[1] The reimposition of the statutory foundations of a confessional state in the 1660s, and the partial compromise of that order after the 'Glorious Revolution', have been regarded as sequential responses to the problem of religious diversity created by two decades of practical freedom after the outbreak of civil war in 1642. Anglican magistracy attempted to put the 'spirit' of religious diversity back in the box. Mark Goldie has laid out a series of important arguments exploring the theories of intolerance and rival claims of tender conscience and the 'science of toleration' after the Restoration. Conscientious defences of the legitimacy of persecution were matched with practical schemes for eradicating dissent in the early 1680s. At a grassroots level, dissenting communities fought back, countering clerical terrorism with campaigns of engaged public discourse, acts of civil disobedience and clever legal strategies that aimed to compromise the efficacy of persecution.[2] The persistence of languages of comprehension, schism, conformity and toleration into the 1700s suggests that the ideological debate between churchmen and dissenters was right at the core of political conflict.[3] Arguments about the nature of 'godly rule' that had driven political conflict since the sixteenth century remained at the heart of public debate into the eighteenth century.[4] Prompted by the revolutionary decades of the mid-century, gradually political structures were shaped to reflect a context of godly diversity.

One of the immediate and most intractable consequences of the revolutionary decades was a fundamental dispute about the meaning of words. In the communal sphere of the pulpit, and the print culture of the sermon and pamphlet, much of the political conflict of the times was shaped by trying to accrue public legitimacy to a number of national and local religious and political institutions by capturing the intellectual and emotive value of a key vocabulary. The urgency of defining the true meaning of words and concepts like 'true religion', 'popery', 'conscience', 'church' and 'order', and perhaps more importantly attaching them to specific practices and institutions, was profound. Driven by what John Pocock has called the idea of the 'politics of incarnation', such definitions were shaped by theological foundations. There were clearly rival understandings of how Christ's grace and God's will were instantiated in the world: the different theologies of the 'flesh' and the 'word' empowered very distinct sets of ecclesiastical institutions. Whether one believed that true religion was incarnated in the church or in the 'spirit' meant a commitment to believing that diverse forms of clerical and political institutions were godly. Religious belief and commitment were prompted by the experience of participation within those institutions (the variety of sacramental functions and ritual ceremonies, pulpit preaching and 'inner light' prophecy outline some of the variants). In each of these cases, the theological doctrines that underpinned the politics of incarnation had very precise institutional consequences: grace made flesh in the form of Anglican ministry was a different form of 'church' power from that of those who emphasised that inspiration was by the word alone (as in 'faith comes by hearing').[5]

The legacy of the fracturing and contested experience of the 1640s and 1650s meant that there were very different communal contexts for the definition of the primary vocabulary of religious truth. Put simply, bishops saw the world in a different way from the perceptions of sectarians. They employed the commonplace language of religious truth to describe this world, investing their *episteme* with legitimacy. The fundamental difficulty was that others – Quakers, Presbyterians, Baptists and later still 'men of reason' – used the same words with different meanings. This was no mere semantic or philological dispute confined to the world of discourse, but was intimately related to the lived experience of each man, woman and child in the country. The language of orthodoxy, translated into civic policy by conformist Anglicans after 1660 was, from the perspective of Quakers in Southwark, Baptists in Bristol or Roman Catholics in Norfolk, no simple and harmless discursive manoeuvre. The phrase 'anti-Christian persecution' was easily substituted for 'religious truth'. Likewise sectarian claims for tender conscience looked to many conforming clergy and laity suspiciously like seditious rebellion.[6] That these linguistic games were more than simply a question of 'turn' can be illustrated by looking at the long-running debates about the word 'church'.[7]

Defining the nature of the 'church' was both a theological and a political challenge. The Restoration politics of religion was driven by this process of enforced meaning. The 1650s had seen repeated ideological contests over the simple meaning of the word – did *ecclesia* mean 'church' or 'congregation'? Were churches sacred spaces or spiritual communities? Was the church simply the body of ordained ministers or was it the entire collective of Christians (fallen and saved)?[8] After 1660 one of the most significant, persistent and profoundly practical issues, over which conceptual, theological, legal and social conflict converged, was the relationship between 'churches' and 'conventicles'.[9] The restored Anglican regime used public magistracy to render illegal and seditious any voluntary religious meetings. Following the model of the Elizabethan statutes against sectaries, Conventicle Acts of 1664 and, more rigorously, of 1670 provided requisite statutory justification for the intended persecution. The enforcement of these acts was (as with many statutes) dependent on local circumstances; but at times, for example in the early

1670s and 1680s in urban London, the full force of the law was turned against many nonconformist communities. Studies of quarter sessions records and ecclesiastical surveys from the two decades after 1660 indicate a variety of local experiences. When the various civil and religious interests co-ordinated their efforts, they were a truly terrifying force. Exploring some of the diverse understandings of and responses to this issue will throw light on the radical forms of epistemological incommensurability that bedevilled late Stuart society.[10]

The confrontation between definitions of church and conventicle can be seen in a short (but representative) pamphlet by Thomas Ellwood, one of the most engaged and persistent Quaker controversialists of the 1670s and 1680s. A man at the cutting edge of exploiting legal process to escape the persecutory attentions of the established order, Ellwood repeatedly contested the applicability of many of the anti-dissent laws. The Conventicle Acts, applied with renewed enthusiasm after the defeat of exclusion, were the subject of his *A discourse concerning riots* (1683). The work was prompted by the iniquity of imprisoning Quakers under a charge of riot when they were 'only being at a peaceable meeting to worship God'. Clarity of linguistic meaning and precision of legal definition argued that 'riot' (derived from the French *rioter*) was a form of brawl. As Ellwood concluded: 'This is enough to shew how *inapplicable* the word Riot, in its proper and true signification, is to a *peaceable, quiet, Religious Meeting*.' Exploiting orthodox texts like Cowell's *Interpreter* and Lambarde's *Eirenarcha* (as well as standard justice manuals), the point was underscored that a riot was a disorderly meeting contrived for some evil-doing. The important component was the prospect of violence in the performance of an illegal act which was injurious to another. Peaceable worship of God could not be a riot. Cleverly, turning the intention of the Conventicle Act on its head, Ellwood argued that the statute in fact made a distinction between religious meetings and riots when it declared that such meetings were illegal only if the numbers in attendance were four more than the family who lived in the house where the meeting was held. This, claimed the Quaker, meant that the act 'doth not permit Riots: but . . . doth permit religious meetings'. The silent conduct of Quaker meetings also excluded it from the category of riots. Repeatedly declaiming that 'such meetings are not riots', Ellwood implored both grand and petty juries to take note and consider '[h]ow dishonourable a reflection it would be both to the government, and to the religion established thereby, If peaceable, quiet, religious meetings, conscientiously holden only and alone for the worship and service of God . . . should be judicially declared Riots'. Quaker meetings were defined by 'an innocent, meek, passive, and truly Christian behaviour and deportment'. Like many who attended voluntary meetings, Ellwood simply refused to acknowledge that such meetings were anything other than godly. With such an attitude, it eventually became manifest that communities convinced of their theological duty would persist in their conduct.[11]

To Anglican clergymen, such meetings were worse than riots, posing a clear and persistent danger to the established order in church and state. The state papers of the 1660s and 1670s establish that the government was convinced that conventicles were fundamentally seditious. Repeatedly, royal proclamations and episcopal letters enjoined the prosecution of such meetings to protect the nation from the dual mischief of anarchy and sedition.[12] One of the longer and more learned meditations was composed by James Norris, rector of Aldbourn, Wiltshire, in the late 1660s but published posthumously by his son John (later to write against John Toland) in 1685. That the text was still pertinent in the 1680s indicates the persistence of the issues at stake. In defending the legitimacy of prosecutions of illegal meetings, Norris outlined a classic account of the Church of England as the unique instrument mediating divine authority to the community. He mobilised scripture, patristics, and canon and civil law to establish that the church had 'power to make laws to bind all her children'. Making a fundamental distinction between the *ecclesia collectiva* and the *ecclesia representativa*, he clarified: 'by Church I understand not all the number of the faithfull, but those that have lawfull rule and government of the church'. Although acknowledging that outward forms of worship were variable according to the diversity of time and place, he insisted that, once publicly constituted, the church had authority: to disobey the church was to disobey God.[13] Deploying the example of Constantine, Norris argued that all 'souls' (including ministers) were subject to the authority of the crown. Kings were nursing fathers who used discipline and government to uphold God's rule. Like Uzzah, they could neither burn incense nor sacrifice to God, but 'noncompliance' with royal commands was sacrilege.[14]

The parish was the natural form of ecclesiastical administration. These 'scripture Churches' were contrasted with the meetings where 'people scattered about, some here, and some there, in several parts of the Country'. That such people 'should voluntarily associate and combine themselves in a distinct body, under what Ministry they please, and that best suits with their humour, and call themselves a Church' was against God's order. God had decreed the people should be divided into separate flocks, and that each flock should have its own shepherd. There should be no 'random' shifting according to private fancy and lust. God's providence had created pastors with authority. To allow diversity was to encourage a barren schism and profanity. Such unlawful assemblies were prompted by a faith which was 'mere faction'. As Norris explained, this religion was 'but a professed disobedience to their Superiours, and a studied opposition to the truth of that which (through the Mercy of God) is established in our Church'. Their 'holiness' was simply a 'foolish zeal' premissed on 'their own inventions'. Such conviction was not simply damaging to the individuals concerned, but

> as soon as ever they fansie themselves to be converted, they can teach their King how to govern, and their Ministers how to preach. They can tell what Laws are fit for the Kingdom, and what Orders for the Church; yea, they are presently so illuminated, that they can see every blemish in both, when in themselves, their companions and families, they cannot see beams and intolerable Evils.[15]

To allow conventicles to exist was (as Augustine put it) to abandon Jerusalem (the type of the holy city) for Jericho (a type of the world). Like those who helped with the building of the temple under Zerubbabel, who only pretended to be godly, their 'pretext of Piety and Conscience is both the Veil wherewith they hide their unparallelled Pride, Malice and Hypocrisie; and their Bait wherewith they catch simple Souls in their Net'. It was true, Norris acknowledged, that the New Testament had described a variety of public worship based on the diversity of gifts in their teachers (the churches of Paul, Apollos and Cephas, which Hobbes took as a model of primitive independency), but this reinforced the point that each parish had specific authority, rather than any licence of worship. There was therefore – and church fathers, councils and even some contemporary brethren agreed – an absolute injunction against 'the liberty that People are apt to take of their own heads to wander from their own Pastours, to hear Strangers'.[16]

Norris was explicit in his condemnation of those who contrived 'private, irregular and disorderly meetings' against 'publick church assemblies'. Such meetings were the work of Satan. The spaces of the restored church were as sacred and holy as the temples and tabernacles of Jewish antiquity: accordingly, just 'as in Gospel-times we have the like promises of God's special presence in the publick Congregations of his People'. Parish religion was understood as a direct incarnation of God's grace. Public worship was designed to be a place where a community met, confident that it was 'a place where God will vouchsafe to be more graciously present in his worship, than elsewhere'. Exploiting Henry Spelman's writings on the Jewish temple, Norris reiterated the point that while there may have been elements of worship which were historically specific to the ceremonial, Levitical and Judaic law, the third element of 'simple worship, Prayer and devotion' was universal and 'publick, for ever, and not private'. Christ had turned the doves and oxen out of the temple, thereby terminating the sacrificial functions of the Jewish temple, 'yet the sanctification of it to be an house of prayer ever remained'. This was a repeated and explicit claim: the sanctification of antiquity was the same in the present churches, for they were places 'to which God hath by promise assured his own gracious and heavenly presence and blessing'. The presence of the Holy Spirit was the one fundamental distinction between authorised public and illegal private worship: churches were consecrated to holy purpose, private houses were not, and the 'beauty of holiness' did confer grace. Norris noted that Spelman (writing in the earlier part of the century) had been anxious about the proliferation of sectarians who threatened to turn God 'out of Churches into Barns, and from thence again into Fields, and Mountains, and under Hedges: and the Office of the Ministry (robbed of all dignity and respect) be as contemptible as those places; all Order, Discipline and Church-government left to the newness of Opinion and Mens fancies'. Norris confirmed that the civil war had seen exactly that type of diversity, when 'soon after, as many kinds of Religions [did] spring up, as there are Parish Churches within England, every contentious and ignorant Person cloathing his Fancy with the Spirit of God, and his Imagination with the Gift of Revelation'. Order was godly. Injunctions to hear the word of God ('faith comes by hearing') were useless unless the preacher was publicly authorised. Ministers could 'not be successful in their ministry without a church; they may talk as usurpers, but not preach as God's ambassadors'. Ordination gave inward power, but 'external execution' came from the church and its governor. Put very succinctly: 'God calleth ordinarily by his Church, her voice is his.'[17]

In any society there could be only one faith, one church. Christ was head of only one divine body, not two. If there was diversity, only one church may be the spouse of Christ, meaning the other 'must needs be an harlot'. All men and women, 'all soules and companies', were of either the church of Christ or the 'synagogue of Satan'. Those who separated from the established order were 'congregations of evill doers'. 'House creeping preachers' who worshipped in private were like intruders into the house of the holy. Christ had always been 'a publick orderly preacher, and never a private irregular conventicler'. Nor did the apostles ever preach contrary to the public religion. While later churchmen, under the persecution that beset the early church, did preach in private, this was no model for contemporary nonconformity, because then there was no publicly constituted church, whereas now there was. Norris's arguments were hardly original, but they were clear: without public ordinance there was no grace; sacred authority was received by commission, therefore the powers of ministry were 'restrained to lawfull appointment'. What he called a 'ministry of intruders' was not only corrupting of Christianity and politically seditious, but was soteriologically ineffectual.[18]

That Norris wrote, not from a detached position of theological learning, but with a personal conviction and bitterness prompted by his own experiences of the 'sinfull and pernicious effects' of dissent in Wiltshire is clear from his concluding reflections. Noting that, 'as a King cannot endure a rival with him in his Kingdom, nor a husband in the Marriage-bed, so neither can a minister in his Parish', Norris looked back regretfully to the early 1660s when 'my parish was a Virgin, pure and undefiled, free from all invadours and underminers of her Chastity'. Until 1665, his parish (of about 1,000 souls) had been entire, unanimous and 'constant at all parts of public worship, more free from all inclination to schism, separation, or any of the raigning Epidemical faults of this age'. Unfortunately Satan had erected '*altare contra altare*' and a 'conventicle against the Church'. The consequence was disunity and chaos: the congregation was 'miserably divided' – a chaste wife had fallen into the unlawful embraces of strangers. 'Many who had been regular attendants had totally gone off . . . and for the space of several years, have not set their foot over the threshold of God's house'. Others refused even to let their children receive public baptism. Those who persisted in such 'clanclary and irregular conventions' had made 'a Rupture in the body of Christ, and . . . divide[d] Church from Church, and . . . set up Church against Church'. This was to 'introduce all manner of confusion in Churches and Families; and not onely disturb, but in a little time destroy the power of Godliness, purity of Religion, peace of Christians, and set open a wide gap to bring in Atheism, Popery, Heresie, and all manner of wickedness'. Norris's anxiety, reflected widely among the established church and enshrined in the intentions of the statutes, was that such dissent would become (as in the 'late years of war and confusion') a 'great

Engine to pull down the powers then in being'. Echoing Hobbes's account of the successive sectarian rebellions of the civil wars, Norris underscored the dangers of Presbyterian nonconformity, which could all to easily deteriorate into sectarian anarchy and even atheism.[19]

The central theme of Norris's work, the identification of the conventicle as both a politically subversive and a spiritually contaminated institution, was a staple of Anglican royalist thought. While periods of 'indulgence' in the early 1670s and mid-1680s established that a measure of licence would not see the nation plunged into disorder, most of the political nation remained to be convinced, not just of its practicability in terms of policy, but of its godliness. The question of disciplining the spaces of nonconformity was ultimately an issue of state power: here theories of state-building were mixed up with languages of ecclesiology. Defining the relative limits of religious and civil authority had traditionally been undertaken to preserve the priority of godly rule: the political problem of dissent and nonconformity raised in a very apparent way the difficulties of basing authority on a unitary conception of church and state. The practice of religious diversity after 1660 prompted a reconsideration of those traditional ecclesiological discourses. By exploring an example of how one man negotiated the difficulties of marrying order and conscience it will be possible to tease out some of the permanent tensions between the discourses and the practices of governance.

To Isaac Archer, the stark choices confronting him in the early 1660s were a direct consequence of the turmoil of the revolutionary decades of the 1640s and 1650s. Born in the year of the Irish rebellion, Archer was brought up under the radical influence of his father. An Independent preacher, William Archer had approved of the execution of Charles, an act he replicated in minor, as his son recalled, by cutting out the king's head from a portrait. Educated at Cambridge, Isaac, despite his hostility to the Book of Common Prayer and the manifest disapproval of his father, sought accommodation and a living within the restored Church of England. As his diary shows, Isaac was torn between the need for financial security, the demands of conscience, filial duty to his father and his theological commitments. He acknowledged that without his father's financial support he 'had no other way to live but by the ministry'.[20] In conforming to the established church (thereby, in his father's view, supping with the anti-christ), he compromised the obligations of son to father and made the issue of conscience even more complex. Displaying the characteristic uncertainty revealed in spiritual diaries of the period, Archer looked constantly for 'signes' to confirm that he was taking the providentially appropriate course. For example, he pondered the fact that his stammer made it difficult to read out the set liturgy, whereas when he extemporised in prayer or sermons his impediment was absent – evidence of divine judgement. Sensing the youngs fellow's vacillation, Henry Ferne, master of Trinity and bishop of Chester, intervened (at the prompting of Henry Dearsly) to ease the stricter requirements of conformity, allowing Archer exemptions from subscribing.[21]

Archer determined that it was God's providence that had given him 'favour in the eyes of some from whom I could not expect it'. Unfortunately this was not the way his father understood the events. Noting that 'I had promised my father I would not conforme, meaning thoroughly (for I only heard service, neither meddled with the surplisse etc.)', Archer 'somewhat dubiously and fraudulently' (his words) confirmed his integrity. Unfortunately his father had been primed by a listing of 'nonconformists' on which his son's name did not appear. This created an unhappy breach that persisted in one way or another until his father's death in 1670, and almost certainly was the reason Isaac was disinherited. William 'brake out into many passionate words', but offered to support his son if he desisted from conforming. Isaac, vexed and with an unruly temper, refused to speak: as a consequence 'he told me also that I should not see his face till I had humbled myself for my disobedience to him, and sin against God'. Consulting with his Cambridge friends, Isaac was convinced that his father had no authority over his conscience, thus in resisting his demand any error was not compounded with filial disobedience. A sharp and saucy correspondence followed, with father berating son 'that he never thought that one sprung from his loynes would plead for Baal; and that if he thought I adored those abominable idols, and danced to that molten calfe etc. he would come and stampe it to powder, and make me drinke it etc.'. Isaac, shaken by the anger of his father's letters, made ready to quit Trinity College and be accommodated 'in a nonconformist's house'. Deeply troubled by the dispute with his father, 'the workings of my conscience were great, and strong, yet would not my proud stomach come down or yield'.[22]

The trials of this young man, a scholar, drawn to the ministry but compromised by his loyalty to his father and his own conscience, are emblematic of the difficulties that faced many in the 1660s and 1670s. Faced with the opprobrium of his father, but also with the practical difficulties of supporting himself, the issue of conformity was complex. Unable to live in company with his father, and cut off financially, Isaac eventually took the decision (aided by counsel from Trinity men) to conform at Easter 1662, by taking the sacrament. This was momentous for him: 'It was so solemnly done that never any thing moved my affections as that did, in so much I could not forbeare weeping at the receiving of it.' His father did not lightly give up the battle for Isaac's conscience and, writing repeatedly, finally in August (having read the Act of Uniformity and presumably horrified at the prospect of the danger his son's conformity might bring) offered to maintain him at home. In response to the charge that he was disobeying the fifth commandment, Isaac 'pleaded the power and command of the King, whom we should both obey'.[23] Turning away the man sent to collect him from Cambridge, he invoked conscience, which his father dismissed as 'pride and not tenderness'. In contrast to the commands and entreaties of his father, Trinity College offered money and a position. On top of £5 from a benefactor (which he readily accepted), offers of a school at Wilmington and Ely or a readership in London were temptations that Isaac resisted. Instead, despite the fact that he was not old enough (though Isaac was tall for his age), he resolved to be ordained by the visiting Laudian Bishop Matthew Wren. His father must have been appalled. Through Ferne's good services the question of his age was ignored in his ordination examination. Although willing to waive the age requirements, the examiner was keen to confirm the orthodoxy of the young ordinand. Asked to prove that the scriptures were God's word, the examiner pressed him to 'tell him The argument, as he called it'. Finally twigging, 'at last I said the authority of the Church was a good outward argument'. As a taste of his subscription to the authority of the Church, the examiner insisted (citing Augustine) that it was the 'best argument . . . who said that he would not believe the scriptures to be the scriptures except the Church had said so'. Having submitted to this authority, Isaac was given his holy orders and presented with a college living at Arrington, just outside Cambridge.[24] That was the start of his pursuit of a financially viable and theologically acceptable living.

In one sense, then, this account gives us a model of how, breaking away from the conscientious circles of his father, a young man made his way by subscribing and conforming: a miniature of the process of restoring the church in the 1660s. Some of the elements are emblematic of the difficulties that faced many: the tension between conscience and place; the anxiety about providential encouragement; the burden of the memory of the struggles of the previous two decades. This conflict between father and son about the right actions, and the meaning of conformity, describe the sorts of incommensurable worldviews that prompted religious dissonance. What Isaac saw as acceptable compromise William dismissed as bowing to idols. What Isaac saw as duties to his king William regarded as ungodly disobedience of the magistracy of 'family government'. What is also exemplary is the tone of the relationship between father and son: by turns, passionate, angry, apologetic, vacillating. William banished his son and welcomed him; each in turn refused to speak. Persistently engaged, the dialogue between the two consciences underscores a point we often forget – belief was a process constantly readdressed and revisited. Certainly Isaac wavered in his commitment, while William, undeviating from his belief that the Book of Common Prayer was a device of Baal, repeatedly relented concerning the exile of his son.

Throughout Archer's diary there is a fragile conviction that God's providence protected him for service: whether surviving the plague or serious injury at the hands of rolling horses or friendly rapiers, Isaac believed that God had marked him out for special favour. He was doing the right thing. His ability to conform while maintaining the integrity of his own conscience allows a window on to the flexibility of conformity after the Restoration. Archer did not simply relinquish his intimacy with the 'non-conformist' circle, and enact and impose the Book of Common Prayer. In fact, just as he had done in Cambridge, he tried to balance the demands of the established order with conscientious pursuit of other 'meetings'. Edward Fowler's ministry in St Giles Cripplegate in the 1680s establishes that there were patterns of 'accommodating' conformity. Archer too (and one suspects he was not unique) made his ministry comfortable for those with tender consciences (he noted, 'I did not signe with the crosse because it gave offence'), while himself attending other more godly places. In another instance he baptised a child without the canonical provision of godparents, nor 'by the service book'. It turned out that the family was Quaker, and indeed was so impressed with Archer that the father invited him 'to preach to them, of his family sometimes privately'. Acknowledging that ''twas forbidden by authority, and because it would keep them the more from hearing in publick, I refused to hearken to it'.[25] He knew the limits of accommodation. Certainly Archer took his public ministry seriously: for example, he took great pains at Chippenham, where he discovered the sacrament had not been given for twenty years. He preached twice about it, 'laying downe such qualifications as the strictest divines make use of, and went to the houses of such as would receive, to speake with them concerning so weighty a busines'. Having explained these 'grounds', he noted: 'I left it to their owne consciences what to doe.' In other cases he organised catechism for the young, or berated individuals who spent more time in the alehouse than in church. His flexibility sometimes attracted the attentions of more rigorous conformists who, for example, informed the local justice of the peace about his failure to keep holy days.[26]

The diary in the 1660s shows that he constantly revisited the question of his conformity: his chief design, he admitted, 'in being a minister, next to God's Glory, was that I might be more at leisure for the good of my soule by making that both my generall and particular, which others made their generall calling'. If conformity was implicated in compromising this ambition, he was willing to abandon it. He had agreed to preach in the 'private place' of Sir John Russell, which allowed a greater godliness. Inspired by conviction that he should not 'act against my conscience by baulking any truths of God to please men', he 'left off conforming' briefly in March 1665, although he still offered to preach to his parishioners. Indeed, he managed to make an arrangement whereby he eventually held a living (and more importantly an income) while employing another to read services from the Book of Common Prayer. For most of the 1670s and 1680s, Archer had ministerial duties in a variety of parishes, where he came to an accommodation either with the local community or the godly patron. The device of employing a reader (and thereby avoiding accusations that he did not employ the Common Prayer, while preserving his own conscience) was connived at by ecclesiastical superiors. In the case of one reader, John Goodwin, Archer ultimately dispensed with his services, because he was 'so violent against [the behaviour of] nonconformists' which dissuaded them from attending the church.[27] Such is the evidence of how religious diversity could not be contained by the restored church.

That Archer is emblematic of the tension between order and conscience is further illustrated by his response to the brief prerogative indulgence of diversity in 1672. His diary recorded that this opportunity did not dissuade him or his friends from attending the established church ('none forsook the public'). Indeed he had anxieties that the project was 'dangerous as to the growth of popery'. Despite insisting that he was 'more satisfied in the Church of England than ever', a licence was obtained for a Presbyterian meeting in his house in Chippenham.[28] There Archer took advantage of the indulgence to regularise a practice of private meetings that he and others routinely undertook. There was a long tradition of participating in such voluntary gatherings, alongside public provision. Very often those meetings supplemented the sermons and prayers of the established church. That Archer was able to cross over between the public and the private meeting without apparently compromising either his conscience or his status in the eyes of either his parishioners or ecclesiastical superiors tells us something significant about the flexible nature of conformity. Archer acknowledged that by some he was thought a 'fanatick' (partly because of his father's reputation), but he remained committed to the church of England, even after the act of 1689 made nonconformity tolerable.[29]

From 1689 to the 1720s the legal foundations of the confessional state shifted from a bedrock of statutory coercion to one of a compromise between privilege and voluntary persuasion. There was an adjustment from the assumptions embodied in the writings of Norris to the state of practical accommodation described in Archer's dairy. In one sense, the experience of the half-century after the execution of the king in 1649 had established that the traditional ecclesiological structure was both dangerous (it might easily be captured by enthusiasts or papists) and redundant (it was incapable ultimately of successfully imposing conformity throughout the kingdom). Political thinkers like Hobbes and Locke have been characterised by some historians as developing theories of political sovereignty and liberty applicable to a post-confessional society. Such historical accounts, however, do considerable damage to the integrity of both men's writings – and to our understanding of the nature of their society. Hobbes's subtle and complicated war against priestcraft persisted to the end of his life, and indeed had a powerful afterlife in the writings of men like Charles Blount, John Toland and Matthew Tindal, and the clandestine scribal texts of the 1700s. One might plausibly argue that Locke's writings on toleration exercised more influence over the shape of the late Stuart polity than that of the *Treatises* on government. In a political culture where the most powerful national institutions of governance were a protestant monarchy, the Church of England and parish office-holders, ecclesiological definitions were by default central to 'constitutional' debate. For many contemporaries the starting point for thinking about the nature of public authority and the duties of individuals was ecclesiastical. The nature of the church and the authority of churchmen (and the religion they embodied) was the first and last thing any individual encountered: theories of the church were arguably more significant than theories of the state.

The period did see a complex and subtle restructuring of ways of experiencing and thinking about society and religion. There developed an intellectual distinction between a view of the sacred which assumed there was only one 'true religion' and a more relativistic perception that there were many 'religions'. The experience of ecclesiastical diversity during the decades of the Revolution and its persistence after the Restoration meant that many people at all levels of society knew that there were (and indeed could be) more than one church. What the

Revolution did was compromise the purity of a singular 'church–state': a society either with a different church or perhaps with many churches was no longer unthinkable. That these possibilities were still acute is manifest in an episode that convulsed the political nation shortly after the accession of George I.

In 1717 one of the most controversial assaults of the eighteenth century was launched against the legitimacy of the Church of England. Despite being the 'the most bitter ideological conflict of the century', it has received very little historical attention.[30] The immediate political consequence was the suspension of the constitutional institutions of the church. Clerical convocation, the fount of stentorian, polemical hostility since the mid-1690s, was dismissed and neutered by regal injunction. In the following year the radical commonwealth ministry led by Sunderland and Stanhope enacted statutory reform of the legislation that infringed the civic identity of dissenting communities. Although many of the historical accounts of the period barely allude to the crisis, it was a moment of real constitutional meaning, disentangling at an institutional level the intertwined interests of church and state. The paradox of the affair is underscored when one considers that the controversy was launched, not by an irreligious deist or incendiary atheist, but by a clergyman, royal chaplain and bishop. Benjamin Hoadly, the bishop of Bangor, had by his writings 'done more harm to the Church of Christ and the Protestant cause than any man living', said one contemporary.[31] The suspension of convocation in 1717 was not simply a political act, but an ecclesiological one: it brought to a conclusion an attack on the church that had been initiated in its most bloody form by the execution of Archbishop Laud in 1645.

Hoadly was a churchman. Often abused as a turbulent Whig, he was, nevertheless, a conforming minister and a moderate episcopalian. In disputes with presbyterians, he insisted on the function of episcopal ordination against the rival claims of the dissenting interest. When defending the 'reasonableness of conformity to the Church of England', Hoadly described the limits of claims of conscience against the rival authority of a national establishment. Contrary to many on the episcopal bench, he combined subscription to a moderate political conformity to the practices of the state religion with an emphasis on the prerogative of private, individual judgement in matters of belief. Following in the traditions of the 'latitudinarian' churchmen of the Restoration, Hoadly enjoined the arguments of Thomas Hobbes as a suitable model for understanding the relationship between obligation and conscience. Public religion was a matter of political sovereignty and decent order, while conviction, faith and salvation were private issues between God and the individual. The example of Namaan, who bowed his knee to the idol of Rimon as an act of civic obligation, while retaining true belief in God, was advanced as a suitable model for the conduct of Christian life.[32]

The paradox of Hoadly was one that ran deep in the seams of Augustan society: the anti-clerical priest challenging sacerdotalism in the name of true religion.[33] The anti-clericalism of Hoadly was not unique. As studies of Whig ideology have established, attacks on the 'priestcraft' and intolerance of the Church of England were fundamental to the development of party identity from the 1690s.[34] This was not simply a hostility towards specific clerical institutions, but one engaged with assumptions about the 'politics of incarnation'. The successive ecclesiolog-ical crises of the 1700s, which found violent expression in the turbulence of the Sacheverell trial and its aftermath, were driven by a convinced, but devout, hos-tility to the *de jure divino* claims of the high church, repeatedly couched in terms of a defence of true religion. In contrast to the practical atheism of the high Enlightenment, the thrust of this polemic in the English context engaged directly with the nature of public religion. It was a crisis of clerical authority rather than a more fundamental crisis of religion. Men like Hoadly recognised that there was an intimate connection between claims to a spiritual *ordo* in the parish and the exercise of social power in the constitution.[35]

The sermon, published as *The nature of the kingdom, or church, of Christ*, was delivered by Hoadly before King George I, at the royal chapel in St James, on Sunday 31 March 1717. Published 'by his Majesties Special Command', in London, Dublin, Edinburgh and New York, the sermon achieved well over fifteen editions in 1717. William Law described it as an attempt 'to dissolve the Church as a Society'.[36] Taking the utterance of Christ recorded in John 18.36 – 'My Kingdom is not of this world' – as its fundamental text, Hoadly applied Hobbesian historical linguistics to the meaning of the phrase. As Hobbes had illus-trated at great length in *Leviathan*, taking the use of words like 'spirit' and 'angel' in scripture as his subject, such 'names' tended to lose their original meaning over time. Hoadly wrote of 'the alteration of Meaning annexed to certain sounds' so that the 'signification' of a word came to stand for a 'complication of notions, as distinct from the original intention of it, nay, as contradictory to it, as Darkness is to Light'. The remedy lay in a return to 'the original of things', found in the words and practice of Christ. Although 'words and sounds' had a powerful effect on people's minds, their mutations did not change the nature of things. Working through key vocabulary – 'religion', 'worship', 'prayer' – Hoadly drew a distinc-tion between original Christianity and contemporary practice: virtues and integrity, spirit and truth had been supplanted by a variety of self-interested and corrupt modes. Recovering the language of the New Testament was the best method for finding the 'original intentions of such words'. This was especially important for correct understanding of the 'kingdom of Christ'. Originally this phrase had identified those small number of people who believed Christ to be the Messiah 'or those who subjected themselves to Him'. Importantly the 'kingdom' was 'not of this world'.[37]

Building on this scriptural vocabulary, Hoadly expounded a reading that under-mined claims by the clergy to exercise a sacred authority derived from Christ. He was unambiguous: it was clear that Christ 'hath, in those points, left behind him, no visible, humane *Authority*; no *Vicegerents*, who can be said properly to sup-ply his place; no *Interpreters*, upon whom his subjects are absolutely to depend; no *Judges* over the consciences or religion of his people'. As contemporaries were swift to note, this undercut the very notion of a Christian authority delegated to a human institution for the distribution of saving grace. In remodelling the economy of incarnation, Hoadly had struck out the sacred foundations of all clerical institution: by removing any fundamental claims to *ordo*, Hoadly purposively compromised any independent claims to *jurisdictio*, in the process deliberately revising the relationship between magistracy and *sacerdos*. The lower house of convocation rebutted Hoadly's arguments: the sermon tended 'to subvert all government and discipline in the Church of Christ, and reduce his kingdom to a state of anarchy and confusion'. The Church of Christ was left defenceless and bereft of authority, 'without any visible human authority to judge, censure, or punish offenders in the affairs of conscience and eternal salvation'.[38]

Hoadly's immediate intention had been to un-pick the common assumption that the Church of Christ was coincident with the established Church of England. In particular his target was the resurgent assertion that the defining essence of the established church was its sacramental capacity. Provoked by the clericalist arguments of non-juring polemicists like George Hickes who asserted that the Church was Christ's body on earth, that the clergy were his vicegerents and baptism was a means of entry into a spiritual corporation, Hoadly rejected the contention of churchmen that they 'stand in God's stead'.[39] Although the controversy had enormous implications for the relationship between church and state (could the civil state deprive recalcitrant priests?) and church and laity (could clergymen discipline dissenting parishioners?), the thrust of the argument focused on the status of the established church. For men like Hickes, establishing the visibility of the church from the days of Christ to their time was essential: ministerial priests derived their 'function' from the spiritual authority of the Holy Spirit and administered the kingdom of Christ in both 'his kingly as well as his priestly office'. The succession of ordination by the laying on of hands was unbroken.[40]

Like the Whig controversialist Matthew Tindal, Hoadly intended to rescue 'the Church of Christ from ecclesiastical tyranny'.[41] The basis of this argument rested on a Hobbesian reading of Christ's sovereignty over his own kingdom. The principle of 'whosoever hath such an *Authority* of making laws, is so far a King' meant that if Christ has delegated his authority to a body of 'interpreters' he would have lost his authority. Christ's laws and sanctions related to 'another state after this'. The associated economy of rewards and punishments was 'not of this world'.[42] For Hoadly, true faith was freely chosen and not the product of coercion or threat of punishment: for that reason, rewards and punishments in this life could not be effective or instrumental for salvation. Christ alone was 'King, Lawgiver and Judge'. Those who argued from the example of other 'visible societies, and other visible kingdoms of this world' that Christ's kingdom was similar were simply wrong. For men to claim Christ's legacy was both deceitful and wrong: 'they have set up to themselves the Idol of an unintelligible Authority, both in belief and worship and practice; in words under Jesus Christ, but in deed and in truth over him'. The attempt of the Church of England to set up a rival jurisdiction over the conscience and conduct of the laity 'destroys the Rule and Authority of Jesus Christ, as King'.[43] Concluding with a swell of invective against the false traditions of clerical jurisdiction, and delivered before the new monarch (perhaps encouraged by the king himself), Hoadly's sermon acted as a platform for radical ecclesiological reform. The suspension of convocation and, in the following year, the repeal of the Occasional Conformity Act and the projected suspension of the Test Act were high-water marks in civil retrenchment of clerical authority.

To churchmen like Francis Atterbury writing in the 1690s and 1700s, any assault on the 'rights, powers and privileges' of the church was not only impiety but blasphemous.[44] Christian institutions and officers were material incarnations of the divinity of God. The visible marks of the true church, embodied in the high and non-juring traditions after 1689, were badges of soteriological efficacy. With its Cyprianic emphasis on episcopacy as the benchmark of correct sacramental administration this ideology regarded clergyman as ministers of Christ, mediators 'empowered and authorised to negotiate and transact for God'. This idea of the unbroken apostolic succession of bishops, priests and deacons as the stewards of God's mysteries was directly contrary to the vision advanced by Hoadly. As the example of the trial in 1710 of Henry Sacheverel and its aftermath indicates, the clash between the distinct ecclesiologies had massive political resonance. The belief that the church was a key institution in the religious and political administration of society lay behind the attempt to reinvigorate its legal and economic status. Only too aware that the 'church was in danger' from Whig ministries in the 1700s and 1710s, counter-proposals to refurbish the disciplinary powers of church courts and to improve the material life of churchmen were made when Tory ministers were in power. Although these attempts were couched in the languages of *renovatio* and refurbishment, they were in effect a serious attempt at the modernisation of clerical power. When Hoadly claimed then that the 'kingdom of Christ was not of this world' he was engaging in an overtly political debate.[45]

The example of Hoadly allows us to rethink the consequences of 1649, and the relationship between Christianity and Enlightenment in England. In his writings, especially in the sermon of 1717, it is possible to see radical anti-clerical language, side by side with a sincere scriptural piety. The purchase of Hoadly's polemic underscores that the problem of public religion was not simply a conceptual matter, but a parochial one too. Reforming the practice and beliefs of churchmen was the way to establishing a true and virtuous polity. The conflict, then, among a variety of Christian discourses was ultimately an institutional battle, rather than a straightforward confrontation between the godly and the ungodly or between reason and religion. Whereas the earlier discourses attempted to negotiate between civil *jurisdictio* and priestly *ordo*, the later discussion displaced the immediate concern with the sacred powers of the 'church', to focus on the relationship between conscience and community. At the core of this shift was both an argument about the priority of claims of conscience and also, importantly, a redefinition of the nature of clerical institutions. *Sacerdos* implied no public *auctoritas*; or, as Hoadly put it, the church had no corporate authority and therefore no public role in shaping religious ceremonies and duties.[46]

As the controversy over Hoadly's sermon indicates, the language of religious truth was the forum, rather than the butt, of these disputes. Historians have attempted to document how the Reformation debate about the relationship between church and state (*regnum* against *sacerdotium*) modulated into negotiation between the claims of conscience and order. Both sets of conceptual discourse were ecclesiological, but between the 1640s and the 1690s there was a subtle but distinct shift of emphasis, best understood in the change of vocabulary from church and state to religion and state.

Despite the persisting authority of Christian discourses and institutions, after the Revolution the religious culture of the nation became pluralistic and adaptative rather than monolithic and inflexible. Post-1660, the increasing emphasis on a 'reasonable' religion was accompanied by competing assertions of the pastoral, sacramental and divine nature of Christian institutions. As 'nonconformity' became dissent so the varieties of 'Christianities' multiplied. The relationships between these different, converging and competing forms of religious experience and expression were complex. The cultural motors of this religious change have been identified in a number of ways: the languages of a 'second' reformation, of secularisation and of 'enlightenment' have all been used to describe the transformation. The dynamic of debate was not simply about the relative merits of reason and revelation or conducted between deist and priest. Dialogue rather than confrontation, appropriation rather than rejection and redefinition rather than invention are the appropriate vocabularies to describe the relationship.

There is no doubt that the institutions of ecclesiastical authority came under considerable political attack after the Revolution of the 1640s and 1650s. Ecclesiological controversy underpinned the successive political crises of the 1670s, 1680s, 1700s and 1710s: behind the legislation of the Clarendon Code, the repeated Declarations of Indulgence, the Toleration Act, the politics of occasional conformity and the convocation crisis lay a series of doubts about the relationship between religion and society. The intellectual engagement between those who saw true religion as intimately bound up with a visible communal institution and those who argued that the only true expression of belief was internal and individual was fought out in many fora: the parish, parliament, the world of print culture, the court, the public spaces of coffee houses and salons. That this war of ideas took place signified a changing culture of public religious expression. After the 1650s the problem of government became more complicated simply because different groups of people were 'believing' in different ways. The public claim to represent the authority of 'true religion' became a badge of political identity rather than an unconscious aspect of lived religious meaning.[47]

Notes

1 See T. Harris, 'The legacy of the English civil war: rethinking the revolution', *European Legacy*, 5 (2000), 501–14.

2 M. Goldie, 'The Hilton gang and the purge of London in the 1680s', in H. Nenner (ed.), *Politics and the political imagination in later Stuart Britain* (Woodbridge, 1998), 43–73; 'The political thought of the Anglican revolution', in R. Beddard (ed.), *The revolutions of 1688* (Oxford, 1991), 102–36; and 'The theory of religious intolerance in restoration England', in O. P. Grell, J. I. Israel and N. Tyacke (eds), *From persecution to toleration: the glorious revolution and religion in England* (Oxford, 1991), 331–68.

3 See J. Spurr, *The restoration church of England, 1646–1689* (New Haven, CT, 1991); and 'Schism and the restoration church', *Journal of Ecclesiastical History*, 41 (1990), 408–24.

4 See W. Lamont's still fundamentally important *Godly rule* (London, 1969).

5 J. G. A. Pocock, 'Religious freedom and the desacralisation of politics: from the English civil wars to the Virginia statute', in M. D. Petersen and R. C. Vaughan (eds), *The Virginia statute for religious freedom* (Cambridge, 1988), 43–73.

6 See J. Champion, 'Willing to suffer: law and religious conscience in seventeenth-century England', in J. McLaren and H. Coward (eds), *Religious conscience, the state and the law* (New York, 1999), 13–28.

7 A case study of contestation can be seen in J. Champion and L. McNulty, 'Making orthodoxy in late restoration England: the trials of Edmund Hickeringill', in M. J. Braddick and J. Walter (eds), *Negotiating power in early modern society* (Cambridge, 2001), 227–48, 302–5.

8 For a discussion of the historical arguments, see J. Champion, *The pillars of priestcraft shaken* (Cambridge, 1992), esp. ch. 3, 'Arimathea to Cranmer', 53–98.

9 T. Harris, *Politics under the later Stuarts* (London, 1993); and 'Was the Tory reaction popular? Attitudes of Londoners towards the persecution of dissent, 1681–1686', *London Journal*, 13 (1987–88), 106–20.

10 A. Fletcher, 'The enforcement of the Conventicle Acts 1664–1679', in W. J. Sheils (ed.), *Persecution and toleration* (Oxford, 1984), 235–46.

11 T. Ellwood, *A discourse concerning riots* (1683), 3, 11–12, 13–14.

12 R. L. Greaves, 'Conventicles, sedition, and the Toleration Act of 1689', *Eighteenth-Century Life*, 12 (1988), 1–14; and 'Seditious sectaries or "sober and useful inhabitants"? Changing conceptions of the Quakers in early modern Britain', *Albion*, 33 (2001), 24–50. There are around eighty works devoted to the debate, c. 1664–84.

13 J. Norris, *A discourse concerning the pretended religious assembling in private conventicles* (1685), 10–11.

14 *Ibid.*, 10, 38, 51, 54.

15 *Ibid.*, 62–5, 72–3.

16 *Ibid.*, 77–9, 83.

17 *Ibid.*, 98, 109–14, 122–3, 131.

18 *Ibid.*, 158–9, 198, 238–9.

19 *Ibid.*, 240, 249–50, 259, 306.

20 See 'The diary of Isaac Archer, 1641–1700', in *Two East Anglian diaries, 1641–1729*, ed. M. Storey (Woodbridge, 1994), 1–26, 48–9, 101–3, 115.

21 *Ibid.*, 68.

22 *Ibid.*, 71–2.

23 *Ibid.*, 80–1, 82.

24 *Ibid.*, 83–4, 113.

25 *Ibid.*, 92, 110, 111, 113, 114.

26 *Ibid.*, 89–90.

27 *Ibid.*, 148.
28 *Ibid.*, 25.
29 *Ibid.*, 143; P. Collinson 'The English conventicle', in W. J. Sheils and D. Wood (eds), *Voluntary religion* (Oxford, 1986), 223–61, at 239–42.
30 J. C. D. Clark, *English society 1688–1832* (Cambridge, 1985), 302; see P. B. Hessert 'The Bangorian controversy', Ph.D thesis, University of Edinburgh (1951); H. D. Rack, ' "Christ's kingdom not of this world": the case of Benjamin Hoadly versus William Law reconsidered', in D. Baker (ed.), *Church, society and politics* (Oxford, 1975), 275–91. The *ODNB* entry on Hoadly, by Stephen Taylor, is the starting point for modern study.
31 See N. Sykes, 'Benjamin Hoadly, bishop of Bangor', in F. J. C. Hearnshaw (ed.), *The social and political ideas of some English thinkers of the Augustan age* (London, 1928), 112–56, at 120.
32 J. Champion 'Le culte privé quand il est rendu dans le secret': Hobbes, Locke et les limites de la tolérance, l'athéisme et l'hétérodoxie', in Y. C. Zarka, F. Lessay and J. Rogers (eds), *Les fondements philosophique de la tolérance*, 3 vols (Paris, 2002), i. 221–53.
33 See J. Champion ' "Religion's safe, with priestcraft is the war": Augustan anticlericalism and the legacy of the English revolution, 1660–1720', *European Legacy*, 5 (2000), 547–61.
34 M. Goldie 'Priestcraft and the birth of Whiggism', in N. Phillipson and Q. Skinner (eds), *Political discourse in early modern Britain* (Cambridge, 1993), 209–31.
35 See P. Harvey, 'The problem of social–political obligation for the Church of England in the seventeenth century', *Church History*, 40 (1971), 156–69.
36 Sykes, 'Benjamin Hoadly, bishop of Bangor', 143.
37 B. Hoadly, *The nature of the kingdom, or church, of Christ* (1717), 3–5, 6, 9–11.
38 'A representation of the lower house of convocation', in E. Cardwell (ed.), *Synodalia*, 2 vols (Oxford, 1888 [1842]), ii. 829–30.
39 Hessert, 'Bangorian controversy', 41–3, 64.
40 *Ibid.*, 117–19.
41 See M. Tindal, *The rights of the Christian church* (1706), lxxxviii, 80, 84–5 151, 310, 370.
42 Hoadly, *The nature of the kingdom*, 18–20.
43 *Ibid.*, 24, 27.
44 See R. Cornwall, *Visible and apostolic: the constitution of the church in high church Anglican and non-juror thought* (Newark, DE, 1993), 78.
45 See A. M. C. Waterman, 'The nexus between theology and political doctrine', in K. Haakonssen (ed.), *Enlightenment and religion: rational dissent in eighteenth-century England* (Cambridge, 1996), 193–218.
46 See Pocock, 'Religious freedom and the desacralisation of politics'.
47 J. Champion, ' "To govern is to make subjects believe": anticlericalism, politics and power, c. 1680–1717', in M. Cragoe and N. Aston (eds), *Anticlericalism in Britain, c. 1500–1914* (Stroud, 2000), 42–66.

Index

absolutism 1–5, 12, 57, 95, 105
addresses to monarch 170–3
Admonition Controversy 54
Ainsworth, Henry 68
Allen, Benjamin 120
Allen, Thomas 16
Allibond, John 48–9
altars 46, 101–2, 131
Anabaptists 118, 131–2
ancient constitution 2–4, 13
Anglicanism 5, 18, 62, 72, 76, 134,
    139–40
Anne, queen 172
Antinomianism 35, 113, 118
anti-popery 30, 46–7, 52
Apollos 189
Arabic 33
Aragon, Catherine of, queen 87, 89
Archer, Isaac 191–5
    flexible conformity of 193–5
Archer, William 191–3
Argyle, Archibald Campbell, marquis of
    153, 161, 163
Arminianism 17, 46–7
Ascham, Roger 52
Ashe, Simeon 112
assizes 15, 83, 103
Aston, Sir Thomas 47–8
astrology 33
Atking, Margaret 85
Atterbury, Francis, bishop 199
Augustine, St 188
Aylerugg, Maurice 45

Bacon, Francis 7, 55–6
Bacon, Nathaniel 16
Baconians 36
balance of property 2, 5, 7–8
Bagshaw, Edward 19
Baillie, Robert 117
Bancroft, Richard, archbishop 2, 55, 57
Baptists 68–9, 112–14, 123, 136, 138–9,
    186
Barebone, Praisegod 113, 120, 123
Bargrave, Isaac 12
Barne, Sir George 15
Barrington, Sir Thomas 49
Bartham, Robert 85
Bassett, Elizabeth 87
Bate, Randall 71
Baxter, Richard 100, 131, 136
Belewe, Thomas de 89
Bellamy, John 120, 122
Bentham, Joseph 70
Benyon, George 121
Berkshire
    Abingdon 44
    Maidenhead 172
Best, Paul 124
Blasphemy Act (1648) 124, 137
Blount, Charles 195
Blundell, William 66
Blunstone, Jane 90
Boleyn, Anne, queen 87, 89
Bolingbroke, Henry St John, first viscount
    175
Bolton, Robert 70

bond of association 169
Book of Common Prayer 71–5, 105,
    131, 133–4, 138, 141–2, 155, 164,
    191–4
Book of Orders 107
Booth, Sir George 47, 58
bourgeois revolution 1, 6, 8
Bowle, John, bishop 68
Brabourne, Theophilus 73
Brereton, Sir William 47, 53
Bridgewater, John Egerton, first earl of
    32–3
Brooke, Humphrey 111
Brooke, Richard 50
Brooke, Robert, second baron 114–15
Brownists 12, 67, 132
Buckingham, George Villiers, first duke of
    44, 46
Burghley, William Cecil, first baron 15,
    52, 169
Burnsall, John 90
Burroughs, Jeremiah 112, 121
Burton, Henry 114
Butter, Nathaniel 34

Cadiz 55
Calamy, Edmund 121
Callander, James Livingston first, earl of
    161
Calvinism 6, 51–2
Cambridge
    Arrington 193
    Chippenham 194
    Trinity College 191–3
Capel, Arthur, first baron 151, 154
capitalism 4, 6–8
Capstocke, John 87
Careuth, John 88
Cartwright, Thomas 17, 50, 54
Caryl, Joseph 117, 123
Castle, John 32–3
Cecil faction 53
Cephas 189
chapels 68
Charles I, king 3, 11
    credo of 152
    Eikon Basilike 19–20, 150–68
    martyr cult 158

Personal Rule 43–5
    trial of 150
Charles II, king 85, 88, 145, 162–4
    as prince of Wales 151, 154, 158,
    160–2
Chaunseler, Margaret 89
Cheshire 44, 47, 49, 58
    Holt 31
Chillingworth, William 157
Chinese 33
Church, definition of 62, 124, 128, 140–3,
    185–91, 197–200
church papists 44, 64, 69
Cicero 51
citizens 108–9
civic humanism 47, 52
Clarendon, Edward Hyde, first earl of 2,
    10, 20, 22 n.32, 100, 154, 160–1
Clarke, Anne 85
class conflict 1–3, 5–6, 17–20, 97–8,
    105–8, 129
classical republicanism 51
Cleves, Anne of, queen 87
Clifton, Fulke 117
coat and conduct money 43
Cockayne, George 123
Coke, Sir Edward 12–13
    puritan links of 24 n.69
Coles, Peter 116
Collinson, Patrick 70
commerce 3–4
Commons, House of 5, 10–11
    Apology (1604) 18
commonwealth, idea of 16–17, 20, 45–7,
    51, 53, 62, 99, 106, 111
community, definition of 147 n.10
comprehension (religious) 142, 163, 185
confessional state 37, 185, 195
conscience 12, 101–2, 108, 152, 155,
    191–4, 196, 199
    church of 140, 142–3
Constantine, emperor 188
constitutional conflict 7, 12, 14
Conventicle Acts (1664 & 1670) 141,
    186
conventicles 70–1, 187–91
Convocation, suspension of 196, 198–9
Cooper, J. P. 8

Cope, Sir Anthony 49
Copley, Lionel 38
Coriolanus 84
Cornwall 15
corruption 52–3
Cottington, Francis, baron 160
country 53
court 45–6, 49, 52–3, 145
Cowp[er], Harry 86
Cowper, Lady Sarah 181
Cowper, Sir William 181
Cox, Benjamin 121
Cranford, James 111, 118, 121
Crompton, Walter 88
Cromwell, Oliver 33, 114, 121
Cromwell, Richard 122
Cromwell, Thomas 84
Cressy, David 20–21
Crew, John 17
crowds 19, 96–8, 101
crown finances 4, 13–14
Culpeper, Cheney 37, 116
Culpeper, Sir John, first baron 16, 153,
    160
Cust, Richard 2

Darcy, Eward 15–16
    connexion with Raleigh 25 n.87
Darley, Mary 85–7
Davenant, Charles 179
Davenant, Sir William 179
Davison, Richard 144
Davison, William 144
Dearsly, Henry 191
Defoe, Daniel 178
democracy 54, 100
denominationlism 19
Dering, Sir Edward 44, 48
Descartes 33
Devon 15
    Bradninch 172
    Exeter (recorder) 45
Diggers 36, 106, 123
dissolution of the monasteries 5–7, 10
Dixon, Margaret 88
Dod, John 17
Double, Tom 179
Dowsing, William 132

Drake, Richard 15
Duffield, Stephen 88
Duppa, Brian, bishop 156–7, 164

Easter communion 69, 73–4
ecclesiatical courts 13, 19, 130–2, 134,
    144–6
economic history 7
Edgehill, battle of 132
education 9–10
Edward I, king 3
Edward II, king 3
Edward VI, king 88
Edwards, John 177, 181
Edwards, Thomas 29, 35–6, 112–13,
    115–20, 134
elect nation 69–70
Elizabeth I, queen 13, 89–90
Ellesmere, Thomas Egerton, baron 11
Ellwood, Thomas 183 n.36, 187
Elmes, Thomas 44–5, 48
Elton, Geoffrey 10
enclosure 7, 97–8, 101, 106
Engels, Frederick 6
English Revolution
    idea of 1–2, 4–8, 36–7
    legacies 20–1, 27–42, 62, 76, 108–9,
        124, 129, 146
Enlightenment 3, 197, 199
enthusiasm 3
episcopacy 57, 130–1, 151–3, 155, 164,
    186, 196
Essex 43–5, 48–9, 89, 95, 101, 103, 132
    Bocking 153
    Boxted 142
    Earls Colne 105, 132, 136
    Terling 107
Essex, Robert Devereux, second earl of 17,
    53, 55–6
Essex, Robert Devereux, third earl of 33,
    117
Etherington, John 71, 113
Evelyn, John 68
Ewer, Edward 89
excise 14, 17
excommunication 66, 69
ex officio oath 12
Exodus 101

Familism 71, 113
Farthing, John 118
fast days 111–12, 117
Feltwell, John 89
Ferne, Henry, bishop 191–2
feudalism 3–4, 9–10, 13
fictionality 179–80
Fiennes, Nathaniel 155
Firth, Richard 38
fiscal-military state 14, 20, 36–7, 170, 174
Fisher, John 49, 56
Fleming, Sir William 161
Folfarr, Anne 85–6
forced loan 12, 17, 58
forest fines 46
Fowler, Edward 193
Fox, George 136
France 173–4, 176
freedom of speech (in parliament) 4, 12, 50, 56–7
French Revolution 1, 4–7
Frijhoff, William 65
Fuller, Nicholas 12, 16
Fuller, Thomas 14
Fuller, William 180

Gardiner, Samuel Rawson 1, 7, 10
Gardiner, Stephen, bishop 85
Gataker, Thomas 117
Gauden, John, bishop 151–4, 156–7
  views of 153
Gell, Robert 113
gender 19–20, 81–94
gentry 4, 9, 68
  rise of 8–10
George I, king 197
  as cuckold 87
Gerrard, Charles, fourth baron 160
Gibson, Samuel 68–9
Gilbert, Richard 86
Glorious Revolution 6
Gloucester diocese
  consistory court 138
  visitation 139
Gloucestershire 43, 45
  Aschurch 144
  Bristol 119, 121, 186

Fiddington 144
Gloucester 48
Natton 144
Pamington 144
Stoke Orchard 139, 143
Tewkesbury 138–9, 142, 145
Winchcombe 138–9
Goldie, Mark 185
Goodwin, John 111–12, 118, 123–4
Goodwin, Thomas 112
gossip 81–2, 87
Gowche, Barbara 85–6
Gowche, Robert 86
Gowing, Laura 90
grand jury 103
Grand Remonstrance 29, 122
Great Contract 56
Great Rebellion, origin of the term 6–7, 22 n.32
Green, John 113
Greenhill, William 112, 121
Greville, Sir Fulke 50
Grindal, Edmund, archbishop 82
Grosvenor, Sir Richard 47, 53
Guizot, Francois 4–6
Guy, John 57

Habermas, Jürgen 170
Haines, Richard 144
Hallam, Henry 4, 7
Hamilton, James, first duke of 153, 160
Hammond, Henry 157
Hampden, John 17
Hampshire, Basing House 33
Hare, John 56
Harley, Sir Robert 132
Harpur, Sir John 46
Harrington, James 2–3, 5, 7–8, 10, 22 n.17, 37
Harrington, John 50
Harrison, Roger 82
Hartlib, Samuel 116
Hastings, Sir Francis 16
Hatton, Sir Christopher 44, 46
Hawes, Thomas 118
Hebden, James 85
Henderson papers 160

Henrietta Maria, queen 88, 90, 153, 162, 164
Henry III, king 3
Henry VIII, king
  as adulterer 87
  as cuckold 88
Herefordshire, Allens-Moore 66
Hertford, William Seymour, first marquis of 156
Hesilrige, Sir Arthur 17
Hexter, J. H. 8–9
Heylyn, Peter 48, 133
Hickeringill, Edmund 142
Hickes, George 198
high churchmen 173, 176, 181, 197
High Commission, Court of 12–13, 113, 130
Hill, Christopher 1, 8–9
Hoadly, Benjamin, bishop 20, 196–200
Hobbes, Thomas 33, 37, 129, 189, 195–8
Hooker, Richard 7, 38, 62, 68
Hooker, Thomas 71
Hopton, Ralph, baron 160
Howell, James 73
Hoyle, Joshua 121
Hughes, Ann 2
Hult, Lawrence 85
Hume, David 3–5
Hunt, Barbara 83
Hyde, Robert 45

iconoclasm 101–3, 132–3
impositions 12, 17
Independents 112, 115, 121–2, 135, 138–40, 143–4, 154, 156–9, 191
Ireland 151, 154, 159, 162, 172
  confederate Catholics 159, 161

Jacobites 87, 180–1
James I, king 3, 56–7
James II, king 85, 88, 180
Jermyn, Henry, first baron 153
John, king 3
Jones, Mary 87
Josephus 34
Josselin, Ralph 105, 132, 136
Juxon, Thomas 117
Juxon, William, archbishop 156, 158

Kent 44, 46–8, 58, 89, 116
  Beckenham 89
  Canterbury 67
  Dover 44, 88
  Maidstone 67
  Sandwich 67
Kent, Henry Grey, sixth earl of 68
Kett, Robert, rebellion of 83
  wife of 83
Kiffin, William 113, 118, 120–1
Knightley, Richard 17
Knollys, Hanserd 121

laissez-faire 7, 23 n.36
Lake, Peter vii, 18, 28, 54, 57, 170
Lambe, Thomas 113, 122, 124
Lanark, William Hamilton, earl of, second duke of Hamilton 161
Lancashire, Little Crosby 66
Lane, Henry 144
Larner, William 124
Laslett, Peter 8–9
Laud, William, archbishop 7, 17, 74, 95, 133, 137, 196
Lauderdale, John Maitland, second earl of 160–1
Laudians 3, 19, 45, 74–5, 101–2, 130–1
Law, William 197
lay pastors 113
Lechmere, Nicholas 112
'Legion memorial' 178
legitimation crisis 19, 27–8, 35, 171
Leicester, Robert Dudley, earl of 19, 27–8, 35, 90, 171
Leicestershire 46
Leslie, Alexander, first earl of Leven 33
Levellers 19, 36, 38, 104, 111, 122
liberty 2–5, 9, 15, 54–6, 100, 176–7
  of conscience 135, 157
lieutenancy 43–7
Lilburne, John 116, 119, 124
Lilly, Wiliam 33
limited monarchy 1, 3, 5, 7, 12
Lincolnshire 44, 46
  Boston 14
Locke, John 37–8, 177, 195

London 48, 95
  Bell Alley 113
  Cheapside 117, 132
  Christ Church, Newgate 117, 119
  Common Council 112, 116, 120
  Cornhill 116–17, 120, 124
  Court of Aldermen 120
  Dutch Church 67
  Exchange 118
  Evil May Day 84
  Gatehouse 124
  Gazette 169
  Guildhall 118–19
  mayor and corporation 15–16
  Middle Temple 16
  recorder 45
  St Botolph Aldgate 69
  St Dunstan's in the West 123
  St Giles Cripplegate 193
  St Leonard East Cheap 132
  St Martin Outwich 123
  St Mary Abchurch 123
  St Mary Aldermanbury 117
  St Mary Aldermary 113
  St Michael Bassishaw 111
  St Stephen Coleman Street 112, 117
  Sion College 117
  Spittle 116
  Stationers' Company 120
  Stepney 112, 117, 121
  Taylors Hall 117
  Three Cranes 116
  Windmill Tavern 116
Long, Sir Robert (secretary) 160
Long Parliament 2, 7, 9, 13, 16–17,
  20
Lords, House of 5
Losh, James 90
Louvre group 152–4, 164
Lowdall, Robert 85–6
Lucas, Sir John 106
Lucian's *Dialogues* 111
Luttrell, Narcissus 178

Macaulay, Catherine 22 n.7
Macaulay, Thomas Babington 5
Machiavelli 52
Magna Carta 3–5, 12–14, 24 n.62, 102

Maidley, Richard 89
Manchester, Edward Montagu, second
  earl of 33
Manning, Brian 97
Marprelate, Martin 49, 55, 169–70
Marshall, Stephen 112, 117
Marx, Karl 6
Marxism 1, 6, 8–9, 97–8, 100
Mary I, queen 85–8
Mary, queen of Scots 49
Mary of Modena, queen 88–9
Massee, John 89
May, Thomas 2–3
Maynard, William, first baron 48–9
Medowe, Dorothy 83–4
Medowe, Thomas 84
Meredith, Christopher 120
Miles, Alison 86
Miles, Margery 85–6
Millington, Edwin 139
Milton, John 35, 112
Mockett, Thomas 105
monopolies 4, 12–17, 47, 56
  fish (salting, drying and packing)
    15–16
  leather 15–16
  playing cards 16
  proclamations 16
  salt 14–16
  statute 16
  vinegar 15
Mompesson, Sir Giles 16
Monmouth, James Scott, duke of 88
monstrosity 28, 33–4
Montrose, James Graham, first marquis
  of 159, 161–2
Moore, Francis 16
moral economy 99
Morice, James 12

Namaan 196
Naseby, battle of 29, 117
national debt 174
necessity, language of 37
Neile, Sir Richard 85
Neville, Alexander 83
Neville, Henry 48–9, 58
Newbury, second battle of 33

New Model Army 122, 155–6, 159
Newport, treaty of 150, 154–7, 161, 164
news 32–3, 95
newsletters (manuscript) 32, 43–5
Nicolson, William, bishop 140, 142
nobility 2–6, 8–9
Norfolk 177, 186
  Aylsham 84
  Diss 85–6
  King's Lynn 14, 16
  Norwich 12, 67, 105
Norman Conquest 3, 106
Norris, James 188–90, 195
Norris, John 188
Northampton, Henry Howard, earl of
  53
Northamptonshire 43–4, 46
  Fawsley 17
  Higham Ferrers 44
  Northampton 44
  Okeham 78 n.38
  Oundle 68
Northumberland, Newcastle, 85
  North Shields 85–6
Notestein, Wallace 10–11

Oates, Samuel 136
oath of association 169
oaths 104–5
Ormond, James Butler, first marquis of
  154, 159–64
Oxfordshire, rising 97
Overbury, Sir Thomas 53
Overton, Henry 120, 122
Overton, Richard 124

Pagitt, Ephraim 35, 117
parliament 7, 10, 14, 16, 53, 57
  constitutional revolution (1641) 7, 20,
    31
  elections 20, 43–5, 47–9, 54, 59 n.1,
    171–3
  franchise 18, 49
  impeachment 16
  opposition 11, 56
  party 11, 14, 18, 20, 48
  procedure 10–11
  representation 18, 53–4, 171, 180

parish 188–9
  church 63–76, 123–4, 189
  communities 38–9, 62, 123–4, 129–49
  offices 123–4, 172
Patient, Thomas 113
patriarchy 38
patriots 4, 46–7, 51–4
Paul, St 189
Peak Country 83
penance 130
Percy, Henry, baron 160
Perwiche, Alice 88
Peter, Hugh 111, 113, 116, 119
petitioning 19, 103–4, 171–3
Philip II, king 87
Pickering, Sir Gilbert 44–6, 48
pillarisation (*verzuiling*) 18, 64–70
Pliny 34
Plumb, Sir John 178–9
Pocock, John 185
political culture 27–8, 46, 95–110, 147
    n.15, 170–2, 175, 180, 195
  definition of 36
  national 174–5, 180
political language 176–7
political lying 177–8
politics
  of incarnation 185–6, 197
  of religion 129–49
  party 170–81
  popular 11, 15, 18, 20, 43–6, 81–94,
    110
Pollini, Girolamo 2
popish plots 30, 58, 105, 131, 145–6
popularity 15, 20, 30, 47–51, 54–8, 60
    n.28, 152
post-revisionism 1–2
Powell, Alexander 31
predestination 6
Presbyterians 111–12, 115, 118, 120–3,
    139–40, 154–7, 159, 162–3, 186, 194,
    196
presbyterianism 13, 17, 54–5, 122, 133,
    143–4, 151–3, 155, 157
prerogative 14–15, 17, 56, 58
press 20, 29, 170, 181
  'collapse of censorship' 31, 62, 103,
    115, 171

Price, John 114, 118
Price, Richard, mercer 119
Price, Richard, scrivener 111, 120, 123
priestcraft 38, 170, 195–6
privy chamber 15
privy council 45, 83
privy councillors 10, 53
progress 1–4, 9–10
Protestation 95, 104–6
providentialism 33–4, 191–2
Prowde, Johan 84
Prynne, William 35, 133, 155
public
    credit 170, 174
    judgement 170–1, 173–5, 180–1
    opinion 14–15, 18–19, 46, 103, 158,
        169
    sphere 18, 20, 38, 45, 49, 55–6, 58, 59
        n.12, 82, 108, 170, 174
puritanism 1–5, 7–8, 11–13, 16–18, 24
        n.59, 45, 48–9, 52, 69–71, 119
    seigneurial 17, 26 n.95
Puritan Revolution 1–2, 7, 21 n.9
purveyance 13, 56
Pym, John 9, 17, 23 n.44

Quakers 29, 123, 136, 138–9, 143 , 186–7,
        194
    sufferings 143
quarter sessions 103
Questier, Michael 28, 170

Raleigh, Sir Walter 16, 25 n.87
Randall, Giles 113, 116
Ranters 36, 81
Rapin-Thoyras, Paul de 3, 5, 178
Rattsey, Jane 87
Rawlins, Thomas 177
Rayning, Peter 85
regicide 19, 191
religious diversity 18–20, 35–7, 62, 76,
        111–28, 141, 185, 190–1, 195–6
republicans 2, 54
resistance theory 31, 35, 55, 57, 102
revisionism 1, 8–12
revolution 2–4, 7, 36, 38
    (1848) 5
Rich, Sir Nathaniel 17

Richard II, king 3
Ricraft, Josiah 32–3
riots 96–8, 181, 183 n.36, 187
Robinson, Thomas 105
Roman Catholicism 12, 18, 63–7, 104,
        186
root and branch
    bill 130
    petition 130
Rosier, Edmund 113, 123
royalism, popular 108
Royston, Richard 151–2, 156–7
Rupert, prince 160–1
Russell, Conrad vii, 1, 8–13, 17
Russell, Sir John 194
Russian Revolution 1
Rutland 136
Ryves, Bruno 33

Sacheverel, Henry 197, 199
Salisbury, Robert Cecil, first earl of 56
Salisbury diocese 139
Saye and Sele, William Fiennes, first
        viscount 17, 118
Scotland 151–3, 155, 159–64, 172
    lairds 13
    nobility 17, 118
    parliament 13
    presbyterianism 13
    rebellion (1637) 13, 29, 43–4, 48, 58,
        95, 102, 117, 121–2
    triennial act (1640) 13
Scott, James 107
Scott, Jonathan 37–8
Scott, Thomas, of Canterbury 12
separatism in religion 19, 28, 36–7, 67–8,
        115, 135, 143
sermon gadding 68, 111–12
Seymour, Jane, queen 88
Shakespeare, William 7
Sheldon, Gilbert, archbishop 140–2, 144
Sherland, Christopher 17
ship money 12, 17, 44–6
Short Parliament 13, 18, 43
Skipwith, Sir Henry 46
Smith, John 85
Smith, Ralph 116–17, 120
Solemn League and Covenant 32, 122

Somerset, Robert Carr, earl of 53
Southampton, Thomas Wriothesley,
 fourth earl of 156, 164
Southwark 186
 St Olave's 123
 St Saviour's 69
Spanish marriage 56, 58
Spelman, Sir Henry 189
Spencer, John 113–14
Spinoza 33
stadial theory 3
Stamford, battle of 33
standing armies 4, 100
Stanhope, James, first earl of 196
state formation 36–8, 129
Stone, Lawrence 8
Stonehouse, Sir George 44
stranger churches 67
Strode, William 133
Stubbes, John 52–3
subscription (clerical), to articles and
 prayer book 17–18
subsistence 38, 99, 107
Suffolk 89, 132
 Ipwich 95
Sunderland, Charles Spencer, third earl of
 196
superstition 3
Sussex, Henry Radcliffe, second earl of 85
Swift, Jonathan 177

taxation 10, 14–15, 17, 36, 174
Tawney, R. H. 7–9
Taylor, Bartholomew 89
Taylor, Jeremy, bishop 157
Tew, Nicholas 120, 124
Thomason, George 119–22
Throckmorton, Job 18, 49–51, 53
Thurgood, John 89
Tichborne dole 38
Tindal, Matthew 195, 198
Toland, John 188, 195
toleration 100, 111, 114, 123, 137, 177,
 185, 191, 194
 act (1689) 20
Tombes, John 112, 118, 120
Tories 20, 149 n.82, 170, 172–3, 176–81,
 199

Townshend, Hayward 16
treason 32
Trenchard, John 173
Trevor-Roper, Hugh 8
Triennial Act (1694) 181
Trinity, doctrine of 124
Trumble, Isabel 85
truth claims 28, 32, 151, 171, 175–80, 186
Turner, Abigail 85
Twysden, Sir Roger 46–8, 58
Tyacke, Nicholas 21 n.5

Umble, Richard 84
Uzzah, king 188

Vane, Sir Henry, the elder 44, 47, 58
Verney, Sir Ralph 160
Vines, Richard 112
vox populi vox dei 18, 47, 50, 174

Wales, marches of 102
Walker, Garthine 83
Wallington, Nehemiah 112, 132
Walwyn, William 111, 114–16, 119–20,
 122–3, 135
Warner, Henry 15–16
Wars of the Roses 3
Warwick, Robert Rich, second earl 44, 48,
 58, 117, 153
Warwickshire 37, 50
 Birmingham 172
 Warwick 18, 49–51, 56
Webbe, Thomas 120
Weber, Max 6, 8
Wellington, Alice 66
Wells, Francis 142, 145–6
Wenden, Thomas 89
Wentworth, Peter 4–5, 12, 22 n.20
Westminster 69
 abbey 132–3
 Assembly 155
 Directory 133–4, 155
 Hall 119
Wharton, George 33
Whitehall 133
Whig historians 1–2, 4, 7, 9, 120
Whigs 20, 149 n.82, 169–70, 172–3,
 176–81, 196, 199

Whitgift, John, archbishop 54–5, 57
Whitmore, William 49
whores, queens denounced as 19, 87–90
Wilbraham, Sir Richard 47, 58
Wilby, John 85
Wilkes, Thomas 14–16
William I, king 3
William II, prince of Orange 162
William III, king 169–70
Williamson, Janet 83
Willoughby, Francis, fifth baron 160–1
Wilmot, Henry, second baron 160
Wilson, Charles 9
Wilson, Rowland 123
Wiltshire 190
  Aldbourn 188
  Salisbury 45
Winstanley, Gerrard 123–4
witenagemot 3

Woodford, Robert 46
Worcester, battle of 163
Worcestershire, Kidderminster 135–6
Wren, Matthew, bishop 193
Wrightson, Keith 81, 129
Writer, Clement 118
Wroth, Sir Robert 16
Wyndon, Ralph 89

Yorkshire
  Bridlinton 82, 119
  Egton players 67
  Hull 15
  Leeds 172
  Rotherham 38
  York (St John's parish) 83

Zaret, David 121, 171, 182 n.7
Zerubbabel, king 189